STILL MISSING

Also by Susan Ware

Forgotten Heroes: Inspiring American Portraits from Our Leading Historians (editor)

Letter to the World: Seven Women Who Shaped the American Century

Beyond Suffrage: Women in the New Deal

Holding Their Own: American Women in the 1930s

America's History (coauthor)

Partner and I: Molly Dewson, Feminism and New Deal Politics

Modern American Women: A Documentary History

Susan Ware

Amelia Earhart

and the Search

for Modern Feminism

S T I L L   M I S S I N G

W · W · Norton & Company

New York   London

The text of this book is composed in Bembo,
with the display set in Futura Medium and Bernhard Italic.
Composition and manufacturing by the Maple-Vail Book Manufacturing Group.
Since this page cannot accommodate all the copyright notices,
pages 287–88 constitute an extension of the copyright page.
Book design by JAM Design.

LIBRARY OF CONGRESS CATALOGING-IN-PUBLICATION DATA
Ware, Susan, 1950–
Still missing : Amelia Earhart and the search for modern feminism
/ Susan Ware.
p. cm.
1. Earhart, Amelia, 1897–1937. 2. Women air pilots—United
States—Biography. 3. Feminism—United States—Biography.
I. Title.
TL540. E3W37 1993
629. 13´092—dc20
[B] 93-9468

ISBN 0-393-31255-0

W. W. Norton & Company, Inc. , 500 Fifth Avenue, New York, N. Y. 10110
W. W. Norton & Company Ltd. , 10 Coptic Street, London WC1A 1PU

3 4 5 6 7 8 9 0

In Memory of
Barbara Miller Solomon
(1919–1992)

Mentor, Colleague, and Dear Friend

Contents

Preface
and Acknowledgments

I chose *Still Missing* as the title of this book because of its multiple—
and open-ended—meanings. The most literal, of course, is the fact
that no conclusive evidence of Amelia Earhart's remains or the
wreckage from her plane has been found since she disappeared on
a round-the-world flight in 1937. The unsolved mystery has spawned
numerous theories about her fate, with new scenarios, planned search
expeditions, and supposed "facts" surfacing almost monthly. Amelia
Earhart may be even more famous today than she was at the height
of her flying career, and the fascination shows no signs of abating.

Amelia Earhart is "still missing," I would argue, despite the
numerous biographies and books that have studied her life. Unlike
Charles Lindbergh, who has been the subject of many historical
treatments, until now the telling of Amelia Earhart's life has been
the province of journalists, aviators, family members, and more
than a few crackpots and publicity seekers. None of these books is

grounded in the specific historical context of the 1920s and 1930s or tries to relate her life to broader trends of twentieth-century history. Yet Earhart was very much part of the history of modern America. She was an influential figure in the development of mass culture and the merchandising of popular figures. She participated in the emergence of aviation as a major transportation industry. And she symbolized the new opportunities for women in modern life.

It is through the lens of women's history, especially the expanding field of feminist biography, that Earhart's life looks the richest and most compelling. A feminist interpretation of Amelia Earhart's life, one that she herself would have endorsed, does not dramatically change the details or the outcome of her life—she still is born in Kansas, flies the Atlantic twice, and disappears on her last flight—but it shifts the field of focus, with particular aspects of Earhart's life emerging as markers, as places worthy of pausing and lingering, while more familiar parts of the story can be quickly sped over. In such a retelling, for example, the actual details of her record-setting flying career give way to an emphasis on her quest for a full and productive life and her role as an inspiration to other women. This slight shift in priorities opens up previously unexplored connections between the life story of this unique individual and the broader patterns of twentieth-century women's lives.

There is a third level at which Amelia Earhart is "still missing," and that involves probing the meanings of her all-too-brief but very public career between 1928 and 1937. Amelia Earhart's story has broad implications for assessing the fortunes of feminism in the postsuffrage era. To make a play on the title of Nancy Cott's recent book, it speaks of the grounding of modern feminism in the first three decades of the twentieth century, which can mean both its theoretical underpinnings and a sense of running aground in the 1920s. When Amelia Earhart is placed more prominently in the story of modern feminism, the metaphors and images for feminism are the exact opposite: they encompass taking off, flying, and the soaring of women's aspirations. In the 1920s and 1930s independent and individualistic heroines from popular culture—women like

Amelia Earhart—personified a model of women's postsuffrage achievement that was widely, and sympathetically, reported in the media and spread by popular culture. These popular heroines kept feminism alive in a period usually thought to be barren of gender consciousness. The survival of this feminist impulse after 1920 provides an important element of continuity, indeed a bridge, between suffrage activism and the revival of feminism in the 1960s and 1970s.

Even as my retelling restores Amelia Earhart to her rightful place in the history of modern American feminism, there is still one final, indeed ironic, twist to the title. The equality and opportunities that Amelia Earhart tirelessly promoted for women are, alas, "still missing." Just as the search continues for relics of Earhart's plane from the vast expanses of the Pacific Ocean, so, too, does the quest for women's equality.

In the course of writing this book, I overcame my lifelong fear of flying, a somewhat unexpected by-product of studying an aviator who likely died in a plane crash. I cannot claim that this was due entirely to my newfound affinity for feminism and flight. Since 1986 I have commuted weekly from Cambridge, where I live, to New York, where I teach at New York University. My thanks to the pilots and crews of the Pan Am and Delta Shuttles for getting me back and forth safely, and for giving me some spectacular views of the two very different places I spend my time.

The Schlesinger Library of Radcliffe College once again provided me with a congenial place to nurture this project, especially during 1990–1991, when I was an honorary visiting scholar there. Archivists Eva Moseley and Kathy Kraft provided expert help with the library's various Earhart collections. Director Patricia Miller King and Joan Challinor, chair of the Advisory Committee, took a special interest in the project, for which I am especially grateful. I would also like to thank Helen Schroyer, curator of special collections at Purdue University, for her help during the research stage. The Schlesinger Library, Purdue University, the Oral History Collection at Columbia University, and the Seaver Center for Western

History, Los Angeles County Museum of Natural History graciously gave permission to cite from their manuscript collections.

Friends, colleagues, and my graduate students at NYU all expressed much-appreciated interest and support for the project. Joyce Antler and Ingrid Winther Scobie, both skilled biographers in their own right, read the manuscript and gave me thoughtful and constructive critiques, and I hope Joyce Seltzer sees glimpses of her thoughtful organizational suggestions. Lola Van Wagenen gave me the *Mid-Week Pictorial* magazines that inspired the opening of Chapter 6, and Melanie Gustafson enriched my A.E. memorabilia; Wendy Holliday's research on women screenwriters in Hollywood was especially helpful in Chapters 5 and 6. Don Ware provided support and encouragement throughout the entire project, including careful readings of several drafts; if I still cannot tell the difference between "that" and "which," it is not for his want of trying. Steve Forman of W. W. Norton kept alive a connection dating back to graduate student days at Harvard and figured out that Norton was the perfect place for this book long before I did. I'm glad that he persevered and that he linked me up with my editor, Amy Cherry, whose enthusiasm and careful readings of various drafts enriched the final product. And I would like to acknowledge the friendship and interest of Nancy Porter and Jane Feinberg, with whom I often compared notes while I was finishing my book and they were producing their documentary on Amelia Earhart for PBS's "American Experience" series.

This book is dedicated to the memory of Barbara Miller Solomon. I knew Barbara for almost twenty years, practically half my life and my entire professional career. I would not be the historian I am today, indeed, I might not even be in the historical profession at all, were it not for her sustained and inspired support over the years. Barbara really believed in this book, and she read a good chunk of it in the last summer of her life as she battled cancer. I solved the last major interpretive riddle of the text on the morning of the day she died; somehow she hung in there until I got it right. The dedication only begins to repay the debt I owe her.

"Lady Lindy"

On May 20, 1927, twenty-five-year-old Charles Lindbergh soloed the Atlantic in the *Spirit of St. Louis* and overnight became the most famous person in America. Lindbergh's flight to Paris was one of the defining moments in the history of aviation, the cult of popular heroism, and the decade of the 1920s. Historians still debate why Lindbergh touched off the tumultuous acclaim he received and puzzle over how his feat became a self-propelling media event in which the news about him was precisely that there was so much news. To be sure, Lindbergh had his share of heroic attributes: relatively obscure status, boyish good looks, personal modesty, and impeccable reputation. Those elements which did not easily fit into the emerging myth—the financial backing he received, the methodical way he planned and executed the trip, the availability of a technologically advanced airplane—were conveniently overlooked. Soon the adulation approached deification.[1]

Just a little more than a year later another Atlantic crossing captured the popular imagination, although not quite on the scale of the Lindbergh mania. This flight was not out to capture a prize, nor was it solo. Why did anyone care when the three-member *Friendship* crew landed in Wales after more than twenty hours in the air? Because on board was thirty-year-old Amelia Earhart, the first woman to cross the Atlantic by plane. Even though she was merely a passenger, the flight catapulted Earhart into the kind of public celebrity that had greeted Charles Lindbergh on his arrival in France the year before. "First Lindbergh made a record for the men and now she has made one for women," noted an American closely involved in the flight.[2]

From that point on Lindbergh and Earhart were represented in the media as complementary idols of individual achievement, practically a "his and hers" matched set of manhood, womanhood, and heroism. A young air-minded Gore Vidal met these aviation pioneers, whom he referred to collectively as "Lindbergh-Earhart," through his father, Eugene Vidal, who was involved in the business and governmental sides of aviation in the 1930s. These aviators, but especially Amelia Earhart, had a magical effect on the young Vidal's imagination. "It is hard to describe to later generations what it was like to live in a world dominated by two such shining youthful deities," Vidal recalled, "the god and goddess of flight," who looked "spookily like each other." To Gore Vidal, and many others ever since, these two fliers were "the air age beautifully incarnate."[3]

Even before the summer of 1928 Bostonians who came into contact with a young settlement worker named Miss Earhart noticed her uncanny likeness to Colonel Lindbergh, a coincidence that seemed even more remarkable when they learned she, too, was a pilot. During the final preparations for the first leg of the trip from Boston Harbor to Newfoundland, a deckhand who caught sight of her in her flying gear dubbed her Lady Lindy, and the name stuck. In stories filed from Newfoundland while the crew waited for favorable weather, the Boston papers called her a "veritable girl Lindbergh" while the *New York Times* noted her boyish looks, her unruly

This widely circulated 1928 photograph of Amelia Earhart cemented
A.E.'s association with Charles Lindbergh and became the iconographic
image of the woman aviator.

hair, and her "quick, flashing 'Lindbergh smile,' " all before she had crossed the ocean. According to the Norwegian artist Brynjulf Strandenaes, who had painted Charles Lindbergh from life and was commissioned by the flight's backers to do a portrait of Earhart, "She looks more like Lindbergh than Lindbergh himself."[4]

The comparisons intensified once the *Friendship* successfully landed in Burry Port, Wales, on June 18, 1928. Now Amelia Earhart was compared with Lindbergh not just for her looks but for the dignified way she handled her new celebrity status. As one American editorial intoned, "We delight to honor heroes and heroines. . . . Lindbergh set an example of modesty and restraint for all flying heroes to copy. His feminine counterpart promises to set a similar example for the many women who, undoubtedly, will follow her aloft."[5] American-born Lady Astor, who befriended Earhart during the London festivities, noted, "Really, she is a remarkable girl. She has the same unselfishness and modesty which made Lindbergh so well loved wherever he went." She praised Amelia Earhart as the perfect ambassador of American womanhood: "Every one I have talked to in England thinks this girl is a great credit to womanhood and to her own country. She has charm, intelligence, and above all, character. Every one here feels happy that the first girl to fly the Atlantic has those qualities."[6] Change the pronouns, and that same statement could have been made, in fact probably was, about Charles Lindbergh.

Amelia Earhart was surprised, overwhelmed, and somewhat embarrassed by the reaction to her flight. Though a licensed pilot, she had done none of the actual flying and felt the praise cascading down on her was undeserved. She kept trying to deflect attention to Wilmer Stultz and Louis ("Slim") Gordon, the pilot and the mechanic, but to no avail. Instead she found herself congratulated for refraining from taking the controls of an aircraft she was unfamiliar with, an act that might have jeopardized the safety of the crew. Unselfishly *not* flying the plane became part of the emerging mystique.[7]

In the aftermath of her Atlantic crossing, Amelia Earhart remained acutely disturbed by the comparisons with Colonel Lindbergh, whom she had never met. When told that she had been nicknamed Lady Lindy after landing in Wales, she explained that she would seek the first opportunity on returning to America to apologize to him for "innocently inflicting the idiotic comparison." She dismissed the physical resemblance with "Oh, I've got the kind of face that looks like everybody." As she later explained to Anne Morrow Lindbergh, who married Charles in 1929, "The title was given me, I believe, probably because one of us wasn't a swarthy runt. You understand my dislike of the title isn't because I don't appreciate being compared to one who has abilities such as Colonel Lindbergh has, but because that comparison is quite unjustified."[8]

Amelia was right: such a comparison was unjustified, because at that point she had done nothing in aviation equal to his solo crossing. She rectified that on May 20, 1932—perhaps not coincidentally, the fifth anniversary of his flight—when she became the first woman, and only the second person, to solo the Atlantic. Once again the comparisons with Lindbergh flooded in. Amy Phipps Guest, the backer of the 1928 flight, cabled her congratulations, adding "your likeness to Col. Lindbergh more striking than ever." The French air minister called her "Lindbergh's double." The *New York Times* article filed from Londonderry, Ireland, described her as "more like Colonel Lindbergh than ever" and "very boyish with her mop of flaxen hair" (she was then almost thirty-five years old). At the New York City reception honoring the returning aviatrix, Mayor Jimmy Walker played on the title of Lindbergh's best-selling account of his 1927 flight, *We,* when giving credit to Earhart for her own accomplishment: "Five years ago we believed that the aeronautical 'We' had but one gender; now you've destroyed that. The Atlantic solo has gone co-ed."[9]

These repeated comparisons between Amelia Earhart and Charles Lindbergh were not just a creation of a hyperactive media. The physical similarities between the two aviators *were* striking. Both shared a tall, slender build, a high forehead, and similar coloring, a code for their joint Protestant Anglo-Saxon stock. Furthermore, Earhart's short, tousled hair, toward which the press developed almost a fetishistic interest ("Take off your hat, Amelia, so we can

Charles Lindbergh stands in front of the *Spirit of St. Louis* in 1927 in flying garb. At the time of his record-breaking flight, he was twenty-five years old.

see your hair"), made her look boyish, an adjective that was always used to describe Lindbergh. In terms of demeanor, both forswore cigarettes, alcohol, and profanity; both exuded an aura of personal modesty and simple taste. Each was "self-made"—they had not relied on inherited wealth or position to get where they did—and both professed disinterest in capitalizing commercially on their flights, a stand that brought them widespread commendation.

The two aviators also shared certain personality traits. This is not particularly surprising since there must be a process of self-selection that turns some people into long-distance risk takers and keeps the rest of us firmly on the ground, but the media played up these similarities to the hilt. They both were courageous, seeking the unknown, and unafraid of danger. They both were solitary individuals, who exhibited steadfastness and self-control and welcomed the opportunity to go it alone. Anne Morrow Lindbergh, who came to know her inscrutable husband as well as anyone, was quite struck by the similarities in their personalities, confiding to her diary in 1930 about Amelia: "She is the most amazing person— just as tremendous as C., I think. It startles me how much alike they are in breadth. C. doesn't realize it, but he hasn't talked to her as much. She has the clarity of mind, impersonal eye, coolness of temperament, balance of a scientist. Aside from that, I like her."[10]

Atlantic flying had gone coed, but with a nagging suspicion that heroines were not quite the full equals of heroes. Even though Earhart was compared with Lindbergh constantly, it never worked the other way: he was never told how much he looked like her or referred to as "the male Amelia Earhart" or "Lord Earhart." Even the nickname Lady Lindy had chauvinistic undertones, for it suggested that her feats were most important when linked to, or reflective of, his. No one ever told Lindbergh that he lacked the physical stamina to fly the ocean because of his gender, suggested that marriage might be a more suitable occupation than aviation, or asked him if he knew how to bake a cake. And Lindbergh was certainly never subjected to misogynist suggestions that his flight was a sham, as in a 1932 cartoon where a man thinks out loud, ". . . and the more pitchers I see the more I'm convinced the feat wuz performed by

Lindy, dressed up to look like a gal!'"[11] An undercurrent of hostility still greeted women's achievements, alongside an unspoken double standard separating heroines' achievements from heroes'. It was almost as if anything a woman did had an invisible asterisk beside it, reminding the world that the accomplishment was unusual—and somewhat suspect—precisely because it had been done by a female.

Beyond the gendered nature of popular heroism, history and fate treated these two famous aviators differently. Especially after the early 1930s, their careers—and their status as hero and heroine—diverged dramatically. But even before then their differing reactions to fame separated them. Lindbergh never reconciled himself to the demands of being a public figure, while Earhart accepted her public stature and made it work for her and for women in general.

Charles Lindbergh was always a reluctant celebrity, even under the best of circumstances. In the hoopla surrounding his flight and hero's welcome, he felt uncomfortable around reporters and quickly grew to hate the sight of a camera. The unseemly way that he was badgered on his honeymoon confirmed his dislike of the press long before the 1930s. Once it became obvious that the public shared his enthusiasm about air travel (a prime motive of his flight and subsequent goodwill tour), he avoided public commitments such as ceremonial appearances, radio talks, and lectures. Instead he turned to surveying new routes for commercial aviation, often with his wife as his trusted navigator and radio operator. The opportunities that came his way after 1927 (the consensus is that Lindbergh was the only flier to make big money from a flight[12]) freed him from having to earn a living, and his marriage to the daughter of a House of Morgan banker added another level of financial security. By the early 1930s Charles Lindbergh was in semiretirement, guarding his privacy jealously and still resentful of the changes that his celebrity had forced on his life. Of course, he conveniently forgot all the opportunities it had opened for him. Fame for Lindbergh always remained a one-sided affair.

The March 1932 kidnapping of his infant son forever soured Charles Lindbergh's already tenuous relationship with the press and the public. The discovery of the child's body and the subsequent trial of the accused murderer in a circuslike atmosphere only heightened Lindbergh's distrust of the media. The kidnapping set in motion a chain of events that eventually ended America's infatuation with its aviator hero: Lindbergh's decision to abandon America in late 1935 for the relative anonymity of Europe, his flirtation with fascism, and his outspoken (and highly controversial) support for isolationism on the eve of World War II. By then his adoring public had turned against him. "America can be rough with a loser," noted one historian, "and Lindbergh had chosen the wrong side and lost." Even though Lindbergh served courageously in World War II and mounted something of a comeback in the 1950s with the publication of his Pulitzer Prize-winning *The Spirit of St. Louis* (1953), it was never the same. He devoted the rest of his life to environmental activism.[13]

Amelia Earhart, like all other fliers, male or female, never had quite the blank check that Lindbergh enjoyed. She had to make her own way, which involved working hard at keeping her name in the public eye to ensure that aviation opportunities continued to roll in. Although she was not keen about celebrity either (to be sure, she never faced the intensity of adulation that engulfed Lindbergh), she was not pathological about protecting her privacy. Rather than become a recluse, Earhart traveled widely, never letting herself become a prisoner of her fame. She was on easy terms with reporters and understood that they had a job to do, an empathy which Lindbergh lacked. Journalist Bess Furman captured the difference well: "Looking as much like Lindbergh as a woman can look like a man, and hating the resemblance, Amelia breezily gathered up good will among news writers as easily as Lindbergh collected antagonism."[14]

Amelia Earhart's premature death in 1937 makes it difficult to draw comparisons between her life choices and those of Charles Lindbergh. Even if Earhart had lived, however, it seems unlikely that the public would have turned on her with the intensity displayed against Lindbergh in the late 1930s. The pedestal on which his adoring public had placed him was so elevated that he had much farther to fall than the less famous Lady Lindy. Nor would Amelia

Earhart likely have so offended the American public with her political views. She showed no tendency to flirt with fascism, a philosophy she found abhorrent because of its antifeminist calls to restrict
women to home and family. And though she had spoken out against
war in the 1930s, she was a devoted political supporter of Franklin
Roosevelt and a close friend of Eleanor Roosevelt, both strong
internationalists. No, it is more likely that she would have found
another niche or just faded from public view once her record-setting days were over.

In the end the most succinct way to compare the two most famous
aviators of the 1920s and 1930s is to note the following: both Amelia Earhart and Charles Lindbergh flew because they loved the freedom of the skies, and both flew to promote public acceptance of
commercial aviation. But Amelia Earhart had an additional reason
for flying that she did not share with Colonel Lindbergh: *she flew
for women*. Her feminist commitment made her accept, if not
embrace, the minor inconveniences of being a popular heroine.
Unlike Charles Lindbergh, who saw his fame as a hindrance, Amelia Earhart saw hers as an opportunity to do something constructive
for women. After the 1928 flight Amelia Earhart worked to portray
her individual achievements as an example of women's capabilities
in the modern world and as steps forward for all women. As Eleanor
Roosevelt said of the pioneering aviator, "She helped the cause of
women, by giving them a feeling there was nothing they could not
do."[15] In this way she made herself central to the history of feminism in the twentieth century.

In the 1920s and 1930s Amelia Earhart helped sustain the
momentum of the women's movement in a period without active
feminism. By her widely publicized individual accomplishments
and clearly articulated feminist ideology, Amelia Earhart demonstrated that women could be autonomous human beings, could live
life on their own terms, and could overcome conventional barriers.
This message, while not always specifically labeled "feminism,"
provided a highly individualistic route for exceptional women to
excel. This model of female independence drawn from popular culture kept feminism alive in the interwar period, a time in which it

is often assumed to have been dormant, off course, or irrelevant.

The link between popular culture and the survival of a feminist impulse is strengthened by the recognition that Amelia Earhart was not the only woman in the 1920s and 1930s whose media image personified a model of independence and success. Other popular heroines, many of whom shared Earhart's individualistic approach to women's advancement and who, like her, were pioneering in new fields such as journalism, film, and athletics, conveyed similar messages of female competence and progress. The accomplishments of women as disparate as Babe Didrikson, Gertrude Ederle, Katharine Hepburn, Dorothy Thompson, Martha Graham, and Georgia O'Keeffe were widely reported as evidence of the ongoing advancement of the modern, postsuffrage woman. Individual achievements substituted for, and also sustained, the feminist momentum.

When Gertrude Ederle set off to conquer the English Channel in 1926, she prophesied, "All the women of the world will celebrate, too."[16] Amelia Earhart shared this expansive and optimistic vision. She truly believed that if women proved themselves competent in aviation, and by extension in all aspects of modern life, prejudices would fade and barriers would fall. It did not prove to be so simple, as the course of women's history over the twentieth century demonstrates. But the strand of individualistic feminism represented by popular heroines like Amelia Earhart at least tentatively kept women's advancement on the national agenda at a time when mass-based feminist movements were unlikely to coalesce.

We will probably never know what happened on Amelia Earhart's fateful last flight in 1937, but we can probe much more deeply into the meaning and legacy of her short but enormously rich life. Like Charles Lindbergh, she symbolized the excitement of early aviation and the promise of the new commercial age; like Lindbergh, she captured popular attention for her feats of individual courage and bravery in the air. But at this point their stories diverge, in part because of the quirks of fate but mainly because of what Amelia Earhart often referred to as "the accident of sex." Lindbergh had no wish, or need, to paint his individual accomplishments as breakthroughs or triumphs for men as a group. Amelia Earhart proudly presented her own example as testimony to women's widening contributions to modern life. Seen in this new light, Amelia Earhart's life supplies a missing link in the story of modern American feminism.

STILL MISSING

Chapter 1

A Modern Woman Makes History

"I like to fly—and I'm restless." Amelia Earhart's entire life had that restless quality to it, as if she were searching for her role as a woman in modern America. "She was in rebellion against a world which had been made, for women, too safe, too unexciting," observed an editorial in the *New York Times* when she was lost at sea in 1937. "She wanted to dare all that a man would dare." That quest characterized her whole life, not just her last flight. Amelia Earhart could never have lived a conventional female life.[1]

She was born on July 24, 1897, technically a child of the Victorian nineteenth century but spiritually a modern woman of the twentieth. She recalled "growing up here and there" (a chapter title in her second book, *The Fun of It*) and always felt a bit like a rolling stone. For the rest of her life she could never stay long in one place or be content doing one thing; she was always on the move. "I've had twenty-eight different jobs in my life and I hope I'll have two hundred and twenty-eight more," she boasted. At heart she was an experimenter who liked to try everything at least once. Her sister remembered, above all else, her curiosity, "her great interest in so many different things." Amelia loved to drive fast cars and to fly sleek planes, and she relished the solitude of the open road or the air. At the same time she enjoyed company and was completely at home in a roomful of people. She was a caring person, but one who was loath to confide details of her private life to anyone else. She approached life with zest. Her husband later remembered, "All I knew was that Amelia was more fun to play with than anyone else."[2]

Amelia Mary Earhart's family background and upbringing encouraged her individual ambitions and strivings, but since there was no clear aviation "career path" for women in the early twentieth century (or for men, for that matter), attempts to locate yearnings for flight in girlhood are retrospective at best. What her childhood did give her was a curiosity about life, an ability to adapt, and a desire to stretch and explore. "I got out and did *something*," she remembered, and then drew this lesson: "In fact, I think it is just about the most important thing any girl can do—try herself out, do something."[3]

Her early years were shaped by her parents, Edwin and Amy Otis Earhart, her younger (by two years) sister, Muriel, and Amy's parents, the influential Otis family in Atchison, Kansas. Edwin Earhart worked as a railroad claims agent, but money was often tight. In addition, family life was periodically disrupted by his alcoholism, which made it difficult for him to hold a steady job. As a result, the family moved frequently, and the two Earhart girls spent time with their grandparents in Atchison, as well as lived with their parents in Kansas City, Des Moines, St. Paul, and Chicago. Amelia attended six high schools before she had enough credits to finish the required four-year course. Later, when she met people on her lecture tours who said they were from her hometown, she would laugh and say, "Which one?"[4]

As a child Amelia loved school, although she was a bit too high-spirited ever to become a teacher's pet. Along the way she developed a vivid imagination, mainly from her reading. "Books have meant much to me," she wrote in her autobiography. "Not only did I myself read considerably, but Mother read aloud to my sister and me, early and later. So fundamental became the habit that on the occasions when we girls had to do housework, instead of both pitching in and doing it together, one was selected to read aloud and the other to work." Her imaginary flights through literature were adventures as real to her as later flying the Atlantic.[5]

But Amelia was no book-bound recluse; at heart she was a tomboy who loved the outdoors. Throughout her childhood Amelia struggled, often successfully, against the restrictions imposed on her sex. "Unfortunately I lived at a time when girls were still girls. Though reading was considered proper, many of my outdoor exercises were not." Twenty-five years later she still remembered with "special glee" putting on a new bloomer type of gymnasium suit and going out "to shock all the nice little girls. It seems a trivial thing now, but it was tremendously daring in those strictly conventional days." Also daring was her love for all kinds of strenuous games and exercise, including basketball, bicycling, and tennis. On more than one occasion her exploits on sleds or other mechanical contraptions led to scrapes, near misses, and parental reprimands. But nothing stopped Amelia and her willing sidekick, Muriel, especially not her grandmother's stern rebuke that as a small girl she had done "nothing more strenuous than roll my hoop in the public square."[6]

More than anything else, Amelia's childhood embraced a sense of experimentation and physical freedom. "I have always enjoyed doing new things, *first-time* things," she recalled. "It is a desire I have had as long as I can remember. . . . Whether it was considered 'the thing to do' or not was irrelevant." She then listed a medley of these new things that captured her open-ended approach to life: riding a buggy in the stable; climbing up onto a delivery horse; exploring the caves in the cliffs overlooking the Missouri; inventing a trap and then successfully trapping a chicken in it; jumping "over a fence no boy my age had dared to jump." Hers was a vivid, imaginative childhood, and she knew from the start that "there was

Even as a child Amelia displayed two traits that characterized her adult public persona: she stared directly at the camera, and she smiled with her mouth closed.

more fun and excitement in life than I would have time to enjoy."[7]

When a girl grows up to be famous, it is always tempting to ascribe future choices to the circumstances of childhood or family. Retrospectively Amelia explained her attraction to aviation by three "threads": the many trips she made with her father on the railroad, her love of sports and games usually restricted to boys, and her lifelong propensity to experimentation. She was less conscious of choosing paths very different from both her mother and her sister, no matter how close she was to them during her childhood and adult life. Amy Otis Earhart was a typical self-abnegating Victorian wife, who juggled the needs of her family, their diminishing finances, and an alcoholic husband without much concern for her own needs. Muriel eventually married and had children and worked as a schoolteacher for many years in a Boston suburb. Her career set her apart from her mother, but she, too, put the demands of home and family first. As Muriel said many years later, "Amelia had her planes and I had my children. That was the difference."[8]

Amelia set different goals and priorities. She would rely totally on herself. She would follow her interests where they led her. She would not fall into the trap of Victorian selflessness and domesticity that constrained the lives of women like her mother. She would be self-supporting and skeptical about the institution of marriage. She would live her own life.[9]

Luckily the early twentieth century offered far more opportunities for young women to move beyond the conventional woman's path of marriage and motherhood than had existed for earlier generations like her mother's. For many aspiring women the route to economic independence (a crucial step, since few were wealthy enough to forgo the need to work) involved higher education, with undergraduate and graduate degrees providing credentials for satisfying professional work. The Earhart family, though often strapped for money, found the resources to send Amelia to the college preparatory Ogontz School outside Philadelphia. But while Muriel later attended Smith College, Amelia showed no inclination to go on to college full-time, although she did take special courses at Columbia University and at the Harvard extension school. She never took a formal degree, concluding that she received all she wanted out of her life experiences and her occasional time in the classroom, which, by the way, she thoroughly enjoyed. "Experiment! Meet new people. . . . That's better than any college education," she exclaimed.[10] For other women less confident about their future prospects, such a stance might have been unsettling. But to an amazing degree Amelia Earhart thrived on it, took what came her way, and rarely, if ever, looked back.

As a V.A.D. nurse's aide in Toronto during World War I, Amelia developed both a love of flying and a deep-seated hatred of war.

There were two defining moments for American women in the second decade of the twentieth century: the woman suffrage campaign and World War I. Despite her later interest in expanding women's roles in all facets of public life, Earhart was not engaged by the suffrage campaign, although one can hardly imagine her opposing votes for women. For her the critical moment was World War I. This experience affected her personally, philosophically, and professionally.

While visiting her sister, Muriel, at school in Toronto in December 1917, Amelia impulsively decided not to return to Ogontz but instead to volunteer as a V.A.D. (voluntary aid detachment) nurse's aide at the Spadina Military Convalescent Hospital. Six months after the United States had finally entered the war which had been raging in Europe since 1914, she wanted to take a more active role in the war effort. "It so completely changed the direction of my own footsteps that the details of those days remain indelible in my memory," she later recalled.[11]

Spadina awakened her love of flying, although it was to be several years before the full implications of this new interest became clear. Wartime restrictions prevented her from going up in the air, but she listened avidly to the stories told by military pilots who were convalescing at Spadina from their war injuries. (Aviators call this shoptalk ground flying.) The use of aircraft in combat was in its infancy in World War I, and fliers were the source of great fascination. In contrast with the daily horror of trench warfare and poison gas, which pitted hundreds of thousands of soldiers in futile, destructive standoffs, flying aces fought individual battles, almost like medieval knights in shining armor. No wonder they were glorified in the increasingly depersonalized and brutal conduct of modern warfare. Earhart later characterized wartime's boost to aviation as "one of the few worthwhile things that emerged from the misery of war." For the rest of her life Earhart spoke out for pacifism, her own philosophical legacy of the carnage.[12]

When the war ended in November 1918, Amelia Earhart was twenty-one years old. In the period between the armistice and the launching of her public career in 1928, she was somewhat at loose ends. She seemed unfazed by the lack of focus to her life, but her restlessness and constant shifts of direction remind us how few models there were for modern young women desperate to break out of old patterns but not quite sure what to replace them with. Spurred by her wartime experiences, she enrolled at Columbia for premed courses but decided against becoming a doctor. She then moved to California, where her parents now lived, in the hope she could help them patch up their failing marriage. She would do what she could, she confided to her sister, "but after that I'm going to come back here and live my own life."[13]

In fact, she stayed on the West Coast for four years. She regretted leaving New York but soon fell in love with California, which she remembered as "a country of out-door sports. I was fond of automobiles, tennis, horseback riding, and almost anything else that is active and carried on in the open." It was a short step from such interests to aviation because as she recalled, "Southern California was particularly active in air matters." After her Spadina experience Amelia was determined to learn to fly.[14]

She set about her goal methodically. She enlisted the support of her family, first to pay for lessons and then to help her purchase her own airplane, a Kinner Canary. She sought out a female flight instructor, Neta Snook, because she felt she would be less self-conscious taking lessons from a woman, and began to master the intricacies of flying those highly erratic early craft. She made her first solo in June 1921 and soon was participating in the camaraderie of the airstrip and the hangar with other pilots and mechanics, mainly men. She acquired the proper clothing for flight—riding breeches and a heavy leather coat—and cut her long hair inches at a time so her mother would not notice. Soon it was cut short in the hairdo that became her trademark, just the way bobbed hair marked many other "modern women" of the 1920s.

"In 1922, I certainly didn't think of my flying as a means to anything but having fun. So I turned to other means of making a livelihood." As she put it pithily, "no pay, no fly and no work, no play." She worked at a variety of jobs, including as a photographic assistant and as a clerk at the telephone company. For recreation she had the Southern California outdoors. And she had a boyfriend, a young man named Sam Chapman who boarded with her parents. In 1923 they became informally engaged.[15]

With the formal end of her parents' marriage in 1924, Amelia changed direction once more. She sold her Kinner airplane and bought a fancy touring car, the Kissel; she and her mother spent six weeks driving cross-country to Boston to join Muriel, who was teaching school in nearby Medford. Two women driving cross-country in the mid-1920s were still quite a novelty, especially in a bright yellow car. No doubt the auto mechanic's repair course that Amelia had taken at Smith College right after the war helped with the inevitable punctures and breakdowns. Amelia relished the freedom that the automobile represented for women, as did many other independent-minded women, although she noted that its yellow color, considered proper in California, was a "little outspoken" for staid Boston. Even when she was strapped for cash, she managed to hang on to her car, which a friend remembered she "loved like a pet dog."[16]

In 1924 she was twenty-seven years old, and "Like a great many other girls at this age I had no special plan for myself."[17] Sam Chapman followed her east, where he found work as an engineer. He offered her the option of a conventional middle-class marriage, which she kept putting off. She worked at various jobs because she had to support both herself and her mother, who would have considered it improper for a middle-class woman to enter the paid work force. For the rest of her life she and her sister alternated in providing a home for their mother, who was unable to live on her own. Money remained tight, and whatever spare cash Amelia had went toward her car and occasional flying time at a nearby airport. With no family wealth to back her up, she had to be economically self-sufficient, but a desire for affluence never was uppermost in her mind. She remained casual about money and possessions for the rest of her life.

During this restless, searching, yet satisfying period in her late twenties Earhart began to keep a scrapbook documenting the activities of women in public life. If she was consciously looking for role models, she picked a distinguished and varied lot. The scrapbook was remarkably prescient of the areas toward which Earhart would gravitate during the public phase of her career. The scrapbook also represented a comprehensive survey of the new roles open to women in the first third of the twentieth century. For example, the clippings of women firsts or women in unusual occupations showed women breaking down old barriers and serving as symbols of what women could accomplish. The clippings Amelia chose to preserve in her scrapbook also highlighted women reformers and government appointees, as well as the activities of such women's organizations as the League of Women Voters and the Women's Joint Congressional Committee. She seemed especially interested in stories about women who combined marriage and career and supported the right of other women to do so. Earhart even foreshadowed her later support for the Equal Rights Amendment by penciling a comment next to an article about protective legislation: "The method is not sound. Women will gain economic justice by proving themselves in all lines of endeavor."[18]

Amelia Earhart managed to capture in this scrapbook the broad range of women's postsuffrage activism. Her choice of subjects (no movie stars or flappers for her!) remains highly revealing. She allied herself with the accomplishments of the Progressive-era generation of reformers and suffragists who then went on to forge public careers for themselves, such as in government, settlement houses, and social work. And the articles she selected confirm that the 1920s did not represent a downturn in women's organizational and reform energy; quite the contrary, women's public activity deepened and expanded. Without an organized feminist movement in the 1920s, however, much of this activity remained individualistic—that is, women proving on a case-by-case basis that they could compete equally with men. But this stance suited Earhart just fine. The essence of her evolving feminism was a commitment to opening all areas to women, breaking down artificial barriers, and using the examples of individual women who succeeded as models and inspirations to the rest of womankind.[19]

In 1926 Amelia Earhart was a twenty-nine-year-old woman who still could not quite figure out what she wanted to do with herself; flying was still just a hobby, and an expensive one at that. Less than two years later she was a national heroine. In between she finally found a niche, a profoundly satisfying professional identity as a social worker at Denison House in Boston. Her brief stint at Denison House provided one of the truly formative influences on her life, making an enormous contribution to the development of the public (and private) person who captivated the American public after 1928. In developing the poise and self-confidence with which she handled the demands of her grueling public career, her time at Denison House was probably just as critical as the hours she snatched away at the nearby flying field in Squantum.

The field of settlement work that Earhart happened into was, not coincidentally, one of the most important professions for women in the early twentieth century. Denison House had been founded in

1892 along the lines pioneered by Toynbee Hall in London and Jane Addams's Hull House in Chicago. Headworker Helena S. Dudley, aided by such residents as Wellesley College professors and Progressive reformers Emily Balch and Vida Scudder, was Denison House's guiding spirit until 1912. The settlement house was located on Tyler Street in Boston, at the edge of Chinatown; the neighborhood in the 1920s was a mix of Italian, Syrian, Greek, and Chinese families. In that decade approximately eight hundred individuals a year availed themselves of settlement services, including citizenship and English classes, a demonstration kindergarten, music and athletic events, girls' and boys' clubs, and ethnic associations.

Amelia Earhart had found her way to Denison House by way of another venerable Boston institution, the Women's Educational and Industrial Union.[20] She used the WEIU placement bureau in 1926 to look for a better-paying position than her current employment as a companion at a mental hospital for seventy dollars a month plus board. Her listed work preferences were an unusual trilogy: teaching English to foreigners, serving as a hostess, or anything connected with aeronautics. She offered references from former employers as well as from her erstwhile fiancé, Sam Chapman, who declared earnestly, "Miss Amelia M. Earhart is all right. I have known her four years and she is a very dear friend of mine. She is a good scholar and is capable in any field that she may claim." The application on file assessed the prospective candidate as "an extremely interesting girl—very unusual" and noted, with amazement no doubt, "holds a pilots license!"[21]

The WEIU sent Earhart off for an interview at Denison House, where headworker Marion Perkins was instantly taken by the young woman she described as "tall, slender, boyish-looking" and possessed of a "quiet humor and poise." Despite her lack of settlement house experience, Perkins hired her on the spot for a part-time nonresident position with responsibility for adult education and home visitation. In the fall of 1927 Amelia Earhart was graduated to full-time resident, and she continued her work with young girls, taught an adult education class, and organized a Syrian Mothers' Club.[22]

One of the things that made Amelia Earhart so successful in settlement work was what Perkins recalled as her "unusual mixture of the artist and the practical person." Children, boys but especially girls, responded to her like a Pied Piper. Special treats were the rides in the now-battered Kissel Kar she had driven cross-country in 1924, fondly referred to around the neighborhood by its nickname, the Yellow Peril. As headworker Perkins said in 1928, Earhart's philosophy was "to give boys and girls the experiences that will keep them young and that will develop a zest for life." Few, if any, of the neighborhood residents knew she was a flier, even after she had dropped leaflets advertising an upcoming street fair from the air in 1927. To them she was just the "Miss Earhart" who would stop by for visits and happily watch the goings-on in the neighborhood while sharing a cup of tea or pastry. She hated paper work, however, much preferring to spend her time in direct contact with people than to fill out records describing what she had done. She never reconciled herself to this inevitable aspect of modern bureaucratic society.[23]

Amelia Earhart's hallmark as a settlement worker was an openness to all types of people and an eagerness to learn from them as much as to instruct them. "The people whom I met through Denison House were as interesting as any I have ever known." A catalog of the rewards and drawbacks of her new line of work shows her priorities: "Rewards are gain in knowledge; personal satisfaction in accomplishing what must be done in untangling human complexities; and a feeling that the ultimate reason for life is that it can be a beautiful thing, and that I, as well as others, will reap the reward of that. Drawbacks are lack of time for much of beauty in life—time for study, time for people, time for physical exercise." She added tellingly, "Lack of all these partly due to inadequate pay." But perhaps the statement that best captures how much she gained from her settlement work, and the broader social vision that underlay her commitment to the field, was this candid assessment: "There is a feeling of self-preservation here; for what shuts out happiness for some does so for me and mine."[24]

Appropriately enough, it was while teaching a class at Denison House that Amelia Earhart first had an inkling of the Atlantic crossing that changed her life. As she recalled, "It hinged (can turning points hinge?) on a telephone call in Boston early in 1928—as casual as an invitation to a matinee." A wealthy Philadelphia woman, Amy Phipps Guest, had purchased a trimotor Fokker plane in the hope of being the first woman to fly the Atlantic, but her family had vetoed the plan. Guest then turned to publisher George Palmer Putnam and promoter Hilton Railey to find, in Putnam's words, "an American girl who would measure up to adequate standards of American womanhood." The name surfaced of the Boston settlement worker who described herself as "a social worker who flies for sport," and Denison House was contacted.[25]

Once Earhart learned the details, the woman who would try anything once had no doubt that she wanted to be counted in: "Who could refuse an invitation to such a shining adventure?" Her interview with the promotors, however, had certain comic ironies, which were not lost on Earhart herself: "I realized, of course, that I was being weighed. It should have been slightly embarrassing, for if I

Earhart consciously chose a woman, Neta Snook, as a flight instructor when she decided to learn to fly. In 1921 Amelia had not yet bobbed her hair, and her leather coat looked a little too shiny and new.

were found wanting on too many counts I should be deprived of a trip. On the other hand, if I were just too fascinating the gallant gentlemen might be loath to drown me." One factor which probably tipped the balance in Earhart's favor was her remarkable resemblance to aviator Charles A. Lindbergh, both in physical appearance and in her modest, quiet demeanor. Comparisons with Lindbergh were noted even before the flight began.[26]

Before accepting Putnam's offer, Earhart carefully cleared her plans with headworker Marion Perkins (also swearing her to secrecy) and coordinated the trip with her already planned summer vacation. She never anticipated the trip would amount to anything more than an exciting vacation and assured Perkins, "And I'll be back for summer school. I have weighed the values and I want to stay in social work." Before she left, she composed farewell notes to family members, which she offhandedly labeled "popping off letters." To her sister she wrote, "I have tried to play for a large stake, and if I succeed all will be well. If I don't, I shall be happy to pop off in the midst of such an adventure." Her only regret was leaving behind debts which she was confident were temporary: "In a few years I feel I could have laid by something substantial, for so many new things were opening for me. . . ."[27]

Just a year after Lindbergh's May 1927 flight, the preparations for the first transatlantic flight by a woman were front-page news, especially since several teams were racing for the distinction of being first. After a series of weather-related delays, the *Friendship* team of pilot Wilmer ("Bill") Stultz, mechanic Slim Gordon, and log taker Amelia Earhart took off from Trepassey Bay, Newfoundland, on June 17, 1928. Twenty hours and forty minutes later they landed in Burry Port, Wales. Their pontooned craft bobbed in the water for an hour before attracting the attention of local residents. This was practically the last time that Amelia Earhart went anywhere unnoticed. Soon pictures of her in what became her trademark outfit—leather flying jacket and cap, short unruly hair, jodhpurs and high boots, plus the much-copied silk blouse and necktie—circulated throughout Europe and America.

It is hard today to understand the hoopla that surrounded this

1928 flight, especially since Earhart was quite open about the fact that she had done none of the flying. She was merely a passenger who kept the log or, in one of her more self-deprecating descriptions, "a sack of potatoes." But even if she was only a passenger, it took great courage to risk the flight, since fourteen lives, including three women's, had been lost trying to span the ocean just since Lindbergh's flight. Moreover, flight was still so young, and the memory of Lindbergh's crossing so fresh, that newspapers ate up dramatic aviation news. Even staid papers like the *New York Times* filled their front pages with coverage of expeditions, record-breaking aviation feats, and other noteworthy exploits involving danger, risk, and exploration. As Earhart herself noted from the perspective of 1931, "Three years ago the returned aviator still rated spectacular headlines. He was front-page 'news,' she was even front-pager."[28]

Then there was what Earhart referred to as "the accident of sex." (She captioned a picture of the crew, "Two musketeers and—what is a feminine musketeer?") "I tried to make them realize that all the credit belonged to the boys, who did the work," she insisted in interview after interview. "But from the beginning it was evident the accident of sex—the fact that I happened to be the first woman to have made the Atlantic flight—made me the chief performer in our particular sideshow." On another occasion she admitted that she felt "a little resentful that the mere fact that I am a woman apparently overshadows the tremendous feat of flying Bill Stultz has just accomplished." But she could not make the interest in her disappear because fascination with gender was the major reason for the fervid reception that Earhart, and the popular heroines who preceded and followed her, received.[29]

Despite her casual dismissal of the accident of sex, Earhart was determined that the flight should mean something to women. In interviews, dispatches for the *New York Times,* and radio hookups, she repeatedly stressed that women were capable of ocean flying, that she hoped the flight would "quicken the interest of women in flying," and that "there is no fundamental difference between men and women which would prevent women having the same pleasure out of flying that men have." When she finally met Amy Phipps

Guest, the backer of the flight, she noted, "More than ever then did I realize how essentially this was a feminine expedition, originated and financed by a woman, whose wish was to emphasize what her sex stood ready to do." Establishing a pattern that held true for the rest of her career, Earhart always presented her personal accomplishments as evidence of women's capabilities in the modern world and as a spur to further advancement.[30]

Equally apparent from this first flight was the pattern of individual women identifying with Earhart's accomplishments and connecting them to the wider struggles of women in modern life. She appealed to several generations of women—to the young "modern woman" of the 1920s, who identified with her individual achievement, as well as to the older generations, who applauded her modesty, her forthright candor, and her avowed abstinence from alcohol and cigarettes.[31] Frances Perkins, soon to be named Franklin D. Roosevelt's industrial commissioner in New York State and later his secretary of labor in Washington, observed at a New York reception in Earhart's honor that all women "got a vicarious thrill out of Miss Earhart's flight."[32]

Especially telling was the way in which the elder stateswomen of the suffrage and reform movements embraced this new female celebrity. Carrie Chapman Catt remarked that "in this day of plucky American girls none is braver than Miss Earhart," and Margaret Dreier Robins of the Women's Trade Union League noted, "Is it not in us in America to think that if one of us does something we can do it also?" Lillian Wald of the Henry Street Settlement, along with many other feminist leaders, praised her as exemplary of a style of American womanhood far preferable to the media-hyped flapper: "We feel intimately allied to you and we want to express our pride in you and affection for you. And we want to tell you that you are a very, very nice girl, and that we like you a lot. Especially we do tremendously like your modesty. You represent the spirit of the settlements—always ready for a great adventure."[33]

Throughout all the publicity surrounding her 1928 flight Amelia Earhart consistently identified herself as a settlement worker (or, as she put it jokingly, a "social worker on a bat") more than as a flier.

In fact, she clung to that identity, the one element of continuity in her rapidly changing world. One of the few things that she requested be put on her schedule while in England (it was her first trip after all) was a visit to Toynbee Hall and a chance to talk to British settlement workers. In view of her mounting embarrassment at the praise lavished on her in relation to her fairly modest (in her mind) accomplishment, how refreshing it must have been to hear Lady Astor say, "I'm not interested in you a bit because you crossed the Atlantic. I want to hear about your settlement work." As Amelia noted poignantly, "I was glad to find someone who regarded me as a human being."[34]

All this notoriety was a bit overwhelming for a young woman who genuinely had believed once she flew to England for the sport of it, she would just as casually return to her old way of life. While in London, she began to come to grips with her celebrity:

> Ever since landing in England I have been learning about what it means to be a public person. . . . Today I have been receiving offers to go on the stage, appear in the movies, and to accept numerous gifts ranging from an automobile to a husband. The usual letters of criticism and threats which I have always read celebrities receive have also arrived. And I am caught in a situation where very little of me is free. I am being moved instead of moving. . . . But having undertaken to go through with this trip I have to go through with it. That is the drawback of being a public person—you cannot fall down. People's eyes are on you.

Earhart reassured her public that there would be "no stage appearances nor acting in the movies": "I am not going to commercialize my flight in the Friendship and I will be happier when the pressure of life in the public eye diminishes." But it never did. Like it or not, the 1928 flight had launched her "into a life more full than ever."[35]

Ironically, the celebrity surrounding the 1928 Atlantic crossing made it impossible for her to practice her craft of settlement work anymore; she was far too famous to slip in and out of tenements to chat with her Syrian and Chinese neighbors. But the break between her settlement work and her later public career may not be as abrupt as it appears at first glance. The techniques that she honed in social work and teaching, especially her skill at interacting with many varieties of people, were put to good use once she became a public figure. She herself realized the links when she said in the 1930s, "But I still do social service—by lecturing, writing, speaking over the radio. It may be a different kind of social service from that of a settlement. But after all, my social work there has been more than the mere teaching of the correct use of English."[36]

Amelia Earhart was at something of a crossroads in the summer of 1928. Even though the press consistently referred to her as a "girl," she was almost thirty-one years old, hardly a youth. After dispensing such obligations as celebrations in New York, Boston, and Chicago (had she accepted all such offers, she noted, "I might not have got home for a year and a day"), she cranked out what we would now recognize as an "instant" book to capitalize on her flight. After sorting through various business opportunities, she settled on some lecturing and promotional work, plus an affiliation as avia- tion editor for Ray Long's *Cosmopolitan* magazine, for which she would write a monthly column on aviation and answer questions from readers.[37]

The *Cosmopolitan* job meant that New York, not Boston, became her base of operations. Sad at severing her connections with Deni- son House, for a while she and her mother lived at the Barrow Street settlement house, Greenwich House, headed by noted settle- ment worker Mary Simkhovitch. George Putnam later recalled, "It was *her* kind of place, perhaps the one type of place on the ground in which she could feel, just then, truly at home." But Earhart was unable to put into action her plan of combining her settlement work with lecturing and writing, and that element of her life, so impor- tant in the 1920s, dropped from sight.[38] Even though she had writ- ten in 1928 that "aviation is a great thing, but it cannot fill one's life completely," increasingly her future lay in aviation-based activities, not social service, although she always insisted the two were linked.[39]

In the mythic story of Amelia Earhart her 1928 flight across the

Atlantic catapulted her into the public limelight, where she remained steadily until her disappearance in 1937. In actuality she dropped out of the news for long stretches of time at various points in her career. Her popularity, and her status as a public figure, were not a steady or constant progression but rather a series of peaks and valleys, spurts forward and false starts.[40]

Nowhere is that more clear than in the period between the 1928 flight and her 1932 transatlantic solo. Publisher G. P. Putnam, the promoter of the first flight who continued informally to advise his protégée on her career, claimed that this period "crystallized the purposes and personality of Amelia Earhart."[41] (His statement must be tempered by the fact that she finally consented to marry him during that time.) But with the exception of participating in cross-country races, setting a women's speed record, and soloing in an autogiro (the forerunner of the helicopter), Amelia Earhart did not at first do much to live up to her reputation as the world's most famous woman flier. After the incredible newspaper and magazine coverage that surrounded her 1928 flight, she could not, of course, return to anonymity, as her inability to continue social work showed. But she was hardly front-page news very often either.

There are two ways to explain the gaps in Amelia Earhart's public career between 1928 and 1932. The first is tempermental: even though she had cast her lot with aviation, Amelia was in no hurry to settle down. After her penurious days as a social worker, she wanted to savor her improved financial situation. She had received no direct payment for her flight (pilot Stultz was guaranteed twenty thousand dollars); even the ten thousand dollars she earned for her syndicated story was turned back to the promoters. But her book and lectures and endorsements removed the pressure to hold a steady job. Casually dismissing the job opportunities and offers which had come her way as "incidentals" ("very nice, but never part of my plan"), she reaffirmed, "My plan, always, was to do what I wanted," a phrase which was to recur throughout the rest of her career. The *New York Times* captured her footloose state of mind when it noted dryly, "Miss Earhart apparently plans, as she puts it, simply to 'fly around.' "[42]

The second reason for the gap in the progression of Earhart's aviation career is also fairly straightforward: while Amelia Earhart may have been the most well-known woman flier at the time, she was not yet the most experienced or competent. As she said in September 1928, "I don't profess or pretend to be a flier. I am just an amateur, a dub, flying around the country for the amusement there is in it for me." For most of the 1920s she had never had the time or the money to devote herself to flying. Now, thanks to the opportunities streaming her way after 1928, opportunities in part the result of George Palmer Putnam's continued devotion to promoting her career, she had both. In England she had bought—or rather, Putnam had bought for her as an investment in her future— a small Avian plane from Lady Heath, which she now planned to use for "vagabonding" and "gypsying" around the country. Actually this was a cover for what turned out to be the first transcontinental trip by a woman in the fall of 1928.[43]

Over the next few years, out of the public eye except when a mishap or slip suddenly put her back on the front page (AMELIA EARHART AND G. P. PUTNAM IN PLANE CRASH; BOTH ESCAPE WITHOUT INJURY IN PITTSBURGH), she quietly built her skills as a pilot and established her bona fides among the growing sorority of women fliers. In 1930 she acquired her transport license, only the fourth one issued to a woman.[44] Two years later she felt confident enough to try, and to succeed at, a solo of the Atlantic, sweet vindication for her passenger role in 1928.

It was during the interlude between the two Atlantic crossings that Amelia Earhart took perhaps the most courageous step of her entire life: she agreed to marry George Palmer Putnam. For a woman so free-spirited and so committed to going her own way personally and professionally, the decision to marry was not taken lightly. A conventional marriage, such as that which her parents or her sister, Muriel, had chosen, was out of the question. Sam Chapman had offered that to her, but she could never reconcile his desire for bourgeois respectability and his often expressed disapproval of working wives with her own personal aspirations. Moving into Denison House in the fall of 1927 was in many ways her declaration of independence from him, and their engagement was formally broken in November 1928.[45]

Because of the business interests that Amelia and George shared (the business, of course, being A.E. herself), they had spent quite a lot of time together from 1928 on. When reporters pursued Earhart about her marital intentions after her Atlantic flight, she replied flippantly, "You never can tell what I will do. If I was sure of the man, I might get married tomorrow." Rumors about a possible romantic attachment between manager and client escalated after Putnam and his wife of eighteen years, Dorothy Binney Putnam, were divorced in December 1929. Less than a month later Dorothy married Captain Frank Monroe Upton of New York, suggesting she had her own reasons for ending the relationship. If he hadn't been pursuing Amelia before then, G.P. now stepped up his pitch. Family lore differs on whether he proposed two times or six before she finally accepted. The issuance of a marriage license in November 1930 produced only a flurry of denials from the participants. "Sometime in the next fifty years I may be married," said the potential bride. "As for the wedding, all I can say is that no time has been set," said the slightly more forthcoming groom-to-be.[46]

The wedding finally took place at George's mother's home in Noank, Connecticut, on Saturday, February 7, 1931. The bride wore brown, and the groom slipped onto her finger a plain gold band which she never wore afterward. She kept her own name professionally, although she did not mind being called Mrs. Putnam socially.[47] Both bride and groom were back at their respective desks on Monday morning. Within days Amelia was writing to her mother, who had not approved of the marriage to the divorced Putnam: "I am much happier than I expected I could ever be in that state. I believe the whole thing was for the best. Of course I go on in the same way as before as far as business is concerned. I haven't changed at all and will only be busier I suppose."[48]

But underlying all these protestations of happiness was a woman who was profoundly skittish about the institution of marriage. She had just barely escaped the trap of Sam Chapman's bourgeois domesticity, realizing in time she would never be happy in such a conventional life. Her sister Muriel's marriage in 1929 rekindled her doubts, leading her to remark to the minister after the ceremony, "I think what Pidge [Muriel] has just done took more courage than my flying does." In a 1930 letter to a friend she wrote, "I am still unsold on marriage. I don't want *anything,* all of the time." She compared marriage with a far-too-comfortable den: "A den is stuffy. I'd rather live in a tree," adding, "I think I may not ever be able to see marriage except as a cage until I am unfit to work or fly or be active—and of course I wouldn't be desirable then."[49]

The most compelling statement of her fear of marriage was the letter she presented to her husband-to-be right before the wedding, an amazing document of feminist independence, angst, and a cry for reassurance that what she was doing was not completely insane. To his credit, George Putnam accepted her less-than-enthusiastic entrance into the wedded state and proceeded with the ceremony. The letter paralleled a modern prenuptial agreement, except that it negotiated freedom and autonomy instead of financial assets. It must be quoted in full to appreciate its force:

There are some things which should be writ before we are married—things we have talked over before—most of them.

You must know again my reluctance to marry, my feeling that I shatter thereby chances in work which mean much to me. I feel the move just now as foolish as anything I could do. I know there may be compensations, but have no heart to look ahead.

On our life together I want you to understand I shall not hold you to any medieval code of faithfulness to me, nor shall I consider myself bound to you similarly. If we can be honest I think the difficulties which arise may best be avoided should you or I become interested deeply (or in passing) with anyone else.

Please let us not interfere with the other's work or play, nor let the world see our private joys or disagreements. In this connection I may have to keep some place where I can go to be myself now and then, for I cannot guarantee to endure at all times the confinement of even an attractive cage.

I must exact a cruel promise, and that is you will let me go in a year if we find no happiness together.

I will try to do my best in every way and give you that part of me you know and seem to want.

A.E.[50]

The section of this letter which has drawn the most attention is its endorsement of what later came to be called an open marriage. Earhart's acceptance of sexual freedom within marriage was exceptional, although there is no evidence that either one ever felt the need to exercise the option. But other themes, especially Earhart's cries for autonomy and space within the traditionally patriarchal institution of marriage, were just as important. The letter expressed a deep-seated fear that marriage would destroy her chances of productive work. Other women entered marriage blinded by passion or radiant about the future; Amelia seemed practically immobilized (she had "no heart to look ahead") and could only hope that it wouldn't be as bad as she feared. She expressed her deep need to maintain her own sense of self with her Virginia Woolf–like request "to keep some place where I can go to be myself." (Note the phrase said "be myself," not "be by myself.") Her choice of the words "confinement" and "cage" to describe the institution of marriage was especially telling. In fact, she was so unsure about the outcome that she bound Putnam to the "cruel promise" of letting her go in a year if they were unhappy. The most enthusiasm she could muster was her final tentative statement about trying to do her best and "give you that part of me you know and seem to want." Such lack of self-esteem, very much out of character with her general approach to life, was probably brought on by her deep ambivalence about marriage. It was almost as if she did not think any man would want her as is.

Amelia Earhart had reason to be gun-shy about the institution of marriage. For aspiring women of the nineteenth and early twentieth centuries, marriage usually meant the end of any aspirations for full lives beyond the household. Without access to reliable birth control, marriage meant children, perhaps as many as four or five, who limited women's ability to find independent work.[51] Moreover, society disapproved of married women working, or more accurately, of middle-class women holding employment outside the home. (What working-class women did was not so tightly constricted.) An independent-minded woman of an earlier generation, one born in the 1870s rather than the 1890s, would likely have steered clear of the institution of marriage as death to her chances for making something of herself. The choice was starkly presented as marriage or career, and many aspiring women remained single in order to lead productive lives, often in the company of like-minded women. By the 1920s and 1930s there was more support—and more precedent—for combining marriage and career, but the burdens were still steep. For a woman of independence and ambition to contemplate marriage was still something of a leap of faith.[52]

Why did Amelia finally decide to marry G.P.? He had assured her that he would not be a traditional husband who expected his wife to have dinner ready when he came home each night. Men with enlightened feminist attitudes (and incomes to pay for servants), especially ones who could also help by managing their wives' careers, were in rather short supply in the 1930s. Furthermore, a chain of events in Amelia's family life in 1930 might have predisposed her toward taking the plunge: her father had just died in September, her sister, Muriel, was pregnant, and her mother continued to be unable to live on her own. Maybe she got tired of people challenging her about when she was going to get married. After all, she was already thirty-three years old. (Putnam was forty-three.) Perhaps she married just to get it out of the way, to stop the questions.[53]

Maybe she was in love. An interview that Earhart gave a few years after her marriage, and after the escape clause had not been invoked, gives further clues to the stages leading up to her marriage and her reconciliation to it:

I had no special feelings about Mr. Putnam at first. I was too absorbed in the prospects of the trip and of my being the one to make it. . . . Of course after I had talked to him for very long I was conscious of the brilliant mind and keen insight of the man. . . . We came to depend on each other, yet it was only friendship between us, or so—at least—I thought at first. At least I didn't admit even to myself that I was in love . . . but at last the time came, I don't quite know when it happened, when I could deceive myself no longer. I couldn't continue telling myself that what I felt for GP was only friendship. I knew I had found the one person who could put up with me.

Surprised by her own feelings, she found herself drawn to this charismatic, perpetually in motion man who seemed to accept, even relish the independence and self-reliance that were the core of her being. Perhaps she had opposed marriage in part because she had never seen the possibility of being herself and being married at the same time. And yet, even after she finally met a man who offered this option, she still had trouble describing their obviously mutual attraction in positive terms. Only G.P., she concluded, was willing to put up with an odd creature like her.[54]

Many of the people who observed Amelia and George together, probably a majority, thought that they had a mutually satisfying and rewarding relationship, although most found her much more appealing and likable than him. There was a minority, however, that thought he had married her only because she was his most famous property. Perhaps the best way to understand this marriage is on their own terms: as a mutually beneficial relationship between two hardworking, almost workaholic individuals. Theirs was as much a business partnership as a love match, but it suited them fine. He was enormously helpful to her career. As one Earhart biographer noted, "If G.P. needed to bask in her limelight, she needed him to maintain that limelight." They spent a lot of time apart but enjoyed their time together. Their vision of marriage, and practice of it, remain remarkably modern even today.[55]

Also modern is what seems to have been a decision, or at least a mutual understanding, not to have children. Here Earhart was in line with a pattern found in surveys conducted in the 1920s: between two-fifths and one-half of married professional women remained childless, far above the national average.[56] Amelia was not skittish about children. In fact, she adored them, as her charges at Denison House, her niece and nephew, and her two stepchildren attested. Rather, it just "took too long to make a baby. . . . There are so many exciting flying things to be done." Or as she said another time to her sister, "Well, I've thought about it. And then always the air races come along or something else comes, and I just put it off." (This suggests she was practicing birth control, a cause she publicly supported in the 1930s.) There certainly were examples of women fliers who had children, and even flew with them, so she knew that it was not necessary to quit flying to raise a family. It was more, as her husband once put it, that only a "streamlined stork" with enough speed to catch up to her Lockheed Vega could ever turn Amelia and George into parents.[57]

The issue probably would not have come up publicly at all if the wire services had not quoted George as saying, "I'd rather have a baby," while he watched anxiously as his wife attempted one of her record-breaking flights. What he meant was that it would be easier for him to have a baby than to watch his wife fly off into the horizon. Others interpreted it as an example of thwarted paternity, which they both quickly put to rest. It was left to him to note, "There was a time when I thought such matters were the business of nobody except the people directly affected." But perhaps Muriel hit it on the head the best when she noted, "She certainly would have been a different person if she'd had a baby to tie her down."[58]

One day just a year after they were married, Amelia Earhart shyly asked her husband if he would mind if she flew the Atlantic again. He replied that as long as she felt confident she was ready for it, it was all right by him. She had never forgotten the experience of being merely a passenger on the 1928 flight. For her that adventure had been "incomplete": "I had been on the sidelines when I wanted to play the game itself." Having received far more credit than she felt she deserved in 1928, "I wanted to justify myself to myself. I

Amelia Earhart and the Lockheed Vega she flew solo across the Atlantic
in 1932. This plane is now on display at the Air and Space Museum in
Washington, D.C.

wanted to prove that I deserved at least a small fraction of the nice
things said about me."[59]

On May 20, 1932, the fifth anniversary of Lindbergh's solo flight
to Paris (one wonders if Putnam, ever mindful of publicity, had a
hand in that), Amelia Earhart took off from Harbour Grace, New-

foundland, in her single-engine bright red Lockheed Vega. The weather was so poor that she spent most of the next fourteen hours socked in the clouds, flying blind with her instruments. A few hours out of Harbour Grace her altimeter failed, meaning that she was unable to gauge her altitude. When ice and slush began to build up on her wings, necessitating a descent to a lower altitude, she had no way of knowing how close she was to the ocean's waves as she dropped down through the clouds. She was also troubled by an exhaust manifold that caught fire and noisily reverberated throughout the flight. Nevertheless, she pushed on. No wonder she didn't get sleepy. These mechanical problems made it impossible for her to try for Paris, her original goal, so she landed in the small village of Londonderry, Northern Ireland. After telephoning G.P. ("Oh, yes," she replied sweetly to a reporter, "the first thing I do always is to check in like a good girl"), she flew on to her second tumultuous welcome in London, one which she felt she had finally earned.[60]

Of all of Amelia Earhart's aviation accomplishments, her 1932 Atlantic solo was probably her most noteworthy and most widely praised feat. She was the first person since Lindbergh to fly the Atlantic solo, her crossing was done in record time, and she was the first person to have crossed the Atlantic by air twice. She was honored by the Distinguished Flying Cross from the U.S. Congress; the Harmon trophy; the Legion of Honor from the French government;[61] and the Gold Medal of the National Geographic Society, presented by President Herbert Hoover. The presentation of the society's medal put Earhart in the elite company of the twelve men who had received the medal since 1906, including polar explorers Robert E. Peary and Roald Amundsen, Admiral Richard Byrd, and Colonel Charles Lindbergh. Ten thousand people requested tickets to the National Geographic function, and thousands more listened to the live radio broadcast on NBC.[62]

Characteristically Earhart downplayed the significance of her flight, insisting that it had "meant nothing to aviation," except perhaps to suggest that regularly scheduled transatlantic crossings would soon become commonplace. She repeatedly stressed, "I flew the Atlantic because I wanted to." To her mind this was not a selfish reason.

"To want in one's heart to do a thing, for its own sake; to enjoy doing it; to concentrate all one's energies upon it—that is not only the surest guarantee of its success. It is also being true to oneself." Her justifications show how seriously she took her own motivations as the driving force behind her dazzling public accomplishments: "If there is anything I have learned in life it is this: *If you follow the inner desire of your heart, the incidentals will take care of themselves.* If you want badly enough to do a thing, you usually do it very well; and a thing well done, as society is organized, usually works out to the benefit of others as well as yourself." What did G.P. think of all this? "My husband is a good sport. He does not interfere with my flying and I don't interfere with his affairs."[63]

Those kinds of "follow your own heart" homilies fit well into the American tradition of self-help, individualism, and self-reliance. But Earhart's message had a gendered aspect, a decidedly feminist twist which she mentioned repeatedly and forcefully, but never stridently, in her interviews. The rationale for her flight—and, by extension, for a wide range of female activities—was quite simple: "that women can do most things that men can do." As she said in her 1932 book *The Fun of It* (whose title captured her experimental approach to life): "I chose to fly the Atlantic because I wanted to. It was, in a measure, a self-justification—a proving to me, and to anyone else interested, that a woman with adequate experience could do it." She was especially pleased because her flight disproved the contention of noted British aviator Lady Heath that Atlantic flying was not for women. Again Earhart demurred: "I see no reason why a woman, properly qualified, should not fly the ocean as well as a man, given a suitable plane and favorable weather conditions." At a White House ceremony honoring her for her flight, she succinctly captured the links between aviation and feminism: "I shall be happy if my small exploit has drawn attention to the fact that women are flying, too."[64]

The hundreds of telegrams, tributes, and letters that poured in after the 1932 solo testify that women in the United States, indeed throughout the world, took Amelia Earhart's individual triumph as a triumph for womanhood. Writer Fannie Hurst cabled, "Amer-

Amelia Earhart after completing the first solo nonstop transcontinental flight by a woman in August 1932. Even after nineteen hours in the air, her silk scarf is perfectly knotted and she seems totally in control.

ican women are proud today." Suffragist Carrie Chapman Catt telegraphed, "Your splendid achievement reflects glory on American womanhood," as did hundreds of women's clubs, chambers of commerce, and women's professional groups, which reached out to embrace her personal victory as one for their sex.[65] First Lady Lou Henry Hoover spoke for many of the older generation when she remarked: ". . . if a girl was to fly across the Atlantic and so, in a sense, represent America before the world, how nice it is that [she] was such a lovely person as Miss Earhart. She is poised, well bred, lovely to look at, and so intelligent and sincere." This refrain, first heard in 1928 and echoed throughout Earhart's career, represents a key to her appeal.[66]

This 1932 flight marked the high point in feminist identification of Earhart's accomplishments as steps forward for all women, an interpretation that she herself encouraged and that the media fully promoted. President Herbert Hoover cabled his congratulations in just such terms: "You have demonstrated not only your own dauntless courage, but also the capacity of women to match the skill of men in carrying through the most difficult feats of high adventure."[67] For the rest of her public career Earhart continued to speak out for women's causes and to represent her accomplishments in the air as progress for feminism. But none of her later flights, including her record solo flight from Hawaii to the mainland in 1935 and her world flight in 1937, was ever interpreted in such feminist terms as the 1932 solo.

With all the mythology surrounding Amelia Earhart's last flight in 1937, it is hard to assess her career separately from the ongoing mystery of her disappearance. Without that dramatic denouement, however, it seems likely that Amelia Earhart would have been remembered primarily for the skill, daring, and courage demonstrated in flights like the 1932 Atlantic solo rather than the 1937 flight when her career was winding down. This is the Amelia Earhart we should remember and celebrate, without letting the unsolved mystery of her disappearance cloud our historical memories. It is the life, not the death, that counts.

Gender and Aviation

Two events occurred in 1935 which capture aviation in transition. In January 1935 Amelia Earhart was the first person, male or female, to solo between Hawaii and the mainland. On landing in Oakland, her plane was mobbed by admirers and well-wishers who had gathered in anticipation of her arrival. "My landing was in marked contrast to that of the solo Atlantic flight," Earhart dryly told readers of the *National Geographic*. When she had landed in Northern Ireland after her 1932 solo, her "I'm from America" made no impression on the locals. "At Oakland I did not have to explain whence I came."[1] The feat received front-page coverage throughout the country, a reminder of Earhart's unchallenged status as aviation's best-known female figure as well as the ongoing appeal of record-breaking flights and daring exploits well into the 1930s.

Just ten months later, on November 22, 1935, more than twenty thousand people turned out in San Francisco to watch Pan American Airways' *China Clipper* take off on the first direct transpacific flight. This flight, offering regularly scheduled commercial air service, was the wave of the future. In a fanciful image the two aircraft—Amelia Earhart's small single-engine Lockheed Vega and Pan Am's huge four-engine flying boat, complete with sleeping berths, lounges, and dining areas—could almost have passed in the skies over the vast Pacific Ocean, the one heading east, the way of the past, and the other heading west, the way of the future.[2]

"Ours is the commencement of a flying age," Amelia Earhart noted in 1928, "and I am happy to have popped into existence at a period so interesting." She called aviation "this modern young giant" and noted, "No other phase of modern progress continues to maintain such a brimming measure of romance and beauty coupled with utility as does aviation." In many ways Earhart straddled two eras in aviation: that of the barnstorming, record-breaking, front-page-news pilot whose exploits (his or hers) received as much coverage as the World Series or a championship boxing match and the next stage represented by the emergence of a commercial aviation industry in the United States. Many of the opportunities that came her way, and some of the constraints, were grounded in the broader developments of aviation in the 1930s. One of the most significant was the way in which gender affected the course of modern aviation.[3]

Aviation was a new profession, seemingly free from the gender expectations and sex typing that limited women elsewhere. Women were getting in near the beginning, yet the deck was stacked against them. From hindsight, it is clear that the industry developed along sex-segregated lines that marginalized women. They were welcomed as stewardesses but banned as pilots; they could demonstrate light sports craft but were denied access to heavier commercial and military aircraft; except for an occasional woman in the front office to deal with the "woman's angle," they were frozen out of the business side. To be sure, individual women found opportunities in this new profession, and many embraced the freedom of the skies. The late 1920s and 1930s represented a golden age for the woman pilot. But at the end of the decade women pilots had been excluded from the next stage of development—that of commercial aviation—and their marginalization was cemented by World War II. The postwar world of aviation was very much a man's world, although strong-minded and talented individual women continued to play a role.

In the 1930s, however, Amelia Earhart and the other women pilots who took to the air did not know what the outcome would be, and they were optimistic about the future. If women proved themselves, opportunities would expand and prejudice would recede. "Each accomplishment, no matter how small, is important," Earhart told fellow pilot Louise Thaden. "Although it may be no direct contribution to the science of aeronautics nor to its technical development, it will encourage other women to fly. The more women who fly, the more who become pilots, the quicker we will be recognized as an important factor in aviation."[4] The course of aviation did not prove to be so simple, but that did not keep women like Amelia Earhart from trying—and flying.

Americans in the interwar years were fascinated by flying and aviation. The term "air-minded" was coined to describe this new orientation. Being "air-minded" entailed "having enthusiasm for airplanes, believing in their potential to better human life, and supporting aviation development." This fascination, which predated Charles Lindbergh's 1927 solo, translated into what one historian has called the "winged gospel," a secular creed about the promise of the future which was promulgated with the intensity of evangelical religion. In this world view, aviation would reorder human society and promote world peace by breaking down isolation and distrust. When everyone took to the air, society would be transformed along the lines of democracy, freedom, and equality—and perhaps even women's liberation. The well-known British aviator Lady Heath recited this ditty in 1928: "Woman's place is in the home, but failing that, the airodome."[5]

Amelia Earhart believed devoutly in "air-mindedness," and she used her public platform to advance the creed. She told the public,

"Not to have had a ride in an airplane today is like not having heard the radio." Like so many Americans who subscribed to the "winged gospel," Earhart envisioned a future in which every citizen flew as a matter of everyday life: "To the newer generation a plane isn't much more unusual than an automobile." In addition to aviation as a form of transportation, she saw flying as a sport, just like tennis or horseback riding, adding that "anyone, whether expert or not, who likes sports generally probably will enjoy flying, either as passenger or pilot." Tradition-bound women must work especially hard to become air-minded, if only to keep up with their children. "The year 1929 is ushering in the Flying Generation," Earhart reminded readers of *Cosmopolitan.* "And the stratagem of it all is that the elders must not let themselves be left behind." Said the protagonist in Dorothy Verill's 1930 *The Sky Girl,* one of the many books geared to the youthful female flier: "I am sorry for the girls who lived in the years before flying was possible."[6]

Earhart also envisioned large potentialities for women's advancement through aviation. In a period without an active feminist movement, the woman pilot was an excellent symbol of women's emancipation in the postsuffrage era. In 1930 journalist and amateur flier Margery Brown explicitly linked aviation with women's liberation when she exulted, "Women are seeking freedom. Freedom in the skies! . . . The woman at the wash-tub, the sewing machine, the office-desk, and the typewriter can glance up from the window when she hears the rhythmic hum of a motor overhead, and say, 'If it's a woman she is helping free me, too!' " In Brown's construction, "a victory for one woman is a victory for all. . . . A woman who can find fulfillment in the skies will never again need to live her life in some man's spare moments." Pilot Louise Thaden put it more forthrightly: "Flying is the only real freedom we are privileged to possess."[7]

This wonderfully optimistic, and in retrospect remarkably naïve, view of human progress lasted for only a generation or two. Technological breakthroughs in the manufacturing of aircraft and the expansion of commercial aviation supplanted the individual heroes and heroines of the earlier decades. The rise of militarism worldwide in the 1930s focused attention on the airplane not as a model for beneficent social change but as a potential weapon of destruction, a view confirmed by the course of World War II. With the ebbing of the dream of "mass personal flight," the unrealistic belief that everyone would be as familiar with flying an airplane as driving a car, the "winged gospel" lost appeal.[8]

What is most remarkable, in fact, is the speed with which the aviation industry outgrew its youth and adolescence and, in the metaphor favored by most aviation experts at the time, settled into a young maturity. It took railroads half a century to complete a cycle of pioneering, merger, regulation, and stabilization; the airlines did it in just over a decade, between 1925 and 1938. There were several important milestones, beginning with the 1925 awarding of government contracts for airmail delivery. "Air mail is the very root of the modern airline," according to experts, because such guaranteed revenues provided the margin of profits in the period before transportation of passengers was extensive enough to make an airline viable.[9]

Even after the so-called Lindbergh boom of 1927 to 1929, there still was not much money to be made in aviation. That did not keep people from starting up airlines, however. Between 1927 and 1930 the number of fledgling airlines increased from sixteen to forty-seven, although the number had dropped back to thirty-four by 1932. The impact of the deepening depression and the movement toward consolidation and merger caused the shakedown. By early in the thirties the outlines of major airline dynasties, including United, American, TWA, Eastern, and Northwest, were firmly in place, and these companies were to dominate the domestic and, in the case of Pan American, the international markets until airline deregulation in the 1970s.

The development of modern aircraft, epitomized by the DC-3 which went into service in 1936 and quickly became the most influential piece of aircraft equipment in history, had a huge impact on aviation. Just comparing photographs of the aircraft of the 1920s, which featured open cockpits and canvas wings, with those of the streamlined metal craft of less than a decade later shows how quickly and dramatically the changes occurred. The technological and engineering breakthroughs that produced safer craft such as the DC-3 offered an airline a capacity large enough to generate profits through transporting passengers (the original DC-3 held twenty-one passengers) rather than be totally dependent on government airmail contracts. In conjunction with the improvements in night flying, instrument flying, and the construction of more airports and landing strips (many of them financed after 1933 by such New Deal public works programs as the Federal Emergency Relief Administration, Civil Works Administration, Public Works Administration, and Works Progress Administration), an industry based on transporting passengers for business and pleasure was now possible. These developments went forward even in the face of the Great Depression.

The other major influence on the shape of commercial aviation in the United States was government intervention. Airlines actively sought such involvement, including federal regulation, to bring order to their chaotic industry. The process began in the 1920s, with the passage of the 1926 Air Commerce Act. Walter Folger Brown, the postmaster general during the Hoover administration, used the awarding of airmail contracts to foster his own vision of what American aviation should look like. Instead of promoting a series of short individual lines, Brown wanted an integrated system, with several transcontinental routes at its heart intersected by extensive north-south feeder routes. The next major step by the federal government occurred in 1934, when President Franklin Roosevelt decided to cancel airmail contracts and have the army fly the mail instead. A series of terrible air crashes soon led to a rescinding of that ban, but the resulting confusion and scandal, coupled with the effects of the depression, harmed the industry. The passage of the Civil Aeronautics Act in 1938 was designed to increase public confidence and bring order to the industry, as it did. With its passage the airlines entered the stage of a mature transportation industry.

Amelia Earhart was very much involved in the industry side of commercial aviation. Several airlines sought the endorsement and expertise of this first woman to fly the Atlantic and a public figure

You need celebrities to inaugurate an airline, in this case the first
westbound flight of Transcontinental Air Transport (TAT) on July 9,
1929. Amelia Earhart is on the far left, Charles and Anne Morrow
Lindbergh on the right. TAT, also known as the Lindbergh line, was the
forerunner of the modern TWA.

closely associated with the excitement of aviation. But her roles
were more ceremonial than substantive (she joked about being a
"chronic vice-president"[10]), her activities usually limited to goodwill promotion tours. And since airlines were struggling financially
in these years, the compensation she received was usually along the
lines of a token dollar a year, plus the opportunity to fly free on the
line, actually a substantial benefit during the depression.

Amelia Earhart's first business association was with TAT
(Transcontinental Air Transport, later absorbed into TWA), which
she joined as assistant to the general traffic manager in August 1929.
Traffic departments, despite their somewhat unwieldy names, were

really promotional bureaus set up to obtain business. TAT promised passengers coast-to-coast passage in forty-eight hours by flying during the day and taking the train at night, because night flying, especially over mountaineous regions, was still too rudimentary. Charles A. Lindbergh was one of the line's backers, and TAT built on the goodwill generated by his name by advertising itself as "the Lindbergh Line." Former West Point athlete Eugene Vidal, later head of the Commerce Department's Aeronautics Bureau in the New Deal, and Paul ("Dog") Collins, a former World War I ace and airline leader, were also involved in running the airline. But TAT never really turned much of a profit. It did not save all that much time over the fastest train from coast to coast and was much more expensive. The year 1929 was just too early to make a go of an airline primarily devoted to passenger travel.[11]

Between the fall of 1930 and mid-1931 Amelia Earhart turned her promotional skills to the Ludington Line, a forerunner of modern shuttle service between New York and Washington. The New York-Philadelphia-Washington Airway Corporation, of which Earhart was a vice-president, offered hourly service on the heavily traveled East Coast corridor for a round trip fare of $23.75. The idea was to make it seem no more unusual to fly from New York to Washington than to drive or take the train. But when the Ludington Line failed to get airmail contracts (its short line did not fit the integrated system envisioned by the postmaster general), it was sold to Eastern Transport in 1933.[12]

The third commercial venture with which Earhart associated herself offered air service between Boston and Bangor, Waterville, and Portland, Maine. This airline was a subsidiary of the Boston and Maine Railroad. It started up in 1931, then quickly suspended operations because of the depression. It resumed service in 1933 and 1934 but once again failed to sustain itself, despite the publicity-grabbing strategy of having Amelia Earhart fly on many of the planes as a roving goodwill ambassador.[13]

Amelia Earhart's three commercial affiliations suggest the turn-over and widespread failures common to the airline industry in the uncertain business climate of the early 1930s. Aviation struggled to convince potential passengers that flying was safe, convenient, and not prohibitively expensive. In some ways, aviation had to disabuse the public of the very things—romance, excitement, daredevil feats—that had proved fascinating in the 1910s and 1920s. This proved no simple task. In the early 1930s very few Americans were flying at all—perhaps 500,000 out of a total population of around 125 million. Fear, as much as fare, kept Americans (and American airlines) on the ground.

Many of Amelia Earhart's public activities between 1928 and 1937 were directed at overcoming popular fears about commercial aviation, especially women's supposed resistance to flying. Earhart's job with the traffic department of TAT was specifically created so that she could provide "the woman's angle." "My job was to sell flying to women, both by talking about it and by watching details of handling passengers, which were calculated to appeal to feminine travelers." The very fact that women like Amelia Earhart flew regularly was used to show the public how easy and safe aviation was.[14]

"Vocal salesmanship" was how Amelia Earhart described her extensive speaking tours to promote aviation to women's clubs, college women, professional organizations, men's groups, and anyone else who would listen. She often began her lectures by asking for a show of hands of how many in the audience had flown. (She even did this once in an appearance at a prison, and a surprising number of the inmates' hands went up.) She then asked the nonfliers, Would they go if offered a free ride? How many would not? It was that last group that she was especially interested in, since it was assumed that they would primarily be women or the husbands of women who forbade them to fly. The industry referred to this problem in shorthand as "Father won't fly, if Mother says he can't." Note how convenient it was to exploit gender stereotypes and blame women for what was more likely a generalized, and not unfounded, fear of flying.[15]

To all these doubters Amelia Earhart had a simple challenge: "Try flying!" She was not simply trying to drum up passengers for the airlines. She sincerely believed that American women could play a vital role in the acceptance and promotion of flying and, conversely, that if they were ignorant or uncooperative, they would hold back its promising future. "Sooner or later," she noted, "the big airlines must enlist women's intelligent cooperation, because without them aviation cannot hope for success." As she told a national audience in 1930, "Knowledge concerning the air, the plane and the pilot should be the possession of every intelligent woman."[16]

The best example of the air-mindedness Amelia Earhart had in mind was that of Eleanor Roosevelt. The first lady made a point of traveling by air on official or personal business whenever she could, always making sure to follow up by casually plugging air travel in her press conference or daily newspaper column discussing the event. Eleanor Roosevelt loved to fly and even consulted with Amelia Earhart about getting a pilot's license, until FDR nixed the idea.

Amelia Earhart and Eleanor Roosevelt go skylarking at night after a White House function in the spring of 1933. The first lady wanted to take flying lessons, but the president said no.

But the two women quickly became fast friends, and Amelia and George Putnam were frequent visitors at the White House. After one formal dinner in April 1933, just a month after the inauguration, Eleanor Roosevelt, her brother, Hall, Amelia, and George slipped away to a nearby airport still dressed in evening clothes for E.R.'s first night flight. The escapade was written up in admiring tones in the next day's newspapers by members of the female Washington press corps who went along for the ride.[17]

Amelia Earhart hoped that exposure, knowledge, and patronage from well-known figures would overcome women's supposed resistance to flying, especially now that "aviation has reached a point where it is no longer necessary to emphasize safety." As she noted, a few years before one had had to be a "good sport" to undertake air travel of any kind, with light airplanes open to the elements and rudimentary landing facilities. Now "the utmost in luxury can be obtained on the better air lines in this country," an improvement that was seen as especially relevant to attracting women. As examples of the kind of personal attention airlines now offered, Earhart cited the bottle of formula put on board with the luncheon tray for a mother traveling with an infant or the gardenias TWA presented to every woman leaving the plane. Given air transportation's cost, this attempt to reach affluent travelers was a savvy move, but it unwittingly played into the stereotype that women were primarily interested in frivolous extras rather than safety, convenience, and cost, which were presumed to be more on men's minds.[18]

Many of Earhart's pronouncements on air travel, while superficially pitched to the potential woman traveler, applied with equal force to the entire public. She reassured potential passengers that airsickness was rarely a problem in the newer aircraft and that there was very little sensation to flying, certainly not the feelings of dizziness experienced on roller coasters or atop high buildings. "My mother, by the way, finds flying so unexciting that she takes mystery stories with her to read along the way," she casually informed audiences. And she repeatedly stressed that air travel was much easier on infants and elderly travelers than the train was, adding, "If I had a grandmother who wished to go from one coast to the other, I should certainly send her on what I considered the best air line, confident of its being the most comfortable way for her to go. Not only would she avoid several fatiguing days and nights of train travel, but she would have unexcelled personal service. Further, if I wished to take children—even small ones—on the same journey, I should go by air."[19]

As part of her sales pitch, Amelia Earhart made repeated comparisons between the airplane and the automobile, suggesting once again how much these aviation promoters expected the airplane to become a commonplace part of everyday life. Earhart reassured audiences that traveling by air posed no greater danger than driving a car around the block. She credited women with influencing auto manufacturers to include luxury and comfort in car design, such as upholstered seats, closed cars, and striking colors, and saw a similar "woman's touch" at work in aviation.[20] "What has happened in the automobile industry is now being repeated in aviation. The leaders recognize the fact that not only safety and service but comfort too are essential factors in drawing the interest of women to the industry." But she did not want to convey the impression that "air travel is an effeminate sort of thing": "Men appreciate the things which women will not travel without, and as the amenities are introduced into flying, more and more men are using air transportation."[21]

The obvious fact that aviation, in order to win over the traveling public of both sexes, would have to develop safer and more comfortable planes than the barnstorming machines of the 1910s and 1920s was obscured by playing so blatantly to these assumptions about gender. That a feminist like Amelia Earhart who was dedicated to obliterating all differences between the sexes got caught in the trap of promoting the "woman's angle" to wear down women's resistance to flying suggests some of the contradictions involved in Earhart's stance toward modern women's advancement. In order to get women into the air as passengers, she was forced to rely on traditional gender stereotypes that exaggerated the differences between women and men. This strategy was a very different approach from that of hers for getting women into the air as pilots, which downplayed such differences.[22]

A similar trap applied to women who worked as sales representatives demonstrating planes to prospective buyers. This work could not have been an easy sell during the Great Depression, when private planes cost between three thousand and fifteen thousand dollars and up to forty thousand dollars for a passenger plane. Plus it was cash only, no credit. Far more women proportionally than men ended up in this aspect of aviation, where their sex actually worked to their advantage. As Louise Thaden recalled, "Nothing impresses the safety of aviation on the public quite so much as to see a woman flying an airplane." If a woman can handle it, "the public thinks it must be duck soup for men." Once again, the reinforcement of notions of women's inferiority was an unfortunate by-product, but at least this strategy allowed a sizable minority of women who held pilots' licenses to make a living out of aviation-based activities.[23]

As she traveled around the country, Earhart was often asked about career opportunities for women in the field of aviation. She developed a multilayered set of answers, which were generally optimistic but with a decided undercurrent cogniscent of the difficulties women faced in the aviation field, as elsewhere. "Aviation is not different from any other industry," she argued. "The same hard work is required and the same ability." Earhart's entire attitude toward advancement in the professions, aviation and beyond, was summed up thusly: "I believe if a woman showed the ability that is required of a man, she would be employed."[24]

From Amelia Earhart's statements on careers in aviation it is clear that she had a somewhat broader agenda in mind than just getting a few thousand women jobs in the midst of the Great Depression. This emphasis on opening opportunities for women, showing that women were capable, asking that women be given a chance ran like a refrain through almost all of her public statements on aviation. She was not talking about a battle-of-the-sexes competition with men (she found even the word "competitor" inappropriate, adding, "Somehow it sounds feministic!"[25]); she just wanted a chance to show what women could do.

In some respects aviation was both atypical and typical of the twentieth-century professional workplace. As an entirely new field it was somewhat less encumbered, at first at least, by older traditions and patterns that would have excluded women or minority groups such as African-Americans.[26] "Aviation Invites," Earhart titled a chapter in her first book. As Amelia's sister, Muriel, recalled, "in the aviation field, women have grown up right with the men . . . I think they were accepted in that field much sooner and much more graciously than, for instance, men accepted women doctors. It seems as if it may be because there were women in it from the beginning, and it never was thought of exactly as a man's province."[27] Such situations traditionally work to women's benefit; Hollywood in the 1920s and the New Deal's social welfare programs in the 1930s are two ready examples. But this "grace period" for women in aviation, like the industry's adolescence, was short-lived. As in other areas, old traditions and prejudices quickly asserted themselves.[28]

Most people who queried Earhart about careers in aviation had in mind becoming pilots, the most visible and glamorous job. She always tried to discourage those who were drawn to aviation for the wrong reasons. "I should not advise any girl—or man, for that matter—to take up aviation for just the thrills or the notoriety, or the money." (Ruth Nichols caricatured these thrill seekers as "devoted almost entirely to posing for pictures and using a lip stick while facing death.") Earhart continued, "There must be a sincere interest in the work, a love for it, and a hunger and a longing for it, just as there must be in a nurse before she gives herself over to that work, or an actress, or a surgeon, or a teacher—or a wife. Of course not everyone can find just the right work, but those who can are fortunate; there is nothing more satisfying."[29]

In lectures and writings Amelia Earhart stressed the opportunities in aviation besides piloting. As she reminded her audiences, it took between forty and one hundred people to keep one plane in the air, "and I don't think all those jobs need forever to be held by men."[30] Time and again Earhart tried to route prospective aviation buffs into the expanding field of support jobs critical to the development of modern aviation. But the ones most accessible to women—clerical and office workers, file clerks, interior decorators and designers for the planes—were already stereotyped as "women's work." Was it really that different being a secretary to the (male) head of an airline from being a secretary in a more traditional business? Rarely did women graduate from such jobs into executive positions in the industry; even A.E.'s front-office jobs were more in public relations than in airline management, and she hardly qualified as an industry executive.

In the industry as a whole, men outnumbered women by about forty-four to one. On the manufacturing side, certain jobs were designated as women's—like sewing and cutting the fabric on airplane wings or splitting mica in spark plug manufacture—with convenient stereotypes deployed to explain why women had an affinity for these specific jobs. (This pattern also operated in the electrical and automobile industries, except the jobs designated as suitable for women were different.[31]) But there was no real logic in these assignments; their main function was to keep the lines clearly demarcated between men's higher-status, higher-paying work and the less lucrative jobs open to women. When challenged, one vice-president said candidly, "Well, the women will work for less so you can't blame the factory manager for cutting his costs any way he can."[32]

As the decade wore on, one job went increasingly to women: that of stewardess or hostess (at the beginning the terms were used interchangeably). United Airlines hired the first flight attendants in 1930, and by 1936 there were 264 women flying (and 41 stewards; Pan American preferred men). Prospective attendants had to be unmarried, small (no more than 120 pounds and five feet four inches), and under the age of twenty-five. Since their main function was to allay passenger anxiety about flying and to pamper the predominantly (75–80 percent) male passengers, airlines sought the all-American girl, not Hollywood show types. The initial requirement that they be nurses was not so much because they might need medical training in air emergencies as because nurses were accustomed to hard work, discipline, and responsibility, which would help calm nervous passengers in the air.[33]

At first these hostess jobs were very glamorous; a typical *Literary*

Digest article in 1936 was titled "Flying Supermen and Super-women." (The supermen in the title were pilots, not stewards, but this tendency to put pilots and stewardesses in the same category, with the corresponding presumption that the positions were roughly equal in prestige and adventure, was common.) Those flight attendants who survived the rigorous screening process were seen as "pioneers" in the air, working in an entirely new profession for women devoted to "adventure, excitement and opportunity for achieving insight into human nature with the bars down." But fairly quickly the job of stewardess was revealed as just another nurturing function performed by females to domesticate the skies. Olette Hasle, a hostess on United's transcontinental run, observed in 1932, "By taking our home-making instincts into the cabins of the commercial airlines, we can lend familiar aspects to which travelers may cling." Even though Hasle proudly predicted, "Very soon we are going to be able to say in aviation that 'they can't keep a good girl down!' " the post of flight attendant quickly turned into a dead-end job. Training as a stewardess never led to the cockpit, unless, of course, she married a pilot. But that meant she lost her job since marriage was cause for immediate grounding in aviation as in many other professions like teaching. There was no way to win![34]

Women who wanted to train as pilots faced especially large obstacles, especially if they wanted to make a career out of it. Women were held back by the two *T*'s—tradition and training, or lack thereof. Boys could get their training through the military or by hanging out at the local airstrip, but who wanted a female "grease monkey"? Needless to say, Earhart was critical of the role socialization that made women piemakers and men mechanics: "If women were born into the intensely mechanical world that shapes men, they could probably grind the valves of the family automobile as dextrously as husbands and brothers do now." To overcome the handicap, she hoped for "some genial philosopher" to "provide a huge free shop filled with tools where women could play and build things unhampered and unlaughed at." Only when "the strong opinions of an airminded generation of school girls" united to challenge and overturn the "fallacious barriers" that kept women from vocational training would this "unfair and unjust discrimination" cease.[35]

Until men and women had more equal conditions from childhood, Amelia Earhart preferred not to rise to the bait of whether women would ever be as great aviators as men. Ad-libbed a Boston reporter in 1932: "The temptation to brain the one who puts such a query must be strong, but if Miss Earhart felt such an urge she concealed it magnificently." Earhart replied: "I don't think they [women fliers] have had a fair trial. Until we have the knowledge that an equal number of women pilots have had the same background and training as an equal number of men, it will be impossible to make comparisons."[36]

One key to women's future in aviation was whether they would be allowed to fly the heavier aircraft developed for commercial aviation in the 1930s. Some pilots such as Ruth Nichols believed that women should stick to flying mainly for sport. "Piloting isn't suitable for a girl, any more than taxi-driving," she had argued in 1929. "Tell girls to discriminate between flying and aviation. I don't think many girls can earn a living at flying. Flying should be a sport, to women—that and a quick, convenient means of getting about."[37] Individual or sport flight in light aircraft was not the way of the future, however; commercial aviation was. And here women were frozen out completely.

The story of Helen Richey is painfully instructive. In 1934 the twenty-five-old native of McKeesport, Pennsylvania, beat out seven male competitors for a position as copilot on the Central Airways mail route from Washington, D.C., to Pittsburgh. Richey had more than 1,000 hours of flying experience to her credit without an accident and had set a women's endurance record of 197 hours and 5 minutes with Frances Harrell Marsalis in 1933. Central Airways' pilots were unhappy about a female's invading the male bastion of the cockpit, implying, among other things, that Richey was too weak to fly in the rough weather often encountered over the Alleghenies. But Central Airways stood by Richey, in part because of the favorable publicity her piloting brought the struggling airline. A *Collier's* article opened, "This is Pilot Richey. Yes, she's a

Amelia Earhart used the 1936 Bendix race as a shakedown cruise for her spanking new Lockheed Electra, of which she had just proudly taken possession. Note how much aircraft technology had changed in the space of a few years.

girl. She's young. She's pretty. She's a good flyer. But she's more than that. . . ." The pilots took their complaints to their pilots' association and then to the Aeronautics Bureau of the Commerce Department, which issued an advisory limiting women in regularly scheduled routes to fair-weather flying. (The Commerce Department had earlier considered grounding female pilots for nine days a month during menstruation.) This new regulation effectively made it impossible for Richey to do her job, and she resigned in frustration in November 1935.[38]

Most women aviators, including Amelia Earhart, rallied around Richey and tried to pressure the airlines into hiring women as commercial pilots. "I am not urging the employment of unqualified women in the aviation industry," Earhart had asserted earlier. "All I hope is that those who have ability and who get adequate training by some means will be given a chance to make a living as pilots, *if they wish to.*"[39] In a further gesture of feminist solidarity, Earhart asked Richey to serve as her copilot in the 1936 cross-country Bendix race, in which they finished fifth.

After Richey's resignation women were shut out of the cockpits of scheduled airlines for the next thirty years. What kept them out was not laws or regulations but total stonewalling by male pilots and the aviation industry, which made it clear that women were not welcome as pilots and would not be accepted if they dared try to break in. None did. During the same period token women could make it as doctors, lawyers, journalists, and the like. Not so as commercial pilots.

As the treatment of Helen Richey suggests, women faced outright discrimination, including raw male prejudice and hostility, as they tried to make their way in aviation. When Blanche Noyes was being tested for her transport license (the highest ranking), the male examiner told an onlooker that she had better be good "or I'm going to flunk her on general principles, because she's a woman." Many male pilots ascribed to women the same negative traits given to women drivers: instability, flightiness, nerves. Ran one typical comment: "If a woman had to make a forced landing she would pick out a field, and immediately change her mind; pick out another, get nearly there; change her mind again, start back to the first—and crack up midway between them!" Any kind of personality trait associated with women was automatically held against them, despite levelheaded attempts to show that the stereotypical behavior might actually make women better pilots. "We hear much of women's 'nerves,' " observed Earhart, trying to educate the skeptical. "A woman can sew, watch two or three things on the stove, keep an eye on three or four children, and remain unperturbed. Half an hour in a similar situation for a man completely shatters his nervous system."[40]

At base, widespread skepticism greeted the notion that women were capable of flying, despite all the evidence to the contrary. Earhart noted that if a man and a woman emerged from a plane, the public always assumed that the man had really done the flying: "It always happens that if a man is along, whether or not he has ever been off the ground before and though he may sleep in the cockpit all the time, he is invariably termed a 'co-pilot.' " When male aviators crashed, it was usually seen as an equipment problem or bad luck; when women had mishaps, such as in the first Women's Air Derby in 1929, it was their fault, confirmation that they were inept in the air in the first place. When Wiley Post and Will Rogers died in a plane crash in Alaska in 1935, no one blamed the pilots because they were men. About the only time that being a woman pilot seemed to work to an advantage, according to Ruth Nichols, was in attracting just a bit of extra attention for accomplishing anything since it was still seen as unusual.[41]

If gender stereotypes had not proved so resilient, one might have expected that technology would have neutralized or made moot the differences between the sexes. Flying a modern airplane required keen eyesight, quick reactions, and manual dexterity, not brute strength. To those who questioned whether flying heavy transport planes required more muscular strength than a woman could provide, even as a copilot, aviation editor Carl B. Allen had a good reply: "[N]o plane that can't be controlled by either sex as far as physical strength goes is a safe plane for passenger operation." According to Amelia Earhart, "With the machine age releasing her latent potentialities, a woman with a fundamental bent properly trained is the equal of a man." Or as she said on another occasion, "Women have always had more endurance than men but they have lacked power to their blow. But now in this machine age, with the machine to help them, women can equal, if not better, man's performances."[42] But as the questioning of Helen Richey's capacity to pilot in rough weather and the attempt to ground women during menstruation show, stereotypes, no matter how outmoded or illogical, still found a ready audience when so many people believed deep down that women really were not the equals of men in the air—or on the ground.[43]

For the most part women fliers, including Amelia Earhart, dealt with the ongoing discrimination and double standard by a combination of two tactics: ignoring it and just going about their business, or trying to use their own examples of individual success as a way of breaking down prejudices and stereotypes.[44] They simply wanted to be taken seriously as aviators, to be allowed to excel and compete on an equal basis with men. "Of course my belief is that work should be done by the *individual* best suited to do it, be he a man or she a woman," pushed Amelia. "I feel women must hold to it if they are to progress." But she believed as a corollary that once women had proved themselves, once they had shown they were the equals of men, they deserved equal respect: "Some day, I daresay, women can be flyers and yet not be regarded as curiosities!" That was not so easy to secure. Toward this goal any accomplishment or advance by a woman was yet another piece of evidence that "women are people in the air."[45]

Still, in her darker moments Earhart was well aware that accumulated years of prejudice and discrimination made it difficult for women to get ahead in aviation, no matter how hard they tried. "I hope women keep on trying to enter aviation," she said in 1931. "In doing so they must overcome what they have to in any business and do twice as well as men to get half the credit." Piloting was still considered a male preserve, and Earhart wondered if women would ever be admitted as pilots of passenger or mail planes on regularly scheduled runs. "Contrary to legal precedent," she realized with a sigh, women "are considered guilty of incompetence until proved otherwise," but she preferred not to dwell on the possibility of failure. Women, she noted cheerfully, "have opened so many doors marked 'Impossible' that I don't know where they'll stop."[46]

Compared with the decades before and after, the 1930s did represent a fairly hospitable climate for women in aviation. Amelia Earhart was far from the only female aviator to capture the public eye. Even though no more than five hundred women held pilots' licenses in the early 1930s compared with fifteen thousand men, women received publicity and coverage far in excess of their fairly small numbers. Who were the female fliers? Amelia Earhart claimed they were not any different from those women found in any other group: "There are slim ones and plump ones and quiet ones and those who talk all the time. They're large and small, young and old, about half the list are married and many of these have children. In a word, they are simply thoroughly normal girls and women who happen to have taken up flying rather than golf, swimming, or steeplechasing." In one sample of women pilots, a surprising 20 percent flew professionally, and most of the rest flew primarily for sport. As Earhart noted, many of these women were married, often to other fliers, and quite a few had children. These flying couples (Charles and Anne Morrow Lindbergh are the most famous example) seemed to present an appealing example of the companionate marriage. Being married also protected women from harassment at airfields, as well as squelched the inevitable suggestions that aviators were less than "full women" because of their unusual career choice.[47]

The Women's Air Derby begun in 1929 offered a chance for women pilots to come together without the inevitable comparisons with men. The first race was held in August 1929 with nineteen entrants; sixteen finished. In fact, it was a battle just to get the National Aeronautic Association (NAA) race committee to approve a format the women did not find offensive. One plan proposed a course only from Omaha to Cleveland, so that the women would not have to fly over the Rockies. Another alternative required a male navigator. Amelia Earhart was outraged: "If we can't fly the race and navigate our own course through the Rockies I, for one, won't enter. . . ." The final format featured an eight-day solo from Santa Monica to Cleveland. In a nationally syndicated column describing the beginning of the race, Will Rogers called it the Powder Puff Derby, and the name stuck. Feature writers used such terms as "ladybirds," "angels," and "sweethearts of the air" to describe the contestants. Earhart could only sigh parenthetically, "We are still trying to get ourselves called just 'pilots.' "[48]

Participant and third-place finisher Amelia Earhart pronounced the race "a most interesting and valuable experience": "The derby,

I feel, added considerably to our flying knowledge and at the same time served to increase public interest and confidence in women in aviation." Many of the contestants found the nightly chicken banquets along the way more of an ordeal than the flying itself. Even when one of the contestants, Marvel Crosson, was killed in an accident, the women did not give up. As the eventual winner, Louise Thaden, said, "We women pilots were blazing a new trail. Each pioneering effort must bow to death. There has never been nor will there ever be progress without sacrifice of human life." Seconded A.E.: "A fatal accident to a woman pilot is not a greater disaster than one to a man of equal worth. Feminine flyers have never subscribed to the super-sentimental valuation placed upon their needs." Yet the newspapers portrayed Crosson's crash as her fault and an example of women's lack of fitness to fly.[49]

The Women's Air Derby became an annual affair, and in 1932 Amelia Earhart could note, "Slowly the prejudice against women is lessening, and it appears probable that before long they will compete in major speed events on equal terms." This came to pass in 1935, when women were allowed to enter the prestigious Bendix cross-country race for the first time. Amelia was the first woman competitor, and she finished fifth. The next year Louise Thaden and copilot Blanche Noyes beat the entire field of men. In fact, women's teams took three out of the top five places that year. Jacqueline Cochran won the Bendix in 1938.[50] Yet women continued the Powder Puff Derby, enjoying the camaraderie of an all-female race. In arguments similar to the rationale behind single-sex education, they believed that the absence of men allowed women to excel and build the qualities necessary to compete in the wider aviation world and that such all-women events focused more attention on women's capabilities as pilots and competitors.

Whether women should compete in all-female races, coed ones, or both paralleled the debate over aviation records. Amelia Earhart felt very strongly that there should be separate world records for women, such as those kept in tennis, track and field, swimming, and golf. She argued, "The young woman who stays aloft for twenty hours should be given official recognition, for her feat is a criterion of women's ability. Women are on the defensive and must prove their mettle by doing things." Her reasoning took into account that women did not usually have access to equal equipment or training with men and thus were penalized in open competitions. "Consequently, it is almost impossible now for a woman to have the fun of gaining any official recognition for her best efforts. Which is sad!" So she proposed that men's and women's records be kept and "a sexless thing called a world's record in all activities, flying being no exception." As always, there was the wider feminist agenda: "Records as such may or may not be important, but at least the more of them women make, the more forcefully it is demonstrated that they can and do fly. Directly or indirectly, more opportunities for those who wish to enter the aviation world should be opened by such evidence."[51]

For a certain kind of woman aviator, getting her name in the record books held a special appeal. Setting records offered women a chance to show their stuff to prospective employers and sponsors. It also garnered publicity and exposure. In the first four months of 1929 alone, the endurance record for women changed hands five times among Bobbi Trout, Louise Thaden, and Elinor Smith, who was only seventeen at the time. Amelia Earhart, Louise Thaden, and Jacqueline Cochran competed for women's speed records, either over closed courses or for the fastest elapsed time for a cross-country trip. Women also competed for altitude records in various categories of planes: Ruth Nichols set a world's altitude record for women (28,743 feet) in her Lockheed Vega in April 1931, and Helen Richey established a women's world altitude record for light planes (18,448 feet) in 1936.[52] These records provided friendly competition among the women fliers, gave them an excuse to try out new equipment, and won publicity and potential endorsements. As always, they also served to remind the world that women, too, were flying.

For such an individualistic and competitive group, women fliers exhibited a high degree of gender consciousness.[53] One outlet was the Ninety-Nines, an organization founded by the nucleus of the contestants in the first Women's Air Derby. In November 1929 twenty-six women pilots met at Curtiss Field, Valley Stream, Long Island, to launch a group "to provide closer relationship among pilots and to unite them in any movement that may be for their benefit or for that of aviation in general." The original letter soliciting support stated, "The only purpose so far would be the tacit understanding that it is to interest women in aviation, and be a general clearing house of ideas." The organization, whose membership was open to all women pilots in good standing, "would be neither strictly frivolous nor entirely serious." At Amelia Earhart's suggestion, they took their name from the number of charter members who joined out of the possible 117 active licenses.[54]

From the beginning the group served as a support and advocacy group for the needs and interests of women aviators. It was similar to professional organizations founded by women in law and medicine which addressed women's issues not deemed significant or worthy of attention by general professional organizations such as the American Medical Association or the American Bar Association. Such female professional groups offered women the psychic space to relax and socialize ("Ninety-Nines have a friend in every airport" went a favorite saying) and not have to apologize for being a woman doctor, woman lawyer, or woman aviator.

The Ninety-Nines served a genuine purpose in a profession still defined primarily for and by men. The National Aeronautic Association could not be counted on to represent women's interests, even after Amelia Earhart became the first woman vice-president in 1931. (She resigned in 1933 not over the NAA's treatment of women but over questions about membership outreach.[55]) Nor could the all-male commercial pilots' association, which had shown its true colors by blackballing Helen Richey. The continued need for separate women's professional organizations in the postsuffrage era suggests an in-between stage of women's equality: no longer excluded from male professions but not yet fully accepted into them. Examples like the Ninety-Nines, with its combination of personal and political agendas, show the continuation of gender-specific political strategies despite women's increasing professional integration in the 1920s and 1930s and beyond.[56]

The charter members of the Ninety-Nines were a spunky, energetic, and individualistic group, the kind of women who never were stopped by statements like "No, women can't do that. . . ." The organization was run informally, with information and professional news shared through newsletters and at the yearly meetings around the time of the Women's Air Derby. The Ninety-Nines protested, as part of its goal to promote women's interests in aviation, restrictions on women's participation in races, such as limiting them to small aircraft or requiring male medical personnel to go along. It also pressured the government not to ban flying during menstruation and lobbied for the first woman medical examiner appointed in the Commerce Department. But its protests over the treatment of Helen Richey by the male pilots' organization were to no avail.[57]

Amelia Earhart served as the first president of the Ninety-Nines (1929–1933), a fitting token of the respect and admiration she received from her flying sisters. She won them over because despite all the fame and, to a lesser degree, fortune she achieved, she never was out just for herself. One small example was Earhart's "Hat-of-the-Month" contest to stimulate cross-country flying: each month she

Women aviators came in all shapes, sizes, and styles of dress. Here charter members of the Ninety-Nines gather in 1929; Earhart is the fourth from the right.

donated a Stetson hat she personally designed to the Ninety-Nine who flew into the largest number of airports. The Ninety-Nines appreciated gestures like that and was especially grateful for how Earhart always made sure that the press quoted her concerning the wider implications of her individual achievements for women in aviation in general. Blanche Noyes recalled, "I believe Amelia did more than any other to encourage women in all careers." As Phoebe Omlie said in 1935 about the "trail blazer" Earhart, "She is all woman and one that the other women of America can proudly put up as an example of their contribution to the progress of this great generation."[58]

Fellow fliers also focused on Amelia's warm and giving personality as a reason why she was such a leader and inspiration. Blanche Noyes recalled, "She was one of the most humane persons I ever had known. If she liked you, she liked you. If she didn't, she let you alone, because there was nothing catty about her. I don't think there was a jealous bone in Amelia's body." Jacqueline Cochran, who said proudly, "Amelia Earhart was my inspiration," developed a deep personal rapport with Earhart, who was a frequent visitor at the California ranch owned by Cochran and her wealthy husband, Floyd Odlum. Ruth Nichols, who was a neighbor of Amelia's in Rye, New York, admitted to "occasional twinges of envy" when Earhart beat her across the Atlantic twice but never bore her a grudge: "I felt then, and I feel now, that the achievements of any flyer, man or woman, advance the science and the understanding of aviation, and so are of eventual benefit to all civilization." Even Elinor Smith, who was later critical of Earhart's abilities as a pilot, found her warm and gracious as a person.[59]

With this range of talented female aviators, many of whom were breaking records and winning front-page coverage throughout the late 1920s and 1930s, why did Amelia Earhart emerge as the country's best-known woman aviator and practically the only one remembered today? Was it really more significant to fly solo from Hawaii to California than to win the Bendix race? To have been a passenger on a transatlantic crossing than to have set a cross-country speed record? There is no simple answer. Certainly the events surrounding her disappearance in 1937 added to her mystique, but even before then she had established herself as *the* woman aviator with her 1928 and 1932 Atlantic crossings. As an aviation historian observed in 1942, Earhart "was probably responsible for creating more acceptance for women in aviation than any other woman flyer." A four-year-old boy exclaimed, "There goes Amelia," every time he saw a plane in the sky.[60]

Turn-of-the-century Tammany politician George Washington Plunkitt once said, "I seen my opportunities, and I took them,"[61] and Amelia Earhart and her flying sisters were determined to do the same where aviation was concerned. Yet the opportunities available to women in the 1920s and 1930s were deeply affected by gender. Individual women found opportunities to excel in odd pockets of aviation (like demonstrating light aircraft or marking airways for the Commerce Department in the New Deal[62]), but their individual success did little to challenge the male basis of this developing industry. What role Earhart might have played in aviation if she had returned from her round-the-world flight remains highly speculative.[63]

The limits of custom and prejudice did not stop this talented and exceptional group of female pioneers, who forged ahead with their optimistic vision that doing what they wanted to do would also aid aviation in general and women in particular. Yet lurking within their demonstrated successes and their unbounded enthusiasm for flying were harbingers of why women would not play large roles in the future development of aviation after the 1930s. Women's participation in the ruse of "if a woman could do the flight, it must be safe and it must be easy" had unintended consequences. The theme had played an important role in overcoming the popular image of aviation as only death-defying barnstormers and heroic "bird-men." But once the public had been convinced that flying was safe and easy (what one historian has called women's role "domesticating the sky"), women aviators were no longer in such demand. Ironically, the strategy of using women to break down the fear of flying paved the way for the rise of the stewardess, the one job in aviation where women were truly welcome.[64]

Women fliers were also concentrating in areas of aviation that did not represent the wave of the future. At the time perhaps the lure of the "winged gospel" of personal flight was so appealing that Americans really did believe that flying a plane would be as common as driving a car. Ruth Nichols's casual remark—"The woman who has a car today will have a plane tomorrow"[65]—was widely, if naïvely, held. If that had been the case, women might have had a greater impact on the industry. But it manifestly was not the case, for reasons which from hindsight are far too obvious: the difficulties of landing such craft in urban areas, congestion in the skies, and, most especially, cost. In all the pronouncements about the future of personal aviation, it was rarely mentioned that airplanes were more expensive than cars and that especially in the midst of the worst economic contraction the United States had ever faced, envisioning a future in which everyone could afford not only cars but planes was patently silly. In fact, the whole "winged gospel" was oblivious of the ways in which class and, to lesser degrees, race and gender affected the democratic consumption of the airplane.

Women also found themselves caught in a trap not of their own making. Discrimination and prejudice excluded women from the two major career paths for pilots: commercial aviation and the military. In addition, women faced continuing difficulty obtaining access to the best equipment and newest technology, which manufacturers were loath to put at the disposal of mere women who had no future in the field. As a result, women did not get enough training time on new techniques such as night flying, instrument flying, or the use of radio. Instead they concentrated on lighter, less technologically advanced sport craft. Here they excelled, with their solos, endurance flights, and competitions for women's records, but they were mainly competing against other women. And the chance to compete in something like the Bendix race was open only to the very elite of fliers, male or female. They could be glamorous record setters ("headline fliers"), they could fly for sport or personal satisfaction, but they were not integrated into the emerging aviation industry. Or to put it another way, success by individual women posed no threat to the emerging patterns that structured the devel-

opment of aviation. Women's accomplishments could be celebrated, then marginalized and ignored until the next woman did
something spectacular and the patterns started again.[66]

Yet these women aviators did not feel inferior, downtrodden, or,
for the most part, bitter. Their celebration of individual achievement bound them together and kept them going, despite the odds.
More than anything else, these women wanted to be judged as human
beings, as individuals, rather than women. Listen to their voices.
Bendix winner Jackie Cochran: "But I never really wanted to copy
men or to do what men can or should do better. I only wanted to
be myself. And for me that meant flying." Elinor Smith: "All I
wanted was some way that I could hang in there and fly. And I
wanted to do it on merit, not because I was a girl, or seventeen
years old, or for any of the other reasons the reporters imagined. I
wanted to be judged on my piloting skills alone." Ruth Nichols on
British-born Beryl Markham, who was the first person to fly solo
across the Atlantic from east to west: "It just goes to show that if
women have the chance they can do as good a job as men." Or
Amelia Earhart herself: "I'm not out for any speed record, but I do
want to prove that there is no reason why a woman can't fly from
here to New York nonstop as well as a man." As she said point-
edly, "How is a fellow going to earn spurs without at least trying
to ride?"[67]

"We women pilots have a rough, rocky road ahead of us," Earhart explained to fellow pilot Louise Thaden. "Men do not believe
us capable. We can fly—you know that. Ever since we started we've
butted our heads against a stone wall. Manufacturers refuse us planes,
the public have no confidence in our ability. If we had access to the
equipment and training men have, we could certainly do as well.
Thank heaven, we continue willingly fighting a losing battle . . .
but if enough of us keep trying, we'll get someplace."[68] A determined and proud statement but also, unfortunately, an apt summary of the perhaps insurmountable obstacles that women aviators
faced. Their individualistic philosophy left them no other choice.

It's Hard Work
Being a Popular Heroine

On August 6, 1926, a nineteen-year-old girl from New York named Gertrude Ederle became the first woman to swim the English Channel, besting by two hours the marks of the five men who had previously made the crossing. "I just knew if it could be done, it had to be done, and I did it," she told one of the swarm of reporters covering the attempt. On October 11, 1927, Ruth Elder took off for Paris in a bright orange single-engine Stinson aircraft called *The American Girl* with her flying instructor, George Haldeman, at the controls. After thirty-six hours in the air, an oil leak forced them down near the Azores, where they were dramatically rescued from the ocean just before their plane exploded and caught fire. On June 18, 1928, Amelia Earhart became the first woman to cross the Atlantic by plane and was subjected to the same media madness that had greeted Ederle and Elder. In fact, so interchangeable did these three popular heroines seem to the public that Amelia Earhart was twice congratulated for swimming the English Channel and often asked, "Weren't you lucky to be picked up by that steamer? Near the Azores, wasn't it?" As she put it slyly, "Elder, Ederle, Earhart—how thoughtless for us all to have names that begin with E."[1]

What characterized a popular heroine in America in the 1920s and 1930s? She shared many characteristics with male heroes, such as Charles Lindbergh, Babe Ruth, Richard Byrd, Jack Dempsey, and Will Rogers. At first the recipient of spontaneous homage and acclaim for an act of individual achievement, she soon found herself the object of curiosity, identification, and imitation from fans and followers. Her admiring public honored the heroine's accomplishments through song, poems, and other accolades, grasped for tidbits about the heroine's life and values, and tried to establish personal relationships with its heroine through souvenir hunting, autograph collecting, and perhaps even the chance for a fleeting glimpse of the celebrity at a public function. Like heroes, heroines offered "inspiration . . . for rise in status" and served as "common symbols for identification . . . with whom the group feels a special pride and unity."[2] Amelia Earhart fitted this definition of hero worship exactly.

Because popular heroes and heroines usually burst on the scene with a dramatic feat of individual courage, they often appear curiously disconnected from their ensuing fame and adulation. Each was simply the right person in the right place at the right time. Perhaps this is what happened to Charles Lindbergh, but for all the rest, male and female, celebrity was not handed to them on a silver platter, and many found it difficult to capitalize on and sustain their initial success.[3]

Amelia Earhart's career confirms that there was no easy route to being a popular heroine. She had to make it happen, working on it practically every day of her life after her June 1928 flight had thrust her into the limelight. G. P. Putnam, her husband and manager, captured this when he drew attention to "the sheer, thumping hard work of conscientious heroing."[4] For Earhart, it meant fourteen-hour days of lecturing and receptions, answering hundreds of letters a week from fans, cranking out instant books, dealing with newsreel photographers and reporters the very moment a grueling flight finished so they could make their deadlines, and always being on display wherever she went. By dint of hard work, skill, and luck, she was able to make a viable living out of promoting herself as an aviation celebrity. "I'm really very fortunate," she admitted, "because flying is both my business and my pleasure. I've got a job I love."[5]

But her "job" had a price. Just as Amelia had quipped in the 1920s, "No pay, no fly and no work, no play," she was caught in a similar cycle in which public appearances and endorsements were all part of what was necessary to earn money to allow her to fly. *Newsweek* captured the facts of life perfectly: "Every so often Miss Earhart, like other prominent flyers, pulls a spectacular stunt to hit the front pages. This enhances a flyer's value as a cigarette endorser, helps finance new planes, sometimes publicizes a book." She told an old flying friend in 1933: "It's a routine now. I make a record and then I lecture on it. That's where the money comes from. Until it's time to make another record." She did two major flights in 1935, candidly admitting after Mexico, "I expect to make quite a sum lecturing and writing for magazines about the trip."[6] In the end she sustained public interest in her activities for close to a decade, quite a record of longevity for an American public notoriously fickle about its heroes and heroines.

It is hard to come to any assessment of Amelia Earhart's career without dealing with the overwhelming, if not overbearing, presence of George Palmer Putnam, who first entered her life as a manager in 1928 and added the role of husband in 1931. Aviator Bobbi Trout observed with more than a bit of asperity, "If I had a promotor like Putnam, I could have done the things Amelia did." One recent biographer went so far as to conclude that it was "mainly due to Putnam's brilliant management of the name Amelia Earhart that she is still remembered." The contrast between the well-liked, modest, and gracious Amelia Earhart and the opinionated, domineering, and aggressive George Palmer Putnam confused many who came into contact with them. But after all, she had married him and was a willing, if not always eager, participant in his schemes and promotions. Fellow aviator Elinor Smith emphasized Earhart's active participation in the creation of her own career: "The image of a shy and retiring individual thrust against her will into the public eye was a figment of Putnam's lively imagination. Amelia was about as shy as Muhammad Ali."[7]

From 1928 on Putnam had worked tirelessly and successfully to make the name Amelia Earhart synonymous with "best woman pilot" in the public mind, but his relentless publicizing did not always win him friends. There are legions of stories of his insensitivity if anyone got in the way of his promoting Amelia and of his crassness, sometimes highly embarrassing even to her, as he pushed her career. He came on so strong that many people could not stand to be in the same room with him. "If he went to a dogfight, he'd have to be one of the dogs," observed an acquaintance. Photographers dubbed him "the lens louse" because he always elbowed in on coverage of his famous wife. Anne Morrow Lindbergh confided ominously to her diary in 1933, "Amelia Earhart's husband hovering," while describing the aviator herself as "a shaft of white coming out of a blue room."[8]

Female aviators concurred with Anne Morrow Lindbergh's assessment of G.P. Jacqueline Cochran, perhaps the generation's most talented and versatile pilot, recounted how patronizing Putnam was to her when she first met him, saying, "Well, little girl, what's your ambition in flying?" Cochran testily replied, "To put your wife in the shade, sir." Elinor Smith, an aspiring pilot who had learned to fly at age twelve and held the women's solo endurance record, was convinced that Putnam had deliberately sabotaged her career by making sure that she did not get certain endorsements and contracts. Florence ("Pancho") Barnes, a free-spirited California stunt pilot, went even further, calling Putnam a "Svengali" and complaining of Earhart, whom she did not like, "She was a goddamned robot. Putnam would wind her up and she'd go and do what he said." Barnes's reaction was extreme. Most fliers, and many of their friends, absolved her and tolerated him.[9]

Whatever George Palmer Putnam's character flaws (and they were legion), he was enormously important to Amelia Earhart's career. "I know I'm lucky to have him, for I never could do it without his help. He takes care of everything," Amelia conceded before leaving on her round-the-world flight. If Earhart's interests were more in the aviation field, and Putnam's in the direction of publicity, celebrity, and the life-styles of the rich and famous, they nevertheless managed to strike a balance in their personal and professional partnership. "I'm a very good passenger," said G.P. "He is a very good front seat driver," replied A.E. As aviator Fay Gillis Wells recalled later, "Amelia described it herself as a marriage of convenience. But they both had a wonderful zest for living; and I think they both respected each other. She knew that he was most helpful to her, and he knew he had a marvelous commodity."[10]

George Palmer Putnam was born in 1887 in Rye, New York, into a prominent, but not especially wealthy, New England family whose name is still associated with the publishing firm G. P. Putnam's Sons. "My father was a publisher, and his father before him. My earliest recollections are of books; and of authors, whom I have never held in proper awe since." He attended Harvard College and the University of California at Berkeley but was not graduated from either institution. Choosing not to enter the family business, he set off at age twenty-one to Bend, Oregon, in 1909 to make his own way. Over the next six years he bought and edited the local newspaper, the *Bend Bulletin,* and served as the town's mayor. He also dabbled in politics at the gubernatorial level. In 1911 he married Dorothy Binney, a daughter in the family that had made its fortune with Binney and Smith Crayola crayons. They had two sons: David Binney Putnam (born 1913) and George Palmer Putnam, Jr. (born 1921).[11]

When World War I broke out, Putnam enlisted, but he did not serve overseas. The death of his older brother in the worldwide influenza pandemic in 1918 caused him to change his plans of returning to Oregon. Instead he took his brother's place at the family publishing house, G. P. Putnam's Sons, and settled his family into a spacious mansion in his hometown of Rye. The publishing world showcased the talent he had already shown in Oregon for surrounding himself with lively and interesting people, throwing good parties, and generally being in the middle of everything. He was especially drawn to adventure and exploration stories, for which the public displayed an insatiable appetite in the 1920s. For example, G. P. Putnam's Sons published Lindbergh's *We* (1927), the phenomenal best seller describing the Atlantic solo, and Richard Byrd's *Skyward* (1928), an account of Byrd's exploration by plane of the North Pole.

But Putnam had aspirations toward being an explorer and author himself. "I practiced what I preached. It seemed inappropriate to promote books about exploration without doing a bit of exploration myself. So I did." In 1926 he undertook a six-month expedition to Greenland, writing syndicated front-page stories on the voyage for the *New York Times,* and the next summer he organized a scientific expedition to Canada's Baffin Island. A fellow traveler on one of these adventures captured Putnam's seemingly insatiable need to be at the center of the action with this only slightly overdrawn characterization: "George would have stopped in the middle of a rotten plank over a chasm a hundred feet deep to broadcast his reaction to a waiting world."[12]

One offshoot of his explorer phase was a series of adventure books for young readers. His twelve-year-old son David inaugurated the series with *David Goes Voyaging* (1925), a description of being the junior member on William Beebe's expedition to the Galápagos Islands, followed by *David Goes to Greenland* (1926) and *David Goes to Baffin Island* (1927). Another book by an adventurous young author was sixteen-year-old Bradford Washburn's *Among the Alps with Bradford* (1927), the story of the teenager's hiking and climbing in Switzerland and France. In a quirk of fate Washburn was approached to serve as the navigator for Earhart's round-the-world flight in 1937 because of this prior connection with Putnam, but he was never formally offered the position.[13]

The success of Putnam's publishing ventures in adventuring, especially the Lindbergh and Byrd books, had drawn him increasingly into aviation, as had his association with the production of the successful aviation film *Wings* (1927), which won the first Acad-

emy Award for best picture. In 1928 he heard of a possible transatlantic flight involving a woman under the sponsorship of Amy
Phipps Guest. Soon he was involved in finding the "right sort of
girl" to make the flight, although both he and Hilton Railey claim
credit for discovering the young Boston settlement worker named
Miss Earhart. After the successful *Friendship* flight, G.P. continued
to advise Amelia on her fledgling career, while maintaining his usual
full plate of publishing and promotional ventures. Putnam remained
in his family's publishing firm until 1930, when it merged with
another firm. He joined the publishing venture of Brewer and War-
ren, but left in 1932 to become chairman of the Editorial Board of
Paramount, a New York-based job of somewhat vague responsibilities, which he held until 1935. But long before then Putnam was
basically functioning as a full-time manager and promoter of his
aviator wife.[14]

What George Putnam did for Amelia Earhart was part old-time
promoter (as if she were a boxing star or polar explorer), part press
agent (writing and handing out the press releases), and part public
relations counsel, a new profession in the 1920s and 1930s. As epitomized by Edward Bernays, public relations was a new way of
managing the news—not just getting publicity but constructing and
manipulating events in order to get positive results. Putnam, totally
committed to the public image of his client, was very much a manager and manipulator of events, always seeking an excuse to get his
wife's name in the paper.[15] "Here I am jumping through hoops just
like the little white horse in the circus," Earhart complained during
a particularly strenuous trip in 1931.[16]

"In the routine meaning of the term I was, I suppose, Amelia
Earhart's manager," wrote George Palmer Putnam. "Philosophically, as has been said, she felt no human being of normal intelligence should be *managed* by anyone else. Temperamentally she had
a healthy distaste for the implication of being led around by the
hand. Yet no client of any counselor ever received counsel more
reasonably—or, on occasion, refused with more firmness to act on
it!" Perhaps Putnam was thinking of the time that he had ordered
a batch of children's hats embellished with a facsimile of her sig-

nature, and she had absolutely refused to have anything to do with them because they were so cheaply made. Or of how she, fearful of not living up to advance billing, would never announce her flights beforehand, sheer torture to a publicity freak like George Putnam. But he may have had his way anyhow: three of her major flights (the Atlantic solo, a 1933 transcontinental speed record, and the 1935 solo from Hawaii) all began on Friday, finished on Saturday, and thus made the front pages in the Sunday newspaper editions with the widest circulations.[17]

One of Putnam's main functions as Amelia's manager and promoter was raising money for her flights. "I try to make my flying self-supporting," she told reporters after a record-breaking flight in 1935. "I could not fly otherwise." She never quite did break even, so tapping benefactors and taking advantage of business opportunities were a must. Here Putnam's promotional skills and wide-ranging connections in the worlds of entertainment, sports, and business were enormously useful. "After all, record flying is terribly expensive and we have to accept legitimate returns when we can get them," Putnam once said to business associate Paul Mantz. Amelia used similar words in the wake of her 1932 solo when she told reporters that she would capitalize "in any legitimate way that comes to hand. Any woman who wishes to should be able to do so without stigma." But as Ruth Nichols noted, women were at a disadvantage when it came to raising money: "The people who could finance these undertakings have not believed as we have and have not been willing to back us financially. It has been much easier for men to get backing, for the public has more confidence in the men fliers." Here is where George probably made a crucial difference in making sure that "your client's public-character wife" (as A.E. once jokingly referred to herself) had as many opportunities as comparable men.[18]

In some ways it is surprising that Amelia Earhart endorsed anything at all after her first experience. In return for a fifteen-hundred-dollar endorsement fee, Amelia Earhart "wickedly" (her word) appeared in an ad for Lucky Strike cigarettes after the 1928 flight. The copy read, "Lucky Strikes were the cigarettes carried on the

'Friendship' when she crossed the Atlantic."[19] Amelia Earhart did not in fact smoke, but she wanted to make a contribution toward Commander Richard E. Byrd's upcoming Antarctic expedition in return for his support for her trip. Byrd publicly called Earhart's gesture "an act of astonishing generosity," but others of the general public, for whom smoking by women was still unacceptable in the 1920s, were not so positive. One irate correspondent wrote Earhart, "I suppose you drink too." (She did neither.) The adverse publicity cost the newest aviation celebrity a columnist's job at *McCall's,* but Ray Long at *Cosmopolitan* quickly signed her on. She never endorsed cigarettes again, or alcohol.[20]

Endorsements were big business in advertising and product promotion, but they worked only if done carefully. The most successful ads were ones where "big names," well-known public figures with upstanding reputations, had logical links to the product; less successful, in fact almost totally discredited by the 1930s, were Hollywood types of celebrities who indiscriminately endorsed one product after another with no logical or appropriate connection.[21] Amelia Earhart was often in demand, and she endorsed or appeared in support of the following products: Kodak film, Pratt & Whitney Wasp engines,[22] Stanavo engine oil,[23] Franklin and Hudson automobiles, Lucky Strike cigarettes, women's clothing and luggage, Time Saver note cards and stationery,[24] and a mail-order kitchen firm. The endorsements of aviation products no doubt resulted in contributions of products and services to the latest Earhart-Putnam air venture, and clothing and accessories plugs were logical considering her yearly appearance on the best dressed lists. However, the endorsement that Putnam arranged for mail-order kitchen cabinets in exchange for a set of the products for a new Hollywood house they were building was not very believable; how much time did Amelia Earhart spend in a kitchen? Friends like aviation writer Carl B. Allen thought that this was one case where G.P. went too far.[25]

Less controversial, and more in line with her public image, was Amelia Earhart Air-Light Luggage. Her mother recalled that Amelia "happened to be talking one day to the man she knew who was designing luggage and she made such sensible suggestions that he asked her to give him her ideas." The result was an association with the Orenstein Trunk Corporation of Newark, New Jersey, which began in 1933, whereby Earhart received a royalty for her ideas and the use of her name. A press release called it "the first truly practical and genuine airplane luggage," able to provide both extreme lightness and great strength through its use of the three-plywood aircraft veneer wood suggested by Earhart. Alice Hughes, fashion authority of the Hearst newspapers, commented: "Everything is one-third lighter in weight than the usual travel equipment. Any who have had to pay 80 cents a pound for excess airplane baggage will appreciate this thoughtfullness on the part of Miss Earhart." Even though not that many Americans flew for business or vacation yet, she tapped a potential market for aviation-related accessories that could be used in other forms of travel.[26]

The publicity for the luggage prominently featured the aviator. Macy's did a window display which included a fully equipped model of a pilot's cabin with the displayed luggage and pictures of Amelia. Dressed in her customary traveling outfit of slacks, plaid shirt, and silk scarf, she posed for publicity shots loading the luggage into an airplane. The text stressed how she had adapted airplane technology and expertise to the design of the luggage: "Amelia Earhart, whose knowledge of things aeronautical was unquestioned, drew on available scientific data and from her own experience in airplane and other modes of travel designed the first practical and genuine aeroplane luggage."[27] Few things better capture the changes under way in aviation than a record-breaking solo pilot designing luggage for the everyday use of the airline passenger. The luggage is still being manufactured today, its appeal undiminished despite the fact that its namesake died in a plane crash.

Amelia Earhart also designed and marketed a line of clothing under her name in 1933 and 1934. Why clothing? "I just don't like shopping very much," she told an interviewer, adding, "I hate ruffles, and at the price I could pay that was all I could buy. So I decided to design clothes. They are nothing exciting, just good lines and good materials for women who lead active lives." Even though the models were promoted as sports clothes, she preferred the term

The aviator models one of her own creations. Perhaps the design on the fabric was meant to suggest an aeronautical motif.

"active clothes": "This is an era of feminine activity. The stay-at-home and the hammock girl are gone. Modern women are strenuously active."[28]

As was the case with the luggage, there was a clear rationale behind the association. The clothes had many links to flying, such as using parachute silk for fabric or fashioning buttonholes and fasteners in the shape of airplane hardware. "I have always believed that clothes are terribly important in every woman's life," A.E. said, "and I also believe that there is much of beauty in aviation—color and line that is exclusive to the air, which I have attempted to express in my sports clothes." Again and again the designer turned to aviation for inspiration: "I tried to put the freedom that is in flying into the clothes. And the efficiency too." The logo featured the exhaust trail of a plane bisecting her name.[29]

This foray into "air-minded fashions" turned into "one of the hardest strains she ever went through because she was doing so much at that time," according to her mother. Earhart did not just lend her name and a few rough sketches and ideas. She was very much involved in the development of the twenty-five designs which constituted the collection. When interviewers came to her office suite at the Seymour Hotel, Amelia was likely to be surrounded by clotheshorses, fabric samples, pins (and fan mail, overflowing in a corner). She did not, however, personally stitch up the models. The clothes were manufactured by four New York firms, with hats provided by a fifth. They were sold only in special Amelia Earhart Shops within department stores: Macy's had the New York franchise, Marshall Field held it in Chicago, and Jordan Marsh in Boston. This arrangement, common today, was unusual at the time. Perhaps it was modeled on Macy's Cinema Shop, which opened in 1933 to sell reproductions of clothing seen in current films, complete with the name of the star and the picture in which she wore the original.[30]

The advertisements for the Amelia Earhart line in *Women's Wear Daily* and women's magazines often featured the aviator herself modeling the clothes, and doing quite a professional job, too. The designs were indeed simple, practical, and comfortable, with touches usually reserved for men's tailoring. These fashions were geared to the middle-class shopper, not someone interested in haute couture. A dress cost around $30, slacks $16.75, and a tweed suit went for $55. Besides the unusual aviation details, the blouses, jackets, and skirts were sold separately. This, too, was a novelty.[31]

Yet by the end of 1934 this experiment had failed, the victim not just of the depression but of the vagaries of the women's fashion industry. The fashion industry was just too entrenched, even before the depression had cut back the disposable income of the female consumer, for a neophyte like Amelia Earhart to break into and succeed in this highly competitive, volatile market. Amelia and George didn't lose any money on the venture, but they don't seem to have made any either.

But the venture was hardly a total failure. The line of clothing brought the aviator visibility, it reflected the quality that the public associated with her name, and it allowed her to promote her view of the new active womanhood. Women could do things in these clothes, and that was precisely what she had in mind: "I made my clothes to have good long shirt-tails, that wouldn't come loose no matter if the wearer took time out to stand on her head." Here, as in so many other areas, she was definitely ahead of her times.[32]

No commercial link in Earhart's career took up as much of her time and energy as her fashion designing. Other promotions and endorsements were usually one-shot events or plugs designed for maximum publicity. "If she could find people she believed in, representing something she believed in, which would benefit from the news she could create," her manager rationalized, "she was willing and glad to make that news help underwrite her activities." She christened a new plane owned by the Parker Pen Company, the Goodyear dirigible *Resolute*, and stylish automobiles like the Essex Terraplane. She had her vision tested on top of the newly opened Empire State Building in 1931 as part of a promotional campaign by the Better Vision Institute. She went diving in a deep-sea outfit in Long Island Sound, a stunt which was covered by the *New York Times* and then written up by Earhart as one of her *Cosmopolitan* articles.[33] As might be expected, George Putnam's promotional talents lay behind most, if not all, of these stunts. As he cooed about his wife's demonstration of a parachute jump, "Nothing I have ever touched has, proportionally, attracted such wide-spread national publicity. It has proved a 'natural.' Practically every major paper in the country has carried pictures or a story."[34]

Most of these promotions took up time Amelia would rather have spent flying, so she was intrigued by a scheme George cooked up in 1931 with the Beech-Nut Packing Company. This promotion involved a twenty-one-day cross-country trip in an autogiro, a windmill type of plane which was a forerunner of the modern helicopter. The autogiro had wide commercial possibilities, mainly in advertising, and Earhart's autogiro had "Beech-Nut" written prominently on the fuselage. In addition to the national publicity generated by the trip, the need to refuel every two hours meant frequent stops and local visibility. Earhart remembered fondly the warm hospitality and genuine friendliness which greeted her and her mechanic in the seventy-six places they put down in their long tour. But even if it was fun, it was still grueling work, especially the promotional aspects. "But, alas, my autogiro could not talk, or eat chicken, or speak on the radio, or be interviewed—and its pilot, after a manner, could."[35]

Considering her husband's association with Paramount Pictures, it was probably inevitable that Earhart would find her way to Hollywood. George and Amelia were very much part of the Southern California scene, which was as great a place for flying as it was for making movies. George spent a fair amount of time on the West Coast in connection with his Paramount job, and the Putnams counted film stars like Mary Pickford and Douglas Fairbanks as their friends. On several occasions Earhart was photographed with stars such as Cary Grant, Marlene Dietrich, Tallulah Bankhead, and Gary Cooper (a mutual promotion scheme, no doubt), and it was rumored in February 1933 that she might become an adviser on upcoming aviation films. Carl Laemmle of Universal Studios had gone even further, trying to convince Earhart that she "owed it to her public" to go into pictures, but she just laughed it off. The only pictures she would have considered, she said, were ones that

Imagine the commercial possibilities! Amelia Earhart steps into the cockpit of an autogiro painted to promote the products of the Beech-Nut company in 1931. Jodhpurs, riding boots, leather jacket, and tie are the pilot's uniform.

would advance the cause of women in flying or one in which "they let me play my unromantic self, slacks, engine grease and all."[36] But she was never really tempted to try her hand at acting, no doubt to her husband's disappointment. She simply concluded that Hollywood "isn't my sort of thing" and that "I'm a transport flyer, and I'd better stick to my plane!"[37]

There are many parallels between Amelia Earhart's life as a popular heroine and those of Hollywood stars: cultivating a public image; attending carefully staged promotional events; endorsing selected products; being widely photographed and written about; working very hard at what one does. Like Bette Davis or Katharine Hepburn, Amelia Earhart could not walk down the street unnoticed; like the facts about Hollywood stars, details about her personal life and opinions were picked up by the eager media.

Another similarity was receiving a huge amount of mail. In the single month of April 1928 Clara Bow, the "It" girl, received 33,727 letters, some simply addressed to "It, Hollywood, California." In Hollywood the volume of mail was so large that stars could not possibly answer it themselves, so the studios created elaborate publicity departments to handle the correspondence, most of which consisted of requests for autographs or pictures. Very early the studio executives realized that while expensive, such promotion built goodwill and encouraged fan loyalty.[38]

Just as fans wrote to their favorite stars in Hollywood, so young (and old) admirers wrote to Amelia Earhart about their flying aspirations. The first inkling occurred after her 1928 flight: "I never knew that a 'public character' (that, Heaven help me, apparently is my fate since the flight) could be the target of so much mail," said Amelia with a sigh. Four secretaries were necessary to deal with the telegrams, letters of congratulation, commercial offers, proposals of marriage, and crank mail that poured in.[39]

For the rest of her career Earhart kept up an enormous correspondence, especially after such record-breaking flights as the 1932 solo. Responding promptly and efficiently to fan mail was an important aspect of being a popular heroine, one which the aviator actually enjoyed. Characteristically, according to her husband, "she read nearly everything that came to her." Inundated by so much mail, she tried to keep her sense of humor. She called her personal papers her "peppers" and had files marked "bunk" (for all the songs, poems, and accolades that people sent in) and "cousins" (for those who tried to establish an often fictive family connection).[40]

But the demands of her public often cut into her ability to stay in touch with friends. "I do not have much time to write letters," she told an old friend. "I dream that by working very hard I'll have some time later to watch sunsets." She confessed to an aviation buddy in early 1934, "To take a year in answering a letter is about my average rate just now. My friends suffer most, because I am continually shoving their letters aside telling myself they will understand delay while a business correspondent will not. I know my theory is unjust, for I value friends more than I do the butcher, baker, or candlestick maker, worthy souls though they may be. What to do about regulating my life and letters, I know not. . . ."[41]

But she did, at least, keep in touch with her mother and sister, often dashing off letters in the midst of her cross-country travels. The responsibility she had already assumed for her family before the 1928 flight continued once she became a successful and relatively affluent person. But the tone changed. She became patronizing, opinionated, and dogmatic as she told family members how to conduct their lives in a way she never let anyone rule hers. The now-prominent daughter treated her mother like a small child. Relationships with her younger sister, Muriel, with whom Amy lived in Medford, were not much better.[42]

Amelia was now supporting her mother entirely and helping her sister out financially, and she seemed to think that her financial contributions allowed her to interfere as well. "Please throw away rags and get things you need on my account at Filenes," she told her mother immediately after the 1928 flight. "I can do it now, and the pleasure is mine." She was still badgering her mother about clothes in 1935. "Please remember you and Pidge attract attention as my relatives so spare me blowsies. I'd prefer you to get a few simple decent clothes, both of you, not awful cheapies, so people who don't look below the surface won't have anything to converse about." Amelia, of course, was correct that people would think she was selfish if her family went around looking poor, but the peremptory tone of her request betrayed an edginess and impatience with her family that were characteristic of her dealings with them in this period.[43]

Another recurring source of recrimination was what Amelia called "the family failing about money." Sometimes she sent only half what her mother requested because "I thought if I sent the whole you would spend it on someone else and not have anything left for yourself by the first of next month." She reminded her mother, "What I send you is what I myself earn and it does not come from GP. I feel the church gets some of what should go to living expenses and I have no wish to continue that to Pidges loss."[44]

It is difficult to excuse the offensive and patronizing tone of these letters, but it does seem possible that the stress of her public career adversely affected Amelia's ability to relate freely and unconditionally to her family. Perhaps success did go to her head, but more likely it was the constant oppression of feeling that everybody wanted a piece of her. For self-protection, she had to get away from the demands of people, even her family, echoing artist Georgia O'Keeffe's plaintive cry "I have to keep some of myself or I wouldn't have anything left to give."[45] Often George was left with the task of remembering cards and flowers on birthdays, sending along monthly support checks, and settling petty squabbles and misunderstandings with Amelia's family. These responsibilities continued after her death.[46]

"Today, if you ever figure in any unusual exploit, be it a flight, a voyage in a small boat, or, say, a channel swim," noted Amelia, paraphrasing Alice in Wonderland, " 'There's a publisher close behind you who is treading on your heels.' " Of all the duties surrounding being a public figure, the aviator seems to have derived the least satisfaction from writing. She had written poetry all her life but was unable to transfer her affinity for verse into the autobiography and general nonfiction required of a public figure out to keep her

name in the news. Moreover, she found the deadline conditions
under which she had to churn out her prose especially disruptive to
good writing. As a result, she was rarely satisfied with anything
she produced.[47]

The success of Charles Lindbergh's *We* made it inevitable that
Amelia Earhart would try her hand at a similar account after her
June 1928 flight. (Would the book be called "She"? wondered one
skeptic, who accused Putnam of cashing in on the Lindbergh connection.) Poor Amelia quickly concluded that "the hop . . . was
rather easier than the writing." With a great deal of editorial guidance from George Putnam, she finished a manuscript in three weeks
while staying in Rye. "Finally the little book is done, such as it is."
She was rather unsure of the "airworthiness of the manuscript" but
sounded like a kid at the end of school: "Tomorrow I am free to
fly." Her reward from the drudgery of "writers' cramp"? A cross-
country vagabond in the plane purchased from Lady Heath. But
even that vacation soon found its way into print, as one of her first
articles as aviation editor for *Cosmopolitan.* At times it must have
seemed as if nothing she did didn't need to be recycled for public
consumption. No wonder her letter writing suffered.[48]

20 Hrs. 40 Min. truly was an instant book: Earhart finished it on
August 25, and it was in the bookstores by September 10. Earhart
and her publisher, G. P. Putnam's Sons (not coincidentally her future
husband's family firm), thus reaped the potential profits while her
name was still fresh in the public mind after her June flight.[49]

A slightly different pattern prevailed for *The Fun of It,* the bulk
of which was written in the winter of 1931–1932. Its subtitle,
"Random Records of My Own Flying and of Women in Aviation,"
captured the hodgepodge quality of the book, much of which merely
reworked material from earlier published writing. But no doubt
Putnam had impressed on Earhart the need for something fresh,
like a new book, to attract publicity and keep her name before the
public. Once Amelia informed George of her decision to try the
Atlantic solo, he timed the release of the book to the projected first
week of her homecoming. "Here, at the request of the publishers,
is a final chapter describing the flight itself—a postscript from over-

seas," she told her readers. To capitalize further on the flight, each book contained a small phonographic recording of part of the radio broadcast Earhart had made from London, a very catchy G.P. promotional gimmick.[50]

Both these books received generally good reviews,[51] although sales never approached the Lindbergh book. In fact, none of the later aviation or adventure books did; once again, his reception was unique. Readers enjoyed the autobiographical details Earhart supplied and gained a sense of what learning to fly was like. As usual, the author sprinkled her texts with feminist reminders that women, too, were flying. But in general Earhart's prose was pedestrian and lacking in drama. The books, already printed in very large type and illustrated by many photographs (often the best part), seemed padded with extraneous chapters and recycled material. She was just going through the motions expected of a public figure, and under a deadline no less.

Earhart's magazine articles were somewhat livelier, although they, too, had the sense of being written out of necessity rather than inspiration. *Cosmopolitan* expected one article an issue, so the new aviation editor dutifully circled the fourth day of each month to remind her to meet the dreaded deadline. There were just so many ways that she could write about women and flying, flying and women, women and aviation, however. (On the other hand, she very much enjoyed answering the mail addressed to her care of the magazine.) In addition, there were numerous assignments for fluff pieces in other magazines that George diligently lined up, like their joint "My Husband / My Wife" for *Redbook* or Amelia's article on their summer vacation at a Wyoming dude ranch. Probably the best articles that Amelia Earhart wrote—or rather, the ones truest to her approach to aviation and life—were not the artificially jaunty pieces turned out for national magazines but the longer descriptions of her flights published in serious scientific publications like *National Geographic*. Here she could just tell the story of her flight, what she had actually done, rather than have to entertain an audience.[52]

Her hardest deadlines involved the syndicated first-person accounts she had to write immediately following each one of her record-breaking flights. These very lucrative contracts (the *New York Times* paid twenty thousand dollars in 1928 for the story of the *Friendship,* although her part of the fee went back into flight expenses) were the bread and butter of the expensive sport of record breaking. They were also a staple of journalism at the time. G.P. was enormously successful in lining up exclusive syndication deals for each of his wife's major flights and even for some of her minor ones as well.[53]

In order for these articles to be timely, they had to be written almost the moment her plane landed. As soon as she met with the newsreel photographers and gave a few brief remarks to reporters (not too much, however, because that would detract from the value of her own account), she retired to knock out her story. "Without waiting to change from her flying togs . . . Miss Earhart sat down at her portable typewriter when she reached the Seymour and started pounding out her personal story of the flight for the *New York Herald Tribune,"* said an account in that paper after a record flight from Mexico City to Newark in 1935. "Her only concession to the strain to which she had been subjected was to order a chicken and lettuce sandwich and a glass of buttermilk sent up to her room. She nibbled one and sipped the other while she wrote."[54] If these postflight accounts were more straightforward than thrilling, they reflected the careful preparation she put into her flights, her tendency not to sensationalize or overdramatize her story, and her inevitable weariness at having to write immediately after the strain of a grueling long-distance flight.

The aviator felt slightly more at home on the radio, where she was a frequent commentator and lecturer. She must have been good at it because the Columbia Broadcasting System presented her with a medal for distinguished contributions to radio art in June 1932. Many of the major events in her public career were broadcast: the welcome home parade in New York City in 1928; the first full description of that flight from Madison Square Garden; her speeches to the National Geographic Society in 1932 and 1935. Perhaps her most exciting radio transmission was the live hookup from London over the CBS network after her transatlantic solo in May 1932, although her mother and Muriel claimed the quality was so poor they could hardly recognize her voice. She also appeared on such shows as the Friday night aviation series on WABC and on "The Inside Story," which included a dramatization and interview conducted by the popular radio commentator Edwin C. Hill. Twice she broadcast live from the air: in May 1933 from eight different points over New York City on WABC and in January 1935, when she talked to her husband via commercial radio while flying solo between Hawaii and Oakland. Radio was well entrenched in American households by the 1930s, but hearing celebrities describe their adventures was still enough of a novelty to count as entertainment. It was yet another way that links were forged between a public figure and the American public at large.[55]

But in the days before television, the lecture circuit, even more so than newsreels or radio, was the principal means by which popular figures reached the public. Here was a chance for citizens in Des Moines, Iowa, or Tacoma, Washington, to see what polar explorer Richard Byrd or humorist Will Rogers or first lady Eleanor Roosevelt was like in person. They could hear about the latest exploits of journalist Dorothy Thompson or photographer Margaret Bourke-White. Rather than the vicarious experience of radio or newsreels, lectures provided an opportunity to connect in person with the most influential political, social, and cultural leaders of their times, at least for one night.

Of course, for a public figure to draw a crowd, he or she had to have something to say. Public figures were only as good as their most recent exploit or accomplishment. Whenever Amelia Earhart's standard lecture on "Adventures in Flying" began to go stale, she would do something like make another record-breaking flight or write a new book to give it fresh material. Earhart's talks were geared to a general audience and avoided controversial subjects such as pacifism or politics, which she was freer to discuss in interviews. But she always included references to women in aviation as part of her general talk. Her ever-helpful coach G.P. tutored her to speak from note cards and synchronize her talk to the accompanying newsreel footage, and he taught her how to use a pointer without turning her back to the audience, how to ration time, and the importance of crisp endings. He also kept her posted in their nightly telephone conversations about what kind of crowd she would be addressing (a women's club luncheon, a large public speech in the high school auditorium, a tea or social) and whether she had spoken in that locality before.[56]

Life on the lecture tour was a real grind of "one-night stands" and "one hotel after another." Earhart preferred to drive to her engagements, rather than go by train; occasionally she flew. Although she always reserved the time before her talk to compose herself, she usually was willing afterward to attend an informal reception, sign autographs ("Autographing, I discover, is a national mania"), or submit to the obligatory interview with the local newspaper. She often left a lecture around midnight and then drove on to her next engagement; that way she could get a good night's sleep wherever she was going. "I drove here all the way and arrived about four thirty A.M.," she told her mother from Iowa. "It was a gorgeous night and I thought I'd rather sleep for a few hours after I reached Sioux City than to get up at an early hour and drive from some-where along the way to arrive for luncheon." Always the insatiable tourist, she noted how the roads had improved since she and her mother made their cross-country journey in 1924: "They are ele-gant now and almost as well marked as California." Usually she was on her own, although occasionally she hooked up with her husband. "G.P. meets me at Bowling Green," she wrote her mother from Knoxville. "I am not sure whether it will be more or less strenuous with him."[57]

It is hard to imagine anything more strenuous than these lecture tours. During one stretch in October 1933 she delivered 23 talks in twenty-five days; she logged seven thousand miles by car, much of it alone, in just over six weeks. In 1935 one biographer counted 135 stage appearances, before total audiences estimated at eighty thou-sand. Between September 30 and November 3, 1935, she criss-crossed her way from Youngstown, Ohio, to Michigan, on to Minnesota, through Nebraska, into Iowa, to Chicago, then down to Galesburg and Decatur, into Indiana, back up to Michigan, back down to Chicago, off to Missouri and Kansas, back to Indiana,

Amelia Earhart maintained close contact with her mother and sister, Muriel, after she became famous, and Amy Otis Earhart sometimes accompanied Amelia on her lecture tours. Here mother and daughter pose in North Hollywood, California, in 1932.

finally finishing in Wilmette, Illinois.[58] She earned between $250 and $300 for each lecture, although she was willing to take less for a charitable cause. Seven or eight lectures in a week totaled close to $2,400, a tidy sum in depression America. Lecturing became very quickly her major source of income.[59]

As might be expected, such lecture tours took their toll. Her mother sometimes traveled with her and saw the pressure first-hand: "I remember again and again after evenings when she gave a talk and answered questions, and people thoughtlessly arranged a reception for her afterward or neighbors and friends pressed in to speak or to talk to her, she came home dead tired, saying to me,

'No talkee, mother, my cocoa, good night." The stress of the 1935 tour landed her in the hospital with a flare-up of an old sinus problem and pleurisy, and she was uncharacteristically bedridden for ten days, probably one of the longest stretches she stayed put in her entire life.[60]

Not surprisingly, husband and wife often had diametrically opposed perspectives on these lecture tours. George could write blithely during the middle of one such tour, "She, herself, is about mid-way in an extraordinarily successful lecture tour which is bringing her before over 100 major audiences throughout the country—to all of which, of course, she is preaching the pleasures and advantages of flying." Privately Amelia had a less upbeat take on the whole lecture process, calling her schedule at various times "the most strenuous lecture engagement ever undertaken," "signed for the treadmill," and "unescapable." George's central role in scheduling, indeed overscheduling, the tours is clear from this note to her mother: "They were much more intensive than I had planned because the management [G.P.] kept trying to squeeze in more, and in these times I thought I might as well do as much and get as much as I could. Well, anyway they are over." No wonder Amelia loved the solitude of flying—the one time she was free from the demands of her life as a public figure.[61]

It is ironic that this world-famous aviator spent more time on the ground talking about flying than in the air, where she wanted to be. Luckily she did not mind public speaking. "I think it's only fair to say that she like any one enjoyed applause," remarked her sister, Muriel, who occasionally accompanied her on tour, "and when she had completed a lecture and had a crowded audience and had them really on the edge of their chairs, you might say, enjoying it, I think she enjoyed that." But she never craved the public stature of a celebrity. She merely wanted what celebrity made possible. Fellow aviator Fay Gillis Wells confirmed that her friend had no compulsion to be the center of attention: "Some people exhibit an aura of charisma; a brilliance lights up, and bells ring—they are center stage. Amelia wasn't like that. She didn't mind the recognition, when it was earned, but she didn't want to be on stage unless it was essential to reach her goal. If it was money she needed, she would lecture her heart out to get the dues to pay the bills."[62]

The remarkable thing, of course, was how Amelia Earhart managed to conceal from each audience any of the strain, boredom, or stress that had gotten her to that particular podium on that particular day in Anywhere, U.S.A. Clearly she took pride in what she was doing and took her role as a goodwill ambassador for modern aviation and women's rights very seriously. Even though she was not a wildly charismatic speaker, she was effective at establishing a rapport with her audience, and she knew how to work a crowd.

A talk she gave to the Daughters of the American Revolution in 1933 confirms her ease on the platform. The transcript is liberally punctuated by the annotations "laughter" and "applause" as she charmed her audience with self-deprecating stories about her celebrity. For example, she opened with the time a young boy announced after seeing a poster for her upcoming lecture, "Daddy, daddy, Colonel Lindbergh's Mother is going to lecture here." Toward the beginning of the lecture she self-consciously yet humorously gave the audience the "special sermon" she usually preached to women on aviation: "It isn't very long and I might as well preach it here because I feel that the effort will be coming on me," an introduction that provoked laughter from the crowd. She then proceeded to hold them spellbound with the story of her 1932 Atlantic flight.[63]

Further insights into her lecturing come from the recollections of those who heard her speak. "She won the people of Vermont which is not an easy thing to do," noted one satisfied customer. "We all thought Lindbergh was a marvel but our 'Amelia' has shown the world what a woman can do." Another satisfied customer remembered how when the newsreel she was showing of a postflight appearance suddenly turned jerky, she quickly ad-libbed that it really wasn't her first pair of high heels! Alice Kalousdian came under Amelia Earhart's spell at a 1932 Hunter College appearance: "There is nothing in the tilt of her head, or in the warm glow of her eyes that suggests the much interviewed, photographed, and 'autographed' personality. . . . Not for a moment has she the air of one who is being talked about and looked at. She listens, instead, like a spectator of her own career." Many people were probably just as interested in seeing and meeting her as in whatever she had to say. "Her smile and her gracious femininity were unforgettable," recalled one, "but what she said I don't recall."[64]

By 1935 Amelia Earhart had taken her place as a major aviation celebrity and as one of America's best-known and admired women. She had been in the public eye for seven years. Few of the popular heroines, male or female, who flashed briefly into public consciousness in the 1920s and 1930s and then just as quickly disappeared could make such a claim to longevity. But few of them devoted as much energy and hard work to maintaining their public reputation as she did. Nor did most of them have as hardworking and persistent a publicist as G. P. Putnam.

Whether Amelia Earhart would have been able to maintain her stature indefinitely without the unsolved mystery of her disappearance remains unclear. Ironically, this popular heroine who worked so hard at that role in the 1930s now effortlessly generates reams and reams of publicity more than fifty years after her death, and all without George Putnam cranking the handle of the publicity machine.

Feminism and Individualism

In 1935 Eleanor Roosevelt called Amelia Earhart one of the five friends she, the twentieth century's most influential woman, considered a source of inspiration.[1] As early as 1930 journalist Ida Tarbell included Amelia Earhart on her list of the fifty living women who had done the most for the welfare of the United States. Veteran suffrage leader Carrie Chapman Catt cited Earhart as one of the ten outstanding women in 1935, along with Eleanor Roosevelt, Dr. Florence Sabin, Frances Perkins, diplomat Ruth Bryan Owens, Judge Florence Allen, Anne Morrow Lindbergh, and journalist Anne O'Hare McCormick.[2] Margaret Sanger included her in the pantheon of "Famous American Women" invited to the twenty-first anniversary dinner of the American birth control movement in 1935.[3] In a National Council of Women poll citing the twelve women who had made the most valuable contributions to American progress over the last one hundred years, Amelia Earhart found herself in the company of such luminaries as Mary Baker Eddy, Helen Keller, Frances Willard, Susan B. Anthony, Clara Barton, Julia Ward Howe, Harriet Beecher Stowe, and Jane Addams.[4]

Lists of notable women by definition celebrate individual achievement. Every era has put forward and recognized talented women who shaped American history, but individual advancement was especially important to the history of women between the suffrage victory in 1920 and the revitalization of feminism in the 1960s and 1970s. The widely reported accomplishments of popular heroines, outstanding professional women, politicians, Hollywood stars, and sports figures kept alive a sense of progress for women as a group in a period when mass feminist movements were not likely to coalesce. Such celebration of individual achievement cut two ways, however. Even though individual female success stories were uplifting, they did little to inspire women collectively to mobilize for change. Furthermore, individualism as a basis for feminism failed to offer any challenge to the prevailing gender system. As historian Nancy Cott cogently observes, individualism offered no way to achieve the goal of equality other than to act as if it had already been achieved.[5]

Amelia Earhart is a perfect embodiment of the individualistic approach to women's advancement that predominated in the post-suffrage era, with both its strengths and its weaknesses. Never just out for her own personal and professional advancement, Earhart consistently identified her individual accomplishments as victories for women as a whole. This philosophy, in which the emphasis was on individual achievement, equal opportunity, and striving for political and legal equality, represented the essence of liberal feminism, a tradition which dated back to the late eighteenth and early nineteenth centuries. Perhaps the easiest way to think of liberal feminism is as "mainstream feminism," both in the sense of historically being the most common form of feminism and for its goal of integrating women into the mainstream of the dominant culture. Eleanor Roosevelt supplied this straightforward definition in 1935: "Fundamentally, the purpose of Feminism is that a woman should have an equal opportunity and Equal Rights with any other citizen of the country."[6]

Although the inadequacies of this vision are readily apparent (English suffragist Eleanor Rathbone dismissed it as "me-too feminism," and others have called it "piece of the pie" feminism),[7] it was well suited to the generations of women coming of age after suffrage had been won. This appeal was especially effective in the 1920s and 1930s, but it even sustained itself in the far more hostile climate of the 1940s and 1950s. In fact, this kind of individualistic liberal feminism may be more the norm, at least in a country like the United States, than the mass movements of the suffrage era or the 1970s. In this refocusing, Amelia Earhart's strongly articulated message of individual achievement becomes an important piece of the story of the survival of feminism in the postsuffrage era.

Except for her feminism, Amelia Earhart dabbled in politics only selectively. She took no public stand in either the 1928 or the 1932 presidential campaign and assiduously avoided displays of partisanship in her lectures or interviews.[8] But in 1936 she did campaign for Franklin Roosevelt and New York Governor Herbert Lehman. Probably the main reason she came out publicly for the Democrats was her deep friendship with Franklin and Eleanor; whether George Putnam was so enthusiastic about the New Deal is unclear, and Amy Otis Earhart remained stoutly Republican.[9] In support of the president's reelection campaign, Earhart released the following statement: "I am aligned with President Roosevelt because of his social conscience. Throughout his term of office he has fought against odds to reduce human misery. He has realized that obsolescence can affect parts of the machinery of government just as it does the machinery of industry."[10] This rather bland statement represented one of the few times in the 1930s that Earhart even obliquely mentioned the Great Depression, a dramatic example of the distance she had put between herself and her former profession of social work.[11]

The other political candidate whom Earhart publicly supported was her Rye neighbor Caroline O'Day. Like Eleanor Roosevelt, who broke the nonpartisan stance she usually maintained as first lady to endorse O'Day, Amelia Earhart lent her name when O'Day sought election as New York's delegate at large to Congress in 1934. Two years later she seconded O'Day's nomination at the state convention in Syracuse, to the delight of the assembled Democratic women. One bond besides neighborly propinquity was their shared opposition to war. Earhart once told her husband that she and O'Day would likely be packed off to a federal penitentiary as war resisters in the event of hostilities and that rather than put her skills as a pilot to the service of war, she would go to jail.[12]

Earhart's pacifism dated to her V.A.D. service in Toronto during World War I. "I realized what the world war meant," she wrote. "Instead of new uniforms and brass bands I saw only the results of a four years' desperate struggle; men without arms and legs, men who were paralyzed and men who were blind." Pacifism represented the one issue in addition to feminism about which she regularly spoke out. When a 1934 congressional committee chaired by Senator Gerald P. Nye launched a highly publicized investigation into the role of munition makers in World War I, she sent a telegram which stated in part, "I am emphatically opposed to all that has to do with war and activities of munition makers and genuinely hope your committee may curb their devious activities." She upset the Daughters of the American Revolution, a strongly prodefense organization, by opposing the development of aviation for military preparedness. Even more controversially, she told the DAR that she believed women should be drafted in war.[13]

How could a pacifist "utterly opposed to war itself" (in her own words) support the drafting of women? Earhart's reasoning was calculating and revealing. "We are citizens, paying taxes—which are too largely spent for armaments. So why should we not participate in a military system we help support? . . . To kill, to suffer, to be maimed, wasted, paralyzed, impoverished, to lose mental and physical vigor, to shovel under the dead and to die oneself—'gloriously.' There is no logic in disqualifying women from such privileges." But she had another not-so-hidden agenda to accompany her commitment to equal opportunity to experience the horrors of war: "If women go to war, along with their men, the men are just going to hate it! . . . I have a feeling men would rather vacate the arena of war altogether than share it with women." Had she lived to face the need in the late 1930s and 1940s to halt the spread of a fascist system she abhorred, her pacifism would have been sorely tested.[14]

Amelia Earhart was not a joiner. She accepted membership in only a few organizations where she felt she could really make a contribution. But her choices were significant, offering clues to women's voluntarist politics in the two decades after suffrage. The small number of groups she devoted time to had one thing in common: they all were women's organizations. Such groups, with their combination of professional networking and sisterly camaraderie, had a long history, and they proved just as necessary in the post-suffrage era as before. These memberships confirmed that even though Earhart's goal was complete equality with men, she appreciated the paradoxical situation pinpointed by historian Mary Beard: "women who can't avoid being women whatever they do."[15]

The group to which Amelia Earhart devoted the most time, and the only one in which she accepted a leadership role, was the flying group the Ninety-Nines. But she no doubt found similar kindred spirits in the Society of Woman Geographers. This group was organized in 1925 by women "who felt that there should be some medium of contact between women engaged in geographical work and its allied sciences." Membership was open only to those who had done "distinctive work whereby they have added to the world's store of knowledge concerning the countries on which they have specialized, and have published in magazines or in book form, a record of their work." Members included Mary Beard, educator Lucy Sprague Mitchell, anthropologist Margaret Mead, sculptor Malvina Hoffman, explorer Blair Niles, and mountain climber Annie Peck. In solidarity Amelia Earhart carried their flag when she flew from New York to Washington as part of the homecoming celebrations after her 1932 transatlantic solo.[16]

Amelia Earhart supported women's postsuffrage activities in various
ways. Here she joins members of Zonta, a women's professional group,
at a coffee shop after a speech in Springfield, Massachusetts, in 1934.

Earhart also identified strongly with the concerns of professional
women, especially those in business and industry.[17] The professional women's group she was most closely associated with was
Zonta International, founded in 1919 and named for the Sioux word
for "trustworthy." Its main focus was educational and promotional
work for girls and young women, and its membership drew on
women from all professions and industries. After Earhart's death
Zonta honored her memory by establishing a scholarship for girls
to study mechanics.[18]

Professional women really "adopted" Amelia Earhart. Her
achievement in the expanding field of aviation and her unswerving
support for other women in professional life captured their hopes
for the future. In December 1937 the first major fund-raising dinner

for the World Center for Women's Archives, an attempt to collect materials and personal papers documenting women's contributions to modern life, honored Earhart posthumously by accepting the log, charts, and maps of her last flight along with a manuscript of her book.[19] The one discordant note to the Women's Archives event came from Mary Beard, who wanted it to have "some more intellectual aspects" than those provided by an aviator.[20] Amelia Earhart was not the first to be on the wrong side of historian Beard's quirky feminism, or the last. But such criticisms of Earhart from the leadership of the organized women's movement were extremely rare. Far more typical was the introduction supplied by Marie Mattingly Meloney at the September, 1934 *New York Herald Tribune* Women's Conference on Current Problems: "I present to you evidence against a lost generation. No generation which could produce Amelia Earhart can be called a lost generation."[21]

No group adopted Amelia Earhart more enthusiastically or totally than the National Woman's Party. In 1935 the NWP leader Anna Kelton Wiley called Earhart "one of the great women of today and the *greatest exponent* of *courage* and open-mindedness *in our organization.*" Like Zonta, the National Woman's Party established a fund in Earhart's honor after her disappearance. Under the leadership of former suffragist Alice Paul, the NWP was one of the few organizations that self-consciously called itself feminist in the 1920s and 1930s. Its vision of feminism focused on equal rights, the name of its journal, whose masthead proclaimed the organization's intention "to secure for women complete equality with men under the law and in all human relationships." The primary focus of its political energy after 1923 was the passage of the Equal Rights Amendment.[22]

Amelia Earhart's individualistic stance toward women's advancement meshed well with the NWP equal rights philosophy, and she became something of a "pet" of the party in the 1930s. Whenever Earhart did anything of note, the activities of the "ardent young feminist" were praised in an editorial or reported in the "Feminist Notes" section of *Equal Rights*. After the 1932 flight the cover of *Equal Rights* noted that Earhart's "triumphant flight across the Atlantic has given wings to the Feminist movement": "All women hold their heads a little higher because of her heroic courage. Her victory has brought the victory for Equal Rights appreciably nearer."[23] The magazine did this for other prominent women as well, even those like Eleanor Roosevelt who opposed the ERA. At the hands of the NWP there was a feminist connection to practically every event, even Charles Lindbergh's flight. How? His father had voted for woman suffrage![24]

Amelia Earhart put her name and time at the disposal of the National Woman's Party more than any other organization with the exception of the Ninety-Nines. In 1932 Earhart led a NWP delegation to President Herbert Hoover (who just months earlier had presented her with the National Geographic Society medal at a White House ceremony) to plead for equality for women in all aspects of life. The twenty-five-minute session with the president was reported on the front page of the *New York Times*. The aviator told the president: "I know from practical experience of the discriminations which confront women when they enter an occupation where men have priority in opportunity, advancement and protection. In aviation the Department of Commerce recognizes no legal differences between men and women licensed to fly. I feel that similar equality should be carried into all fields of endeavor, so that men and women may achieve without handicap because of sex."[25]

Over the next several years Earhart responded promptly to calls for help from the NWP leadership. When her lecture schedule prevented her from attending the 1933 national convention, she cabled these sentiments to be read aloud to the assembled delegates: "As you know, I thoroughly share the belief of your group that sex should be no barrier to the opportunities open to women in modern life." The convention presented her in absentia with honorary life membership in the NWP. When the party lobbied for a treaty to guarantee that women kept their citizenship when they married foreigners, Earhart cabled Secretary of State Cordell Hull in 1933: "Please help women gain equality in nationality by signing the Montevideo pact. Treaty is simple justice and the easiest means to an end so earnestly desired by advocates of social progress everywhere." At its 1936 convention the NWP released a telegram from Earhart in support of the Equal Rights Amendment: "Today women still stand victims of restrictive class legislation and of conflicting interpretation of statute. To clear the situation their rights must be made theirs by definition—that is, by constitutional guarantee." These messages represented enormous publicity coups for the National Woman's Party, a chance to push its goals with the support of one of the country's most respected women.[26]

Given Amelia Earhart's oft-stated commitment to removing all barriers to women in the air and, by extension, on the ground, her support for the Equal Rights Amendment was not unusual. But her forthright and uncompromising endorsement masks what a controversial issue this was for organized women in the 1920s and 1930s. More than any other, it divided feminists into those who supported equal rights before the law and those who supported protective legislation for women. At base was a differing conception of how best to advance women's interests. In general, professional women were most opposed to such restrictions because they limited women's ability to compete on an equal basis with men, whereas industrial women, and their social reformer supporters, favored protective legislation as a benefit to working women. At times the lines were so starkly drawn that the two sides were barely speaking to each other.

Amelia Earhart had long opposed special treatment for women, as evidenced by her penciled-in comments in the scrapbook she kept on women's public activities in the mid-1920s. In all her NWP statements, she followed this line. In a 1936 interview she said, "Limited hours and limited pay only prolong the infantile period for women and work to the disadvantage of those who want to progress. Wages should be based on work, not sex nor any other consideration." Earhart, in fact, supported minimum wage scales for all workers, a goal which many of the social reformers shared. The conundrum was that a conservative judicial system would not extend such protections to men throughout most of the 1930s. Therefore, either there would be no minimum wage or maximum hours laws at all and female industrial workers would be left at the mercy of their employers, or there would be laws which set women off as a special case, a benefit to most but harmful to the interests of a minority. No wonder the organized women's movement struggled with that question throughout the interwar period. Until the courts changed, no compromise was possible.[27]

The whole question of the Equal Rights Amendment and its impact on protective legislation was so divisive to the organized women's movement that the term "feminism" itself became part of the battle. Because the National Woman's Party had appropriated this term to describe its activities, social reformers went out of their way not to use it to describe themselves. To social reformers like Eleanor Roosevelt and Frances Perkins, feminists were "them" rather than "us."[28]

There were other reasons why the term fell on hard times. As Dorothy Dunbar Bromley captured in a witty 1927 article, feminism had become "a term of opprobrium to the modern young woman." The word suggested either "the old school of fighting feminists who wore flat heels and had very little feminine charm, or the current species who antagonize men with their constant clamor about maiden names, equal rights, woman's place in the world, and many another cause . . . *ad infinitum*." As Bromley noted, "if a blundering male assumes that a young woman is a feminist simply because she happens to have a job or a profession of her own, she will be highly—and quite justifiably insulted: for the word evokes the antithesis of what she flatters herself to be." Instead of identifying with a feminist movement seen as anachronistic, if not downright unattractive, the young woman of 1927 wanted to be treated as a "full-fledged individual," indeed as man's equal.[29]

Amelia Earhart did not share the twenties' view of her feminist foremothers as flat-heeled battle-axes, one reason why she was so warmly taken up by established women leaders. Activists were relieved that at least one member of the rising generation was willing to identify herself with what suffragists had called "the Cause." But Amelia, too, shied away from the term "feminist" in interviews and correspondence, providing a postsuffrage version of the often heard contemporary refrain "I'm not a feminist, but . . ." Her wording to fellow aviator Ruth Nichols in 1927 about the possibility of setting up an organization of women fliers captures the ambivalence she exhibited for the rest of her career, even after she had joined the National Woman's Party: "I cannot claim to be a feminist, but do rather enjoy seeing women tackling all kinds of new problems—new for them, that is." When defending in 1931 the right of women to fly without discrimination, she paused to note, "Doubtless by now I am running the risk of becoming a heavy-handed feminist. In a measure, I'm guilty, as I do become increasingly weary of male supremacy unquestioned." Here she used the term, but only reluctantly and modified by a derogatory adjective. That the number of times that Amelia Earhart used the word "feminist" is barely enough to fill a paragraph suggests how rarely the word appeared in popular discourse.[30]

This semantic muddle has made it difficult to write about the fate of feminism beyond suffrage. If only women who call themselves feminists are included in the story, then the survival of feminism comes down to members of the National Woman's Party, whose numbers were declining throughout this period and whose unswerving devotion to equal rights cut them off from other social and political issues of the day, such as birth control. Such a narrow designation leaves no room for the myriad examples of both individual and organizational activity by women and for women in the 1920s and 1930s, such as social reformers who targeted the needs of female industrial workers or politicians and reformers who worked to advance women's causes within the New Deal. The danger on the other end, however, is to collapse feminism into just "women who did things." As the suffrage-era ditty noted, "All feminists are suffragists, but not all suffragists are feminists."[31] Feminist theory and practice must retain some ideological edge, such as a commitment to ending women's subordination, in order to remain a distinct ideology.

The example of Amelia Earhart helps clarify the parameters of postsuffrage feminism. In *The Grounding of Modern Feminism,* historian Nancy Cott argues that what is usually seen as the demise of feminism after 1920 was really the end of suffragism and the beginning of the early struggle of modern feminism. Cott defines modern feminism in the following way: exhibiting a belief in sex equality, also expressed as opposition to sex hierarchy; believing that women's condition is socially constructed rather than a biological given; and women's perceiving themselves not just as a biological sex but as a social grouping. Within these outlines modern feminism as it emerged in the 1910s and 1920s was characterized by a core of paradoxes: asking for sex equality that also included sex difference, seeking individual freedom through sex solidarity, and embracing gender consciousness at the same time gender roles were challenged. In many ways Amelia Earhart lived out Cott's (or more accurately, feminism's) dilemma of how to make it as a woman and make it in a man's world.[32]

Nancy Cott ends her story of the grounding of modern feminism with the recognition that after the 1960s "feminisms grow toward the plural." A similar insight can be applied to the earlier period. There is not one single manifestation of feminism in the 1920s and 1930s, but multiple manifestations, both in the United States and worldwide. One central strand is liberal feminism, with its emphasis on opportunity, public equality, and individual achievement. Women who fall under this umbrella of liberal feminism—the lowest common denominator of feminist theory—are far broader and more diverse than just the National Woman's Party members.[33] In fact, linking a wider cast of postsuffrage women to the liberal feminist tradition reclaims for the history of feminism women who have previously been dismissed as liberal individualists.[34] This interpretation thus gives liberal feminist messages of equality of opportunity and equal rights a central position in the history of American feminism, especially in periods without mass feminist action.

The kind of individualistic stance toward women's advancement that Amelia Earhart practiced was hardly new to the 1920s and 1930s. Its roots predated the emergence of modern feminism. In fact, they went back to the eighteenth and nineteenth centuries. According to historians, political scientists, and feminist theorists, liberal feminism was an offshot of the classic liberalism that developed in the seventeenth and eighteenth centuries alongside the emergence of modern capitalism. This liberalism, with its emphasis on rationality, individualism, equality, citizenship, and especially liberty, was most closely associated with the philosophers John Locke and Jean-Jacques Rousseau. Starting in the late eighteenth and early nineteenth centuries, philosophers such as Mary Wollstonecraft, Harriet Taylor, and John Stuart Mill called for the extension of the freedoms and responsibilities associated with liberalism to women, who in classic liberal theory had been relegated entirely to dependency on men in the private sphere. Women, too, should be treated as rational and autonomous individuals and citizens in the public realm; they deserved equality, not treatment as a special, and inferior, category. The main strategies employed to achieve that goal were reasoned argument, education, and publicity.[35]

The language in which Amelia Earhart made her pleas conformed closely to the dominant discourse of liberal feminism: a commitment to individualism and self-reliance; a belief in equality of opportunity; a critique of accepted notions of women's inferiority; an emphasis on women's public roles, especially legal rights; and a belief in general liberal values such as economic independence, individual achievement, self-determination, and usefulness. More than any other goal she wished women to be treated as individuals, not as members of the second sex. As she wrote in 1937, "I, for one, hope for the day when women will know no restrictions because of sex but will be individuals free to live their lives as men are free. . . ."[36]

Amelia Earhart's individualist feminist philosophy can be boiled down to two ideas: first, that women can achieve whatever they set out to do, and second, that it should be the ability of the individual, not the sex, that counts. Earhart's whole stance toward opening the field of aviation to women, indeed all public life and the professions, attests to these dual thrusts. Repeatedly she stressed that if women were given a chance to prove themselves, sex would be less of a disadvantage: "Then too, there was my belief that now and then women should do for themselves what men have already done—and occasionally what men have not done—thereby establishing themselves as persons, and perhaps encouraging other women toward greater independence of thought and action." As she hammered away to undergraduate women on a college campus, "A girl must nowadays believe completely in herself as an individual. If you want to try a certain job, try it. Then if you find something on the morrow that looks better, make a change. And if you find that you are the first woman to feel an urge in that direction—what does it matter? Feel it and act on it just the same."[37]

Despite her realization that "society pushes men forward and holds women back," Earhart remained remarkably optimistic about the future. Optimism is an essential component for liberal feminists, who generally are heavily invested in believing that the system is just and will reward women fairly if they perform on an equal level with men. "Because this world has been arranged heretofore so that women could not act as individuals, it has been assumed that they neither wanted to nor ever could be," Earhart noted. "However, so many 'impossibilities' have proved baseless in the last quarter century that there is no telling now where limitations to feminine activities—if any—will be henceforth." Earhart was not one to set artificial boundaries beyond individual aptitude on what men and women could do, but "if women are eventually found in locomotive cabs, building bridges, or chasing bandits as normal occupations, it will be no surprise to me." As Margaret Fuller had said, "Let them be sea captains if they will!"[38]

In 1935 an essay contest in Port Huron, Michigan, offered as first prize the chance to meet the famous aviator at a local air show. The essays submitted on Earhart's contribution to aviation provide evidence that her liberal feminist message was getting through loud and clear, to the occasional boy but especially to the girls. Phyllis Sterling, age fourteen: "She proved to the world that women as well as men may achieve fame and honor in that field." Mary Hobson, age twelve: "Amelia Earhart thinks the most important thing a person can do is try herself out." Charles Cole, age twelve: "She is a pioneer of her sex in the air. She has squarely put it up to the men that women's place is not only in the home but above the clouds. Not chattering like most females, but proves her point."

We do not know who won, but my prize goes to Francetta Cole, age thirteen:

> In these days of progress Miss Earhart leads the way for women who wish to lead freer and wider lives. She is an inspiration to young women who, rather than stay at home in the kitchen, would fly the air as birds. One hundred years ago our great-grandmothers had to keep their wings clipped like discontented little birds. A few ugly ducklings flew from the barnyard to become beautiful white swans. Amelia Earhart, as one of these, led the way so that others might dare follow. We, the women of America, feel grateful that she has shown us a way to make life a more interesting adventure.[39]

The public side of Amelia Earhart's liberal feminism should be clear by now, but it had a private dimension as well. In keeping with general liberal philosophy, however, this private side was far less developed than the public. Just as Earhart used her own accomplishments to lead by example, so, too, did she generalize from her private life when formulating her egalitarian views of marriage as a partnership between equals and individuals, rather than a relationship between master and dependent. "Why should marriage be a cyclone cellar into which a woman retreats from failure in other spheres?" she asked. "I can think of lots of things worse than never getting married," she once announced forthrightly. "One of the worst is being married to a man who tied you down."[40]

Amelia Earhart and George Putnam managed to build a remarkably open and equal relationship for their times, the only kind of marriage she could have survived without becoming claustrophobic. Since she never activated the escape clause of her prenuptial agreement, her anguished fears on the eve of her wedding must have subsided, although they probably never totally disappeared. An apt photographic image is the two of them at their Rye home, he in business suit, she in jodhpurs, knees touching in identical poses, neither subservient to or dominant over the other, each displacing an equal amount of the interior of the circle.

Amelia Earhart and George Palmer Putnam pose at their home in Rye, New York. In *Pat and Mike* (1952) sports promoter Spencer Tracy describes the perfect relationship to his client Katharine Hepburn as "five-oh, five-oh." That kind of equality suited A.E. and G.P. to a tee.

Despite this professed mutuality and support for each other's independent lives, one gets the distinct sense that G. P. Putnam tailored his views to fit the outspoken independence and feminism of his chosen wife. George Putnam was in the publicity business, and he knew how to play a role. During their marriage his role was a combination of "hero's husband," "supportive male feminist," and "the forgotten man."[41] His oft-repeated statements in support of women's equality have an almost scripted, formulaic quality to them, as if they were being served up for public (or Amelia's) consumption. And he occasionally lapsed into some patently antifeminist statements, such as this winner in an article supposedly praising married women's independence: "But I have licked her at plenty of other things [besides flying]. If she were a gloating feminist, always harping on her career and her success and never letting me get my oar in to the conversation, I should probably have to sock her."[42] But such lapses were rare. G. P. desperately wanted to be married to this most intriguing creature, and he quickly figured out that the best (perhaps only) way to Amelia's heart was through mutual independence.

The whole basis of Amelia Earhart's, and liberal feminism's, view of marriage was equality. "I believe both men and women should be in the home some of the time, and out some of the time. Fifty-fifty. It's by no means as co-operative a world as it should be, but it's coming fast."[43] She was convinced that wives with outside interests, including employment, made better marital partners. "I don't even think this is mere 'modern thinking' or 'feminism' or anything of that kind, but just common sense." In general, Amelia thought that women stayed home too much, and men too little. "I believe that a man and woman who are married should each have home responsibilities and should each contribute to the income. In that way a woman will understand a man's business difficulties and he will get a better comprehension of her household griefs." When challenged by a Chicago man who said women could not have both home and career, she retorted, "I spend more than half of my time at home—which is better than a lot of business men do."[44]

A questionnaire that Amelia Earhart distributed to undergraduate women at Purdue University in 1935 captures her approach to careers and marriage quite well. What was Amelia doing at Purdue? She came to the West Lafayette, Indiana, campus at the personal behest of President Edward C. Elliott, who had been so taken by the aviator at the 1934 *New York Herald Tribune* conference on current problems that he asked her to serve as a counselor on careers for women. As Elliott said announcing the appointment of this role model for Purdue's women, who were outnumbered by males by a ratio of six to one, "Miss Earhart represents better than any young woman of this generation the spirit and the courageous skill of what may be called the new pioneering. At no other point in our educational system is there greater need for courageous pioneering and constructive planning than woman's education."[45]

Amelia was not a regular faculty member, but she lived in the women's residence hall when she was on campus and interacted with female students (and a few men) inside and outside the classroom. As part of her duties she distributed an extensive questionnaire to selected female students. Unfortunately the replies are unknown, except for Earhart's statement that 92 percent of the women responding planned to work after college.[46] Under possible responses to why it was advisable to combine marriage and career, Earhart offered these choices:

1. The husband and wife will have a more interesting comradeship
2. It gives the woman more personal independence and self-respect
3. A woman needs continuous activity in her life exactly as a man does
4. Other reasons

(She herself would have checked all of the above.) As for reasons why it was not advisable, she cited that work would interfere "disastrously" with running the home, that a man might be ashamed to have his wife earning money, or that there cannot be two heads of a household. Looking forward to parenting, she asked her students to consider whether it was advisable for married women to work when their children were young, a stance she would have supported under most circumstances. She provided this checklist for what a married man's part in running the household should be:

a. He should not have to have anything to do with it
b. He should do a few simple things—such as keeping his own bureau in order
c. He should do all that he has time for
d. He should have real interest in the running of the household no matter how much or how little he actually takes part
e. If the wife is employed, both husband and wife should take an equal part in the active running of the household

And anticipating the modern phenomenon of house husbands, she even asked students, "If you were the wage earner and your husband ran the home, would you consider his work financially equivalent to yours?"[47]

When Earhart's pronouncements on women's roles in public and private life are analyzed alongside the biographical details of her life, it is obvious how often she is merely generalizing from her own situation. The essence of Amelia Earhart's approach to feminism lay in leading by example—that is, having individual women show that they were capable of participating on equal terms with men, in both the public realm and the private, as an opening wedge toward more equal treatment. But missing from Earhart's ideology was any awareness that there might be women who for reasons of race, class, sexual orientation, or other "differences" would not be able to make the free choices and implement them the way that Earhart had. Far too often a model based on, and mainly available to, privileged members of the white middle class was held up as a universally attainable ideal.

This failure of vision was especially apparent in Earhart's pronouncements about seizing individual opportunities. Statements such as "And to me, fun is the indispensable part of work"[48] must have rung a little hollow in the midst of the Great Depression. Most Americans, male or female, were glad to have any job at all that helped support their families; working at a job that was "fun" was a luxury for all but those in the most self-directed careers. Indeed, how relevant were ideas of economic independence, personal fulfillment, and equal opportunity when at least one out of four Americans was out of work? That the depression so rarely intruded on the consciousness of this former social worker says volumes about how insulated she was from the realities of everyday life. It also shows how inadequate her liberal philosophy was in recognizing the inequality that permeated American society.

A similar class-bound narrowness mars Earhart's prescriptions for domestic accord. At first glance her call for a "fifty-fifty" marriage of equals and partners, at work and at home, seems remarkably modern and simple. Her commitment to women working outside the home, both to make financial contributions to the relationship and to make themselves better people and better spouses, builds on ideas first put forward by early-twentieth-century feminist thinkers such as Charlotte Perkins Gilman. "It is fortunately no longer a disgrace to be undomestic," Earhart noted, "and married women should be able to seek as unrestrictedly as men any gainful occupation their talents and interests makes available."[49]

But supportive husbands like G. P. were few and far between in the 1930s, and the aviator's marriage was based on an exceptional level of financial security that allowed much of the domestic work that usually devolves to women to be conveniently, invisibly relegated to servants. As she noted almost in an aside, "Assistants more skilled than one's self can be employed to substitute in the housewife role, if desirable." The following statement reads quite differently when one realizes that the cheery partnership she describes depends on a houseful of servants: "If George wants to see a new movie we dash out and see it. If I've designed a new dress I try it on and get his judgment. He's so good about the house. We never worry over who ought to do what. More people should try that way of living. Women should know the grind of a job, and men, the drudgery of housework. There would be fewer misunderstandings." Another example (there are many) of how their carefree domestic sharing rested on servants occurred when Amelia once flew off to an engagement in Cleveland, forgetting that they were expecting a bevy of houseguests on her return. *Voilà*—she just picked up the phone and called the butler with instructions for how much roast beef, hearts of lettuce, and ice cream to procure![50]

It is also highly relevant that theirs was a marriage without children. With Earhart flying all over the country for lectures, public appearances, or record setting, and her husband's equally hectic career of promotion, publishing, and Hollywood, they had to work hard to coordinate their schedules for the limited amount of time they actually spent together. This prescription would have worked far less well if there had been children at home. (Putnam's two sons from his earlier marriage did not live with them.) Earhart rarely talked about the changes that parenting would mean for women and men except in the most general terms: "As it is, children often see too much of their mothers and not enough of their fathers. This situation should be equalized." Yet the fact that she and Putnam chose not to have children suggests that at least intuitively she realized her model of unencumbered freedom was at odds with the domestic commitments of child rearing.[51]

Earhart's convenient overlooking of the question of children was symptomatic of liberal feminism's failure to tackle broader issues linked to private life. Sexual emancipation had been an important component of the feminism practiced in Greenwich Village in the 1910s, but that element had totally dropped off the agenda by the 1930s. Earhart never mentioned this issue, beyond a chance remark that "Surely we must have something more to contribute to marriage than our bodies." Nor did she ever discuss the kinds of same-sex romantic friendships and partnerships that had been so important to earlier generations of women.[52]

She did, however, speak out publicly in support of birth control. Under Margaret Sanger's leadership, the birth control movement posted major successes in the 1930s, in the courts and in winning increased public acceptance because of the depression-era need to limit births. Earhart was an easy convert to the cause, since her vision of companionate marriage encompassed family planning as well, both in her own life and for women in general. But although

Amelia and George striding arm in arm toward the future, the perfect picture of a modern companionate marriage. But is there room in this picture for children? Like many other professional women at the time, A.E. found it harder to contemplate combining career with motherhood than just with marriage alone.

she lent her name to Margaret Sanger on several occasions, she never made birth control a priority the way she did equal rights. Earhart's general reticence about the most intimate aspects of women's lives was in keeping with how liberal feminism prioritized the public over the private in the 1930s and stands in sharp contrast with the feminist agenda of the 1960s and 1970s with its insistence that the personal is political.[53]

In sum, liberal feminism encouraged individual women to excel and succeed, while it did little to challenge or change the conditions that keep the masses of women from taking advantage of those opportunities in the first place. This model of success was predominantly, although not exclusively, geared to white middle-class women like Amelia Earhart herself. Such a commitment to equality of opportunity and individualism paid no attention to the ways in which certain aspects of women's lives, such as childbearing, domestic responsibilities, or differences based on race or class, disadvantaged many women from aspiring to the male model of unencumbered individual freedom. (Liberal theory was conveniently vague on *which* men women were to aspire to.) By treating men and women identically, without recognizing the differences that shaped women's lives, women were asked to compete with a handicap in a supposedly open contest.

One of the most critical limits of individualism as a feminist strategy was the difficulty of institutionalizing success. Because this very appealing vision of personal autonomy and independence put such a high premium on individual rather than collective achievement, it presented no real challenge to the more complex structural problems of inequality and discrimination. When women did succeed (and many did), it proved very difficult to pass these highly fragile and historically specific gains on to the next generation. This generalization applies to women's place in aviation and in many other areas, such as Hollywood, politics, and the professions. This inability to institutionalize gains limited the scope of liberal feminism as a strategy for political and social change.

While hindsight exposes telling flaws in liberal feminism, in many ways such a critique misses the point. During the period of Amelia

Earhart's public career, few, if any, feminists were calling for major changes in gender relations in modern American society on either the public or the private level.[54] It seems unfair to criticize Amelia Earhart, and the majority of American women at that time, for not realizing what it took almost fifty years, and a much expanded feminist movement, to figure out. Moreover, this individualistic strategy was not forced on women coming of age in the postsuffrage era. They embraced it willingly, indeed enthusiastically. Instead of harping on the limitations of the feminist ideology adopted by Amelia Earhart and others in the 1920s and 1930s, historians must try to figure out why it was so appealing and what it meant to the generations of women who accepted its tenets.

Given the flush of optimism following passage of the Nineteenth Amendment, the aspirations of these women were neither as naïve nor as unrealistic as they have later been portrayed. Now that political equality had (supposedly) been achieved, it was up to individual women to strive and succeed alongside men. When they succeeded, credit rebounded to their whole sex. On the other hand, if they failed, they blamed themselves, not society, for their disappointments or setbacks. Such an individualistic stance proved especially well suited to the postsuffrage period, when women's issues were in danger of becoming obsolete or irrelevant because of the conservative political climate in the 1920s, which was then followed by the crisis of the Great Depression. This kind of individualism kept the feminist standard alive in a period when a mass women's movement like suffrage was not likely to coalesce.[55]

This stance was also in keeping with women's new modes of political and professional activism. The self-styled modern women coming of age in the 1910s and 1920s had many more opportunities to move directly into the male-dominated public realm than had the previous generations of Progressive reformers and suffragists or their nineteenth-century predecessors. The breaking down of artificial barriers in education, the professions, and politics meant that women and men increasingly worked and played together, a contrast with the more formal (although never total) separation of the previous century. In addition, increased cultural and social imperatives toward heterosexuality by the 1920s made younger women less interested in, indeed almost suspicious of, the homosocial female world which had nurtured earlier generations of activists. Of necessity, twentieth-century feminist practice had to adapt to the emergence of mixed-gender styles of public and private behavior.[56]

If younger women were a bit more likely to refer to women as "they" rather than "we," they did not totally abandon the gender consciousness necessary to a feminist awareness. In Amelia Earhart's case, for example, the main organizations to which she devoted her time were groups of women—aviators, professionals, and feminists—in sum, organizations which very much kept alive the strategy of separatism to advance women's cause. Yet Earhart was using that strategy in a much different political and social context from that in which it had first emerged in the nineteenth century. Now separate female organizations coexisted alongside fairly extensive cooperation and interaction with men rather than as a substitute for that contact.

These individualistic women of the 1920s and 1930s have gotten a bum rap from historians. Compared with the towering figures of Progressive-era reform and suffragism, they seem pale, self-centered, drifting, and uninterested in women's issues. They are practically accused of killing feminism by setting off on the road toward personal fulfillment and the superficial trappings of liberation rather than continuing the older generation's commitment to collective humanitarian reform. But let us try to put ourselves in their shoes. They had witnessed an enormous expansion in opportunities since their mothers' and grandmothers' times, and in the context of their recent enfranchisement, it was not totally unrealistic to think that finally they would be able to go about the world's business as individuals, not just as women. They probably heaved a sigh of relief that women had finally broken into the human race.[57] What a powerful, indeed empowering feeling this must have been for women—especially for the white middle-class women who were the main beneficiaries of the expanding opportunities for their sex. In essence, this was what the appeal of Amelia Earhart was all about.

How aware was Earhart of the impact she was having? The entire record of her public career suggests that she used her own example as a model for other women to emulate. A recollection from Edein French, a Seattle social worker, suggests how the aviator consciously and deliberately spread her feminist message wherever she went.

While on a trip to Washington State around 1932 or 1933, Earhart asked to meet with high school members of the Girl Reserves, a YWCA program for girls. The students were deeply touched that of all the well-known people Earhart could have met in Spokane on her visit, she had asked to meet with them. French added, probably correctly, "I expect that this must have been something she did many times in many cities." French and a few close friends decided that they would not betray her kindness by asking for her autograph, and they hung back while others did ask. Earhart noticed their reticence, and said, "I appreciate your not asking, but really, wouldn't you like one too?" Somehow she had read their minds. "Of course we wanted one. So some place in my possessions is the beautiful tranquil signature of a lovely lady."

But there is more to the story than just that note of graciousness on the aviator's part. Earhart really gave of herself in this unscheduled, and obviously unpaid, appearance, talking extemporaneously with the girls about the "Girl Reserves, life, being a person, and living according to one's ideals." French remembered that the YWCA was very much in the forefront of the "women's movement" in those days and that Girl Reserves believed there was nothing they could not do if they set their minds to it. "And Amelia Earhart was proof." Later she could not remember anything specific that Earhart had said, except that "none of it was stuffy, just natural, sincere and very real," and that she came away "deeply influenced by her presence and determined to try to become a person like her." Reflecting on the incident years later, she concluded, "I think she knew quite well what she was doing, and that this was not a chance generosity to a group of little girls, but rather a carefully thought out plan to pass on some of her own philosophy and by example to demonstrate that women could achieve whatever they set out to do."[58]

An eighteen-year-old factory girl from the Tennessee hills said of Eleanor Roosevelt, "Say, she's swell. Why, I'm not ashamed of being a girl any more."[59] Amelia Earhart had that same effect. For both Roosevelt and Earhart, one suspects that acting as a conscious role model was quite deliberate. It was also the essence of liberal feminism.

Iconography and Representation

In 1929 Charles Lindbergh's image had already been captured in as many as fifty thousand photographs. Amelia Earhart was not the subject of quite such photographic adulation, but the images of her life preserved in photographs and newsreels number in the thousands. This exposure helped make Earhart one of the most easily recognized public figures of the 1930s. She once made a forced landing in an isolated rural area in Mexico. Even though she spoke no Spanish, and the locals spoke no English, "Strangely, they knew who I was." Or not so strangely.[1]

Amelia Earhart had something of an affinity for the photographic image. "Having lived a peripatetic life—never longer than four years in one place, with frequent lengthy excursions away from that, I suppose pictures mean more to me than to some people. They are stabilizers on a shifting world and tend to keep records straight and memories fresh." All her life she had taken photographs, in part, she jested, because of "a predisposition for things to happen when I was around." She worked for a time in the 1920s in a photographic studio, experimenting with photographs of unusual subjects such as garbage cans and artsy self-portraits. When she crossed the Atlantic in 1928, she took pictures from the *Friendship* while lying flat on her stomach, a feat she was unable to duplicate on her 1932 solo crossing, having, as she dryly noted, "only two hands and two feet." The increase in her public celebrity, or, as she put it, "facing too many lenses," somewhat dulled "the pleasure I might have felt as a child in having my picture taken." But she learned to face a still photographer's camera or a newsreel camera with the poise and confidence of a professional model, always willing to provide that "one more picture, Miss Earhart," for the press that followed her activities everywhere.[2]

These surviving photographic images are one of the most valuable texts for reconstructing Amelia Earhart's appeal. In her lectures and articles she hammered away at the promise of aviation and women's roles therein. Photographic images of the pathbreaking aviator reinforced the message in a similar, perhaps equally self-conscious way. A recent biographer has noted Earhart's "unerring instinct for making a physical statement of who and what she was."[3] She presented herself, and was presented in the press, in almost iconographic representations of both WOMAN and AVIATOR. Indeed, her image has stood the test of time remarkably well. If she walked into a room today, she would look perfectly at home, dressed in her comfortable but flattering slacks, silk blouse, with an easy-to-care-for hairstyle and trim, athletic look.

No representations in the media or popular culture are totally neutral; they all have embedded meanings in relation to the dominant social discourse and ideology of the time. Popular culture represents "contested terrain," a site of struggle where dominant ideologies can be challenged and meanings debated. Audiences and subjects receive and decode these messages (or signs[4]) in very individualistic and even contradictory ways. One way of interpreting the constellation of images of Amelia Earhart in newsreels, photographs, and newspapers is to see them as promoting an alternative reading on what it means to be a woman.[5]

This iconographic message was, and is, remarkably powerful. In photographs and newsreels Amelia Earhart is in motion; she flies planes, greets crowds, gives speeches, meets famous people. Even when photographed standing still, she is often surrounded by symbols of action and power usually associated with men: sleek cars, large airplanes, crowds of admirers. But the message she conveys is not simply an aping of traditional male values or even male attire. She appears in flight clothes, but also evening gowns; coveralls, but also silk blouses. By her appearance, manner of presentation, and propensity to stare forthrightly into the camera instead of shyly averting her eyes in the more traditional female gaze, Amelia Earhart helped subvert 1930s gender roles. That gaze was an extension of her own personality and the force of her myriad public accomplishments; its challenge thus opened a window, albeit a small one, toward more autonomy and individual freedom in women's lives.[6]

For Americans reared in the age of television, it is hard to recapture the power of newsreels. For those old enough to remember newsreels, it is impossible to forget it. Even though the individual stories of any given newsreel were very short—often under a minute—they packed a power and vividness that made the image linger and deepen. The fact that newsreels were shown in darkened theaters no doubt added to their mystique.

Newsreels gave moviegoers, especially young people, an enormous amount of information about the world: pictures of places like China, Brazil, and Australia; the world's great cities and their monuments—the Eiffel Tower in Paris, the Colosseum in Rome, the Capitol dome in Washington. Feminist Inez Haynes Irwin noted how newsreels provided moving images of the world's famous figures: "No child but instantly recognizes the faces of King Edward VIII, Queen Mary, Hitler, Mussolini, Stalin, and the leading political figures—and criminals—of the United States; world figures like

Lindbergh, Einstein, and athletic champions of all sports." Eleanor Roosevelt rarely had time to watch the movies shown at the White House, but she always stayed for the newsreels, "for they seem to bring the whole world before us. We can see things which happen hundreds of miles away just as though we were on the spot. I contend that seeing things is almost a necessity in this visual-minded period of our development, and the newsreels are probably doing as much as the radio, newspapers and magazines to make people world-minded today."[7]

Newsreels developed alongside movies, offering a combination of journalism, travelogue, and entertainment before the feature presentation. By the mid-1920s, 85 to 90 percent of the nation's eighteen thousand theaters exhibited newsreels. An enormous boost to newsreels, and so much else, was the Fox Movietone footage of Charles Lindbergh's takeoff in May 1927—one of the very first sound-on-film newsreels. Like the novelty of talking movie pictures, which were being simultaneously introduced, the Lindbergh talking newsreel combined the thrill of the event with the public's fascination with the new medium. By the 1930s the major newsreel companies (Fox Movietone, Hearst Metronone, Paramount, Pathé, and Universal) competed with journalistic organs such as newspapers for the speed with which they could get fast-breaking news to the public. In the 1935 trial of Bruno Hauptmann, the accused kidnapper of Charles Lindbergh's baby, the newsreels even scooped the papers in some regions once the verdict was announced. How did they do this? Companies had prepared two newsreels, one for a guilty verdict, the other for an innocent. When the verdict came in, movie theaters were immediately telephoned with the news and told which trailer to run.[8]

Newsreels were closer to what is now called soft news than hard journalism. As early as the 1920s they had fallen into predictable categories: "catastrophe, international celebrities, pageantry and ceremony, sports, political and military events, technology, and spectacle and novelty." Oscar Levant later characterized the newsreel as "a series of catastrophes, ended by a fashion show." Like all decades, the 1930s were full of sensational news, both hard and soft, so the newsreels had no dearth of subjects. Any major sporting, political, or special event would feature the ubiquitous newsreel cameras recording the story, often perched in a row on top of flat automobile roofs to get a better view. The combination of news footage and narration was incredibly powerful, as the newsreels of the May 6, 1937, crash of the *Hindenburg* dirigible in Lakehurst, New Jersey, attest.[9]

Amelia Earhart was made for the newsreels. Photogenic, pioneering, and considerate of reporters, she was eminently newsworthy, especially when she had just completed a record-breaking flight. Most of the surviving footage is of her aviation feats, especially her flights in 1928, 1932, and 1935, and coverage of the massive search in the Pacific when she disappeared. The most common images of Amelia Earhart, therefore, are of her in flying togs— pants or jodhpurs or a flying suit, leather jacket, and the usual silk blouse or scarf—taxiing before or after landing, then emerging from her plane to be surrounded by a mob of well-wishers. Remember that she had no time to compose herself before she met the press at the end of a long flight. Journalists wanted her reactions right as she stepped off the plane, and she invariably obliged, no matter how tired or disheveled she felt. (In contrast, Jacqueline Cochran always took time to powder her nose and put on lipstick before meeting the press.[10]) If the newsreels could not be on hand for her arrival, as for her unexpected landing in Ireland rather than Paris on her 1932 Atlantic solo, she cooperated by doing something like starting up the plane and taxiing so they could have footage that looked authentic, even if it was not the actual moment of landing.[11]

It is remarkable how at ease she seems in these newsreels. By 1932, one biographer noted, she was so much in control that she was almost the "host" of these postflight interviews. She developed a fairly natural public demeanor that served her well in these situations: she was able to stand still for the cameras and let them keep rolling without the compulsive need to wave, talk, or move. She adopted a sort of bemused tolerance on her face while she let the photographers get their footage. For example, shots of her arrival in London after her 1932 solo show that she knew how to stop before getting into a car to let the crowd, and the cameras, look at her. She did not ham it up like a prizefighter; she just smiled modestly. This was a far cry from her shyness and awkwardness after her 1928 flight. No doubt manager-husband George Palmer Putnam tutored her on how to perfect her public demeanor. She was an apt pupil.[12]

Less successful were the staged newsreel interviews, usually involving her husband, which had an awkward, indeed false tone to them. Before her last flight in 1937 she and Putnam engaged in this "made for newsreel" conversation:

PUTNAM: Tell me, dear, why are you going on this trip?
EARHART: Well, G.P., you know it's because I want to.
PUTNAM: Well, how about taking me along?
EARHART: Well, of course I think a great deal of you, but one hundred eighty pounds of gasoline on a flight perhaps might be a little more valuable.
PUTNAM: You mean you prefer one hundred eighty pounds of gasoline to one hundred eighty pounds of husband?
EARHART: I think you guessed right.

The lines seem pointed and funny today, but they were delivered without spontaneity or conviction, showing the canned and rehearsed nature of this artificial news event. Also awkward, perhaps more understandably so, were the stilted good-byes between husband and wife before major flights, which, like all other last-minute preparations, were conducted in full public view.[13]

Much of the surviving newsreel footage from the 1930s does not have its original sound; in the interests of economy, most newsreel companies disposed of the separate sound tracks when storing old reels, and others were lost in fires or just misplaced. Obviously it would make a difference to how an audience received an image of Amelia Earhart if the text ran, "Amelia Earhart lands at Oakland after a foolhardly, worthless stunt from Hawaii. Why can't women stay at home where they belong?" as opposed to "Amelia Earhart triumphant after yet another feat of heroic flying that shows women

men's equals in the air." Evidence suggests that the accompanying sound tracks were much more of the latter type than the former.[14]

What's in a name? That question captures the dilemma faced by both newsreel captioners and headline writers. Even with sound, the newsreels, like the newspapers, still relied on headlines and titles to capture the public's attention. Was she Amelia Earhart, Amelia Earhart Putnam, or Mrs. Putnam? Was she an aviator or an aviatrix? Was she a woman or a girl flier? There were no consistent answers. Within such semantic muddlings lie further clues to the representation of women and aviation.

Of course, there was no problem with the name in 1928, when she was just plain Amelia Earhart or, on second reference, Miss Earhart. Things got complicated once she married George Palmer Putnam in 1931. The couple were quite clear about how to proceed: she wanted to be known as Amelia Earhart professionally, but in those now-dated phrases of the times, "in private life," "socially," or "at home," she was Mrs. George Palmer Putnam. Despite this straightforward demarcation between public and private, there were inevitable lapses and confusions. In 1932, when President Herbert Hoover presented Earhart with the National Geographic Society medal for her flight, the newsreels recorded his fumbling: ". . . I have the pleasure of bestowing upon you, Miss Earhart—or should I say, Mrs. Putnam. . . ." Similarly, newspapers never adopted a consistent policy, although by the mid-1930s most simply called her Amelia Earhart.[15]

G. P. Putnam thought that eastern newspapers were more stodgy on this issue than those in the rest of the country, and he may have been right. Witness the *New York Times,* which clung to the anachronistic terms "Miss" and "Mrs." well into the 1980s and did no better in figuring out how to describe the country's best-known female aviator. In a front-page article in 1931 the headline refers to her as Miss Earhart, and the text refers to her as both Amelia Earhart and Mrs. Putnam. Most newspapers used Amelia Earhart in their headlines, or at the least the full Amelia Earhart Putnam; the *New York Herald Tribune*'s May 22, 1932, banner headline, MRS.

PUTNAM SPANS SEA . . . was unusual in that regard. But lest there be any doubt that the flier knew her own name, the same *Herald Tribune* story opens by quoting her telephoning the news of her arrival in Ireland to London: "Hello, This is Amelia Earhart speaking." Only occasionally did headlines refer to her just as "Amelia." Although no other prominent figures of the 1930s shared that name, newspaper audiences were not yet on a first-name basis with their celebrities. And no headlines referred to her as A. E., her shorthand signature. Her husband promoted this designation in his own writing after her death, and it has been perpetuated ever since by biographers, but it was not widely used by the press at the time.[16]

This puzzle of how to refer to Amelia Earhart reflects the ongoing public ambivalence about a wife's having a separate public identity from her husband. Even though the Lucy Stone League promoted the practice of women keeping their own names for professional purposes, the media found it difficult to overlook a woman's marital status. In Earhart's case this situation may have been inadvertently inflamed because George Putnam was such a pest that it would have been very hard to forget the man to whom she was married.

The designation of Earhart consistently as an "aviatrix" rather than an "aviator" also shows how gender affected public reception. Very rare indeed would be descriptions of Amelia Earhart as just plain pilot, aviator, record setter, or public figure. She was always referred to by a term that drew attention to her gender, such as aviatrix (by far the most common) or "air heroine." Even "his and hers" terms—aviator and aviatrix—are inherently unequal when the category is male and the female version is seen as an unusual exception. As in references to poetess, woman doctor, actress, executrix, and newspaperwoman, Earhart was always a woman flier, not a flier.[17]

Actually, being designated a woman flier was a step up from "girl flier," and some of the other blatantly sexist terms like "birdwoman" and "No. 1 Ladybird" that recurred throughout her career. The use of the term "girl" dominates the 1928 coverage. Newspapers referred to her as the girl flier, Boston girl, and, in the home-town angle, ex-Chicago girl; headlines read GIRL THRILLED BY ADVENTURE and GIRL'S PLANE FUELED FOR ATLANTIC START. The titles for the newsreels were hardly any more enlighted: "Girl on Atlantic Hop" (Paramount), "Girl Lindy's Triumph" (British Pathé), and "Girl Flyer in London" (Paramount). Even the frontispiece of Ear-hart's own book about the 1928 flight, *20 hrs. 40 min.,* reads, "The American Girl, First Across the Atlantic by Air, Tells Her Story." One of the few newspapers that actually deigned to refer to her as a woman flier was the tabloid *New York Daily News.*[18]

All these references seem a bit incongruous when one realizes that at the time of the flight the "girl" was just one month shy of her thirty-first birthday. How did the press and the public overlook this? She did look young, very young. One of the few references to age in 1928 was this exchange quoted by a British journalist: "She is modest about everything but her age—she boasts she is thirty years old, when it is obvious she is not a day over twenty." No doubt G.P. conspired to underplay his client's age in the hopes of making her seem younger, and thus even more exceptional, for her aviation exploits.[19] Actually the articles throughout Earhart's career rarely mention her age at all, a common practice for women, as well as for men, in a less age-conscious age.

While there are still references to Amelia Earhart as a girl as late as 1935 (EPOCHAL MOMENTS IN CAREER OF GIRL FLYER! blasted the headline of the *Los Angeles Examiner*), by the time of her 1932 solo her name was well enough known that headlines could just say AMELIA EARHART HOPS ATLANTIC and people knew who she was. And the headline terms used in newspapers and the newsreels were a little more befitting her stature—"World Hails Daring Amelia Earhart for Successful Sea Hop"—as were references to her as the "heroine of the skies" and "feminine ace." By the time of her dis-appearance she had been graduated to "First Lady of the Air," "famous woman flyer," and, finally, "premier aviatrix."[20] She would no doubt have approved of the improvement, although always longing to be known just as a pilot, plain and simple.

•   •   •

Like newsreels and newspaper headlines, photographs can be treated as texts containing representations of gender. Photographs, a product of the same technological and economic changes that produced newsreels, play such an important part in modern life that we rarely stop to think about how influential or pervasive they are. The popular images of such figures as Eleanor Roosevelt and Abraham Lincoln, of whom abundant photographs exist, are much clearer than those of George Washington or Abigail Adams, who lived before the photographic process was developed. Such photographs allow a familiarity, an intimacy that is an essential feature of modern life, with a potential impact even wider than moving images. Noted the biographer of Hollywood silent film star Louise Brooks: "Far more people saw Louise's photographs than her movies. . . . For while the films were rather few and rarely played for long, the photos were reproduced in hundreds of magazines and newspapers eager for a fresh face out of Hollywood."[21] Or in Amelia Earhart's case, for the latest aviation star.

Especially when used in conjunction with other more traditional sources, photographs confirm the ways in which repeated imagery (such as a woman flier standing next to an airplane) creates a string of coherent, linked images or iconography. Photographs also hold clues to such illusive matters as style and appearance, to body type, and even to the designation of certain aspects of a public figure's physical appearance as worthy of special attention. (In Earhart's case it was her hair.) Since Amelia Earhart the popular heroine was in part a creation of the public's response to her, especially her female public, and in part her own self-creation, the photographs that dispersed that magnetic image throughout the media and popular culture are central to unlocking the representations of gender in the aviator's life.

Would Amelia Earhart have become such an appealing popular figure if she had been short and dumpy? It is an intriguing question. Luckily she was born with the perfect body for her times. At the turn of the century the preferred female figure was mature and plump, especially full through the bust. Before the World War, however, and especially in the 1920s, a new body look began to

This photograph of Amelia Earhart in an open cockpit was taken two years before the 1928 flight. The juxtaposition of the cap and goggles with the pearls certainly catches the viewer's attention, as do the beauty and strength of the aviator's gaze.

emphasize smaller breasts, slimmer hips, and long legs; in clothing this translated into less focus on the waist and bust and more attention on the legs through shortened skirts. French designers such as Paul Poiret and Coco Chanel were among the first to have the knack to dress this modern woman.[22]

This new body type was youthful, and it emphasized easy, unconstrained movement. No longer did physical activity constitute an affront to womanhood; in fact, in the context of the youth culture of the 1920s and 1930s a certain degree of athleticism became incorporated into the dominant characteristics of modern womanhood. Women shed corsets and other restrictive undergarments in order to engage in dance crazes like the tango or play active games like golf or tennis. A journalist in the *New York Times* noted in 1931, "Any description of the ideal modern girl invariably specifies that she must be good at outdoor sports. A long stride, a strong arm, sunburned hair, a tanned complexion have come to be regarded as part of the picture of American beauty. . . . Today a group picture of women swimmers, golfers, tennis players or fliers generally shows more than its average quota of good looks. And women who abhor physical effort have a reputation for being fat rather than fair."[23]

The movies played a large role in promoting this new style of female physical freedom. Hollywood stars popularized sports and athletic clothes for everyday wear, both on the screen and off. Films showed women in motion far more than paintings or sculpture, or even still photography, ever could. For photographs or moving pictures, as well as athletics, thinness was a definite asset. In art historian Anne Hollander's words, the new "compact and unified visual image" worked best on a "self-contained, sleekly composed physical format."[24]

Amelia Earhart very much had this new athletic body type and its corresponding propensity to motion. She was tall and slim— five feet eight inches tall and 118 pounds. (In 1928 only 17 percent of all American women were both slender and over five feet three inches.) In her own way she was just as "streamlined" in her personal appearance as the airplanes she flew; she and her planes exuded a consciously modern, forward-looking style. If Earhart did not have the rounded curves so distinctive of streamlining in industrial design, she certainly conveyed a form built for speed and efficiency.[25]

Yet Earhart was far from a conventionally beautiful woman. Her legs were very thick, perhaps one reason she was fond of wearing slacks. She was so self-conscious about the gap between her front teeth that she was always photographed with her mouth closed, even when smiling. (Lore has it that promoter G. P. Putnam made that suggestion in 1928,[26] but in surviving childhood and early adulthood photographs she smiles the same way.) She disdained jewelry, except for a favorite bracelet and occasional pearls; she did not wear a wedding ring, which was unusual, or earrings. She rarely wore makeup and had numerous freckles from all her outdoor activities. In the 1920s and 1930s being suntanned was just becoming a fashion statement, inspired by French designer Coco Chanel and the Hollywood film community's affinity for outdoor activities. Earhart's tan was not a status symbol or beauty statement; she merely spent so much time in the sun that she could not help it. By the time of her last flight her skin showed it, having become leathery and wrinkled, with prominent crow's-feet from years of squinting into the sun.[27]

Clothes and adornment have their own language and history, although scholars disagree about what they actually represent. Is clothing a way of making a personal expression, a link in the history of image making, a cultural by-product of capitalist consumer society, an instrument of oppression to women, or all the above? Certainly one's appearance is a form of self-presentation—a vision of ourselves and a recognition that in the eyes of the world clothes are one of the first things people notice. To paraphrase Anne Hollander, clothes make not the woman but the image of the woman. Valerie Steele calls clothes a "guide to identity": "clothing expresses a particular image of the physical body, the individual's self-awareness, and his or her social being." The end result is the presentation of "the ideal self." Dress is also a language system, according to Alison Lurie, whose vocabulary includes not just clothing but also hairstyle, accessories, jewelry, and makeup. Paying attention to the language of clothes is especially fruitful for studying—or, rather, decoding—gender identity and gender roles.[28]

Amelia Earhart by the 1930s exuded an aura of elegance, simplicity, modesty, and an understated but undeniable forcefulness. She had not always had this "together" look, either on the flying field or off. This personal style or self-presentation was learned and acquired, with some coaching from George Putnam no doubt, and also made easier by the increasingly affluent life-style that she enjoyed after 1928. But the real change came from within. In the 1930s she presented to the world an image of self that brought together the various aspects of her life into an integrated whole. She knew who she was and what she wanted to do: preach the cause of aviation to the general public, and preach the cause of feminism to women. This "self" comes through clearly in the surviving newsreels and photographs.

Pictures from her adolescence and early adulthood show a far less arresting Amelia Earhart. Her clothing is obviously more old-fashioned and less stylish. After all, she was born in 1897, and before World War I women's clothes, especially for young women not in major urban areas, still looked closer to the late-nineteenth-century Victorian matron than to the 1920s youthful styles. For example, a picture around 1912 of a fifteen-year-old Amelia dressed in a white waist, long skirt, low-slung belt, and high laced boots, with her hair piled on her head looks dated even for that time. In the 1920s Amelia Earhart was far from a flapper. In her California days her pose as a "businesswoman" in a black suit dressed for success shows none of her later flair. Even her early aviation photos look somehow off. Of course, not having much money certainly affected her ability to look elegant and stylish. But she may have looked less striking in part because her focus in life had not yet gelled.

By 1928 her presentation of self had come together in the flying part of her life—the widely distributed Charles Lindbergh look-alike picture of her in a long leather coat, flying helmet, breeches, and high laced boots has a force to it that cannot be denied—but the rest of her wardrobe still lacked coherence and style. The twen-

ties style of blousy tops and dropped waists, hardly the most flattering to any female body type, looked overwhelming even on a
tall, slim woman like her. In addition, the shorter skirt lengths (just
below the knee) drew attention to her thick legs. One surviving
photograph of Amelia laying a wreath at Medford, Massachusetts,
on her return in 1928 shows silk stockings bagging around her thick
ankles.

She also exhibited a distinct propensity for the most unflattering
collection of cloche hats ever assembled. "Your hats!" George Putnam complained in September 1928. "They are public menaces.
You should do something about them when you must wear them
at all! Some of them are cataclysms!"[29] He was absolutely right.
Especially awful were several of the hats she wore for the 1928
postflight public receptions, including one sequined number that
looked like a bathing cap and another that looked like a helmet.
Totally covering her hair, the hats robbed her of one of her most
distinctive features. From then on Earhart was seen far less often in
headgear. It is hard to imagine her becoming a fashion leader or
popular icon if she had persisted in those hats.

This unstylish, somewhat gawky Amelia Earhart of 1928 quickly
disappeared. By the time of her marriage to George Palmer Putnam
in 1931, in fact, earlier, she was well on her way to developing her
own highly distinctive style, the main hallmark of which was an
ability to wear different kinds of clothes, from flying togs to day-
wear to evening gowns, with equal ease. Her stepson remembered,
"She looked like a bag of bones in a bathing suit, she was so thin,
but she had beautiful clothes and she knew how to wear them.
When she was all dressed up, she didn't look like she had *tried* to be
all dressed up." The dean of women at Purdue, Helen Schleman,
agreed: "Amelia was tall and straight and moved with incredible
grace whether she was in long slim slacks or a floor-length dinner
dress."[30]

This style meshed well with the country's more conservative mood
in the 1930s, resulting from the challenges of hard times. Women's
clothing was more serious and less childlike than in the previous
decade. Suits were heavier and darker, materials thicker, and skirt

lengths much longer. The larger emphasis on curves, the more prominent bustlines, and the increasing use of shoulder pads as the decade developed gave women a more sophisticated and mature mien. Even though Earhart was slimmer than the typical female body of the 1930s, and hardly curvaceous, her understated and simple style fitted the ethos of depression-era America.

More than any other aspect of her clothes "vocabulary," Amelia Earhart's "carefully tousled" hair became her trademark signature. As her husband noted in an uncharacteristic understatement, "as time went on and she wore a hat less and less, her hair became a sort of hallmark." So identified was she with her short, curly hair that whenever she and George wanted a little anonymity, such as sneaking into a restaurant while traveling, she simply pulled a cap down over her curls and escaped detection.[31]

"To bob or not to bob" was a pressing question for women in the 1920s. When fashion-setting society dancer Irene Castle cut her hair in the 1910s, she almost instantly made short hair glamorous and chic. For those who hesitated to cut what many saw as woman's crowning glory, feminist Charlotte Perkins Gilman reminded a 1916 audience: "It was not the Lord who gave men short hair while women's is long. It was the scissors."[32] Soon short hair for women joined other such symbols of modern times as short skirts, smoking in public, and dancing. Mary Pickford's decision in 1928 to bob her hair, a daring move for a movie star whose career had been predicated on her little-girl curls, received front-page coverage. So famous were Pickford's curls that there was talk of putting them in the Smithsonian along with Lindbergh's *Spirit of St. Louis* and other national treasures. Unfortunately the moviegoing public was not ready for a mature Mary Pickford (she was then thirty-seven years old), and her career faltered. But the battle for short hair had been won.[33]

Amelia Earhart had at first been hesitant to cut her hair. When she began to fly in 1920, her hair was still very long, a real bother in the open cockpits of the time. After being told that she did not look like an aviatrix with all that hair, she began to trim it inches at a time but avoided chopping it all off. Her reason? "I had not bobbed it lest people think me eccentric. For in 1920 it was very odd indeed for a woman to fly, and I had tried to remain as normal as possible in looks, in order to offset the usual criticism of my behavior." But by mid-decade the long hair was gone. Surprisingly she looked younger with it shorter, and more attractive, since it filled out her rather high forehead and large head. Yet Earhart's trademark short, curly hairstyle was not the traditional bob, which would have been somewhat longer and softer, its unruliness shaped by a permanent wave. In contrast, Earhart's short haircut did not even need to be styled in a beauty salon, as a photograph of her having it trimmed at the *Oakland Tribune* barbershop right before her last flight attested.[34]

From the very beginning newspaper accounts were fixated on her hair with an almost fetishistic obsession. Stories filed in 1928 talk repeatedly about her "wavy, fluffy hair" and her "tousled" curls, as if no one had ever seen short, curly hair before. "Feminine to the fingertips," wrote the *New York Times,* "she is tall and slender, with a head surmounted by wavy, curling blonde hair, which is surprisingly short when it is plastered down, but unless she has been in swimming, never is." When Earhart addressed the women's committee of the Air League of the British Empire after the flight, Lady Astor requested that she take off her hat, thereby allowing the luncheon guests during the speech "a chance to admire her tousled golden curls." In 1932 a typical description of the recent conqueror of the Atlantic for a second time called her a "tall, slim, blushing girl, her short clipped blonde hair a riot of seeming disorder." Another described her "rebellious short blond hair." By the time of her 1935 flight from Mexico references to the "tousled-haired flyer" had become practically obligatory.[35]

The fact that her hair was so commented on by newspaper accounts, and so prominent in the newsreels, suggests the way in which certain characteristics of public figures become implanted in the public mind. For example, Carole Lombard was identified with her peroxide blond hair, Groucho Marx with his cigar, Eleanor Roosevelt with her prominent teeth, and tennis stars Helen Jacobs and Suzanne Lenglen with shorts and bandannas, respectively. No wonder Amelia hardly ever appeared in public after 1928 in a hat; it would have robbed the public of her most identifiable feature. Only rarely did her unruly hair cause negative comment, but when it did, the correspondent could be blunt: "Dear Amelia. You surly [sic] look like a Zuluwoman. Won't you pleas try to be more cultured by combing your hair before an audience."[36]

A close second to fascination with A.E.'s hair was attention to her wardrobe. One of the interesting things about the many photographs of Amelia Earhart is how many different contexts and settings she appears in, necessitating different styles of dress. Most of the newspaper photographs and newsreel footage, of course, show her in the clothes she wore for flying, which was the occasion when she was most often in the news. But because of her extensive speaking and lecturing engagements, plus the promotions and modeling she did, she was often photographed wearing nonflight garb. This combination of different genres and styles of dress created an interesting, subtle, and ultimately complex representation of Earhart in the media and popular culture. At the very least, crossing these boundaries with different clothes showed that one could be a flier (code: masculine) and a woman (code: feminine) at the same time. But the most important point is that even when dressed in male-inspired clothing or photographed in traditionally male settings, Amelia Earhart was indisputably a woman.

One of the things that struck many who came into contact with Amelia Earhart was what aviation friend Fay Gillis Wells called her "unexpected femininity." Similarly, a Washington newspaperwoman drew attention to two aspects of Earhart's appearance: her "incredibly slim hips" and her "great femininity." This "decidedly feminine" theme appears repeatedly in recollections, no doubt encouraged by the preconceptions that a woman who could fly the ocean would necessarily be large, perhaps burly, maybe even a bit on the masculine side.[37] But as observer after observer noted, Amelia Earhart's appearance was not masculine. Earhart was always a bit surprised when people expected her to look more like a man. "Why should I?" she noted. "Piloting a plane doesn't develop muscle."[38]

This picture, taken around 1930, was one of Amelia's favorites. Pearls, wings, and a velvet evening gown--that's how this pioneering aviator chose to present herself to the public.

It was still unusual for women to be flying in the late 1920s and 1930s, so it is perhaps not surprising that what women wore when they flew was also of interest. Earhart noted that the two questions she was always asked about her 1928 flight were was she afraid (no) and what she wore. "I had no intention whatever of trying to set a fashion in transatlantic air attire," she protested, but her combination of high laced boots, brown breeches, a silk blouse with necktie and scarf, and a leather jacket became the public's iconographic image of what a female aviator should look like. In general, as part of their attempts to make flying seem a part of everyday life, Earhart and many other women pilots like Ruth Nichols and Blanche Noyes tried to avoid special clothing when flying. Amelia flew in either street clothes or pants; occasionally she substituted jodhpurs for slacks. As she said, "I don't get all cluttered up for an automobile ride. Why should I dress any differently for all this?" The sight of the aviator matter-of-factly stepping into her plane just as she might into a car never failed to surprise onlookers.[39]

She took a similar no-nonsense approach to her 1937 round-the-world trip. She packed only the bare essentials: two pairs of slacks, several plaid sports shirts, a leather windbreaker, a warm scarf, coveralls, changes of underwear, low shoes, and, in the words of one newspaper report, "positively no hat." In another account about her packing, the reporter declared, "She has declined all invitations to receptions or social functions along the route—and doesn't expect to wear a dress again until she gets home." That Amelia Earhart's wardrobe was considered news by the *New York Times* in 1937 was a measure of the scrutiny to which female public figures were subjected for supposed traces of female vanity.[40]

One of the most unusual things about Earhart's much-publicized wardrobe was her propensity to wear (and be photographed in) slacks in public. This was an unusual fashion statement at the time. In the 1930s slacks were customarily reserved for the private or informal side of life or for sports activities; a very few women—notably Hollywood stars like Marlene Dietrich and Katharine Hepburn—ordinarily wore pants in public. Not until World War II were women customarily seen on the street in anything other than skirts or dresses, and then only because the rationing of silk and nylon stockings and the increase in female war workers made it more acceptable.[41]

Because she led such a generally active life and spent so much time around airfields or in the air, Earhart had an excuse to dress in pants. She adopted this style wherever possible, although it proved a bit much for Purdue's conservative college community of West Lafayette, Indiana.[42] From photographs it is clear that although she perhaps borrowed occasional pieces of male clothing like belts, she did not wear men's pants. Her slacks buttoned or zipped on the side, a style she could wear well, given her flat stomach and athletic build. Mainly the pants were tailored and trim, sometimes with cuffs, although she also had several pairs of full-legged trousers. She liked sensible walking shoes that tied. Much of her wardrobe no doubt came directly from Abercrombie and Fitch, one of the few places where athletically inclined women could find top-quality sports clothing. So comfortable was she in this "uniform" that many of the publicity shots done for the 1937 flight unapologetically featured her in pants and plaid shirts, enhanced, however, by the inevitable silk scarf which had been her trademark since the 1928 flight.

When Amelia Earhart started making the best dressed lists, it was more for her street clothes than her flying fashions, although the modes were linked in the public mind. In 1934 she joined such well-known women as Eleanor Roosevelt, hostess Elsa Maxwell, artist Georgia O'Keeffe, writer Fannie Hurst, and socialite Mrs. John Hay Whitney on the ten best dressed women list, according to American fashion designers. The choice of Eleanor Roosevelt, known for her general disregard for fashion, suggests that these lists tended to cite the best *known* women as much as the best *dressed*. Like E.R., Earhart measured up on both counts. Earhart was cited as the "smartest dresser in aviation" and praised for the "flawless sports clothes" which she designed herself.[43]

After the fashion mistakes of 1928 the everyday Amelia did cut a stylish figure. She was rarely spotted in the rather severe business suit favored by most professional women at the time, with its long

Hand on hip, hand on prop, Amelia Earhart poses for a publicity shot with her new Lockheed Electra. Looking like a college coed, she was then thirty-nine years old.

jacket, plain skirt, and severe silk blouse. More to her liking were a long skirt (no more short hemlines for her in the more conservative fashion climate of the 1930s) and a short, almost bolero type of jacket cut to her high waist, worn over a simple silk blouse. Dresses were simple, slim affairs, belted but rarely enhanced by shoulder pads. Totally absent were any busy prints, frilly blouses, or unnecessary details or embellishments. These clothes exuded a simple and elegant taste that did not change from year to year. Amelia Earhart was not caught up in fashion for fashion's sake and clearly had favorite outfits or accessories that she wore repeatedly in public. After both the 1928 and 1932 flights, clothing she bought and wore in London she then wore again, without apology, at receptions on her homecoming.

As already noted, Amelia Earhart wore clothes so well that she actually modeled them. She posed for such famous photographers as Edward Steichen, whose 1931 shots in *Vanity Fair* featured Earhart in a plain wool skirt, sweater top, and scarf, looking more like a college coed than a thirty-four-year-old transatlantic flier.[44] She also served as the model for her line of sports clothes in 1933 and 1934. For that, and for the inevitable publicity shots generated to enhance her flying career, she learned to pose naturally, to maintain an unaffected demeanor, and let the clothes drape and fall down her slim frame. This stance was similar to the way she posed for the newsreels.

It is hard to say that Amelia Earhart looked quite so at home in evening clothes. The long, slinky dresses favored in the 1930s and popularized by Hollywood stars overaccentuated her slender figure and lack of curves; no one would ever call her sexy in such clothes. Her plain hairstyle and lack of interest in jewelry or other adornments added to her somewhat unglamorous appearance. If it was a ceremonial occasion, she often awkwardly clutched a spray of flowers while at the same time she dealt with female accessories she usually avoided, like purses. The furs or stoles she wore on fancy occasions similarly looked just a bit incongruous on a woman who preferred Abercrombie and Fitch slacks to an Adrian gown. Yet she still drew praise in the press for her formal clothes, as this 1932 account attests:

"Amelia Earhart Putnam, transatlantic flier, is not always dressed in flying togs. Here she is in conventional attire—and a very pretty gown it is, too, we'll all agree."[45]

Amelia Earhart could change like a chameleon when she moved from evening clothes to flying togs to more conventional female clothing and back again. Of course, on both her transatlantic crossings the transformation was total, since she took no clothing with her and had to buy or borrow a wardrobe once she arrived. As she observed with her typical dry humor concerning all things feminine, "There seems to be a feeling that a woman preparing to drop in on England, so to speak, ought to have at least something of a wardrobe, not to mention those feminine luxuries and knicknacks [sic] in which our sex is supposed to delight." The press always took pleasure in noting that after crossing the Atlantic without any baggage save a toothbrush and comb, she turned to more typically feminine activities, such as buying dresses. As the New York Times told its readers in 1928, "She had also donned a frock and other feminine attire for the first time in days, and was suddenly and miraculously transformed from a daring celebrated aviatrix to a typical, nice American girl having a celebration abroad with a party of friends from home."[46]

In an interesting twist on the tradition of women donning male attire to experience the freedom of movement men enjoy in public, Earhart was free from the attention of the London crowds in 1928 when she dressed in women's clothes, according to one newspaper account. Complete with a "perky black toque" to hide her already well-known hair, "her identity as a celebrity was disguised so completely that she was able to mingle freely in the throngs of London streets without recognition, though pictures of her have been prominent in the London newspapers for two days."[47]

Clearly Amelia Earhart was crossing back and forth over traditional gender boundaries with both her actions and her dress. In general, women are freer to borrow male fashions without social sanctions than men, who, when they choose to dress in women's clothing, upset expected power and gender hierarchies. In fact, women who dress either in men's clothing or in male-inspired dress often look quite dignified, whereas the reverse (transvestism) is rarely true.[48] Yet Amelia bore little resemblance to the stereotyped figure of the upper-class mannish lesbian, which was common in bohemian circles like Paris's Left Bank, New York's Greenwich Village, Harlem and occasionally in Hollywood. These lesbians dressed in tuxedoes and adopted such male affectations as top hats, cigarette holders, and monocles, a style which was foreign to A.E. Nor did she affect the style of working-class lesbians, with their exaggerated role divisions (and corresponding clothes vocabulary) of butch and femme.[49]

Sometimes when a person dresses or acts in a way that blurs gender boundaries, she or he is called androgynous, and that term has certainly been applied to Amelia Earhart. For example, when feminist Susan Brownmiller tried to pinpoint Earhart's ongoing appeal, she called her "America's first androgynous sex symbol." The word "androgynous," according to Carolyn Heilbrun, "defines a condition under which the characteristics of the sexes, and the human impulses expressed by men and women, are not rigidly assigned. Androgyny seeks to liberate the individual from the confines of the appropriate." Certain film stars, like Katharine Hepburn, are sometimes described as androgynous, and the term was also often applied to the boyish flappers of the 1920s.[50]

But an even better term to capture Amelia Earhart's persona is "gender blending." According to sociologist Holly Devor, genderblending individuals "indisputably belong to one sex and identify themselves as belonging to the corresponding gender while exhibiting a complex mixture of characteristics from each of the two standard roles."[51] This definition was formulated to apply to women who are often mistaken for men, a situation which does not apply to Amelia Earhart, but the term has a wider relevance and significance.

Gender blending captures the way in which Amelia Earhart's lifestyle, image, and appeal failed to fit into traditional gender categories. Listen to this recollection by Earhart's friend and fellow airline executive Gene Vidal, which identifies a variety of gendered positions: "She was a very interesting person, a tomboy who liked all

men's games, enjoyed being with the mechanics working on airplanes, and yet was a little girl in some respects. Although often in
trousers, she was very feminine and quite romantic in some ways."
Other examples of the gender-blending aspects of her self-repre-
sentation include photographs of her in flying clothes complete with
man's tie knotted at the neck, but carrying a huge bouquet of roses;
her ubiquitous silk flying scarf, which became the iconographic signature of the female aviator; and her rarely being seen in public
carrying a purse, one of the most widely recognized gender indi-
cators. In each of these cases the usual meanings of things are shifted
or made more complex by the addition (or, in the case of the purse,
the absence) of another prop or affect.[52]

Two of the most striking examples of Earhart's blurring gender
representations involved pearls, one of the few pieces of jewelry
she ever wore. Just before the 1928 transatlantic flight Earhart was
photographed in the cockpit of an open plane, wearing street clothes
but with a leather cap and goggles covering her hair. The "signs"
clearly say "aviator." But the "signs" also say "woman" because in
this pose of a dashing woman in an open cockpit she is *fingering a
string of pearls*.[53] In another photograph taken after the flight, one
often reproduced for publicity purposes, Earhart is dressed in a dark
evening gown with a low neck; she is wearing two ornaments: a
triple string of pearls and the wings presented to her in 1928 as an
honorary major in the 381st Observation Squadron, U.S. Army
Reserve, at San Francisco's Presidio.[54] What these photographs
demonstrate is a juxtaposition and blending of traditional symbols
of femininity, such as silk scarves, pearls, and flowers, against symbols and images more traditionally associated with men: technology like airplanes, clothing like pants and leather jackets, military
honors like wings. The effect is powerful, compelling, yet also
destabilizing, especially in the context of 1930s gender roles.

Many other images of Amelia Earhart contain a jarring note meant
to disturb the too-easy equation of her with the gender status quo.
When modeling clothes, she is not conventionally beautiful or
seductive; instead of averting her eyes in the traditional female pose
of subservience, she usually gazes forthrightly and unapologetically

into the camera. When she is in motion, she strides purposefully toward the camera, a feat made possible by her sensible clothes and flat shoes. When she is photographed with airplanes or other pieces of (male) technology, such as powerful cars, she conveys an aura that she belongs there, wants to be there, is enjoying herself immensely, and has no intention of leaving. She can stand in a bulky flight suit right alongside any man, as his equal, hands on hips just like him. She shows that women can look attractive in a pair of greasy coveralls. Even when she is photographed in pinup-inspired publicity shots (leaning against the propeller of a plane; standing in front of the Electra with her arms raised upward like a chorus girl; looking coyly through a directional signal), she counteracts the usual sexual connotations of such poses with her sure sense of entitlement. Despite the props and poses, she does not look out of place. And by extension, if she is there, then other women belong too.

The distance of these photographic images from traditional representations of femininity is suggested by comparing them with an oil painting of Earhart done in 1937 by the well-known American illustrator and painter Howard Chandler Christy (1873–1952). His rendition is of a much more conventionally "feminine" woman. Earhart's lips are especially full and lush, suggesting the use of makeup (something the aviator rarely used) to enhance their effect. The features of the face are rounder and softer; the hair is more softly coiffed than usual. From the waist up, she is dressed in the recognizable flying outfit of leather jacket, silk blouse, and scarf, but she is uncharacteristically wearing a long, full skirt. In the folds of the blouse and the movement of the scarf, there is even the hint of breasts, a reminder of her sex which is totally absent in most photographs of this very flat-chested woman. Although the painting is recognizable as Earhart, it shifts away from photographic images challenging gender roles to a representation that actually serves to reinforce them.[55]

Another way that Amelia Earhart diverged from traditional representations of femininity was that she was rarely, if ever, presented as a sex object or as exuding any kind of heterosexual attraction. (Whether she meant something else in terms of lesbian iconography is another matter.)[56] Since she did not marry until 1931, she entered public life as an unmarried woman, and an unattached one at that once she had shed her loose engagement to Sam Chapman after the 1928 flight. Yet except for a few obligatory marriage proposals in her fan mail, Amelia Earhart's availability as a love interest, date, or potential wife was rarely played up by the press the way, for example, that the unmarried status of tennis star Helen Wills was. Perhaps it was the more feminine appeal of the game of tennis as played by Wills; perhaps it was her fuller figure that made her seem a more likely candidate for heterosexual attraction. Whereas a New York newspaper editor once observed that every male in America from "six to sixty" was in love with Wills, no one ever said things like that about the transatlantic flier.[57]

Even if no one would likely have accused Amelia Earhart of being a sultry sex goddess or of having "sex appeal,"[58] she did have an allure that was based in part on her physicality. Historian Elizabeth Wilson observes about such Hollywood stars as Marlene Dietrich and Greta Garbo that "the mysterious quality of their allure comes in part from a hint of manliness at the very heart of their feminine presence," and this insight could apply to A.E. as well. Hostess Elsa Maxwell's reasoning for including Amelia Earhart on her 1935 list of the ten most interesting women speaks also to this allure tinged with ambiguity: "Fascination is an elusive quality that is fast disappearing . . . it is hard to find because it has nothing to do with beauty, charm, glamour, riches, or blueblood—only one woman in a thousand has it. Amelia Earhart has everything that fascinates."[59]

Trying to figure out what made Amelia Earhart so fascinating is similar to trying to figure out why certain Hollywood stars were "box office"—that is, why the public would go to any film they were in just to see them. Although studio executives and critics tried to figure out the basis of star appeal, in truth Hollywood had no idea who was going to make it and who would not. It came down to personality—that certain something, perhaps a combination of "beauty plus brains," that sparked on the screen. Elinor Glyn coined "It" in the 1920s to describe a kind of appeal that com-

In Howard Chandler Christy's hands, Amelia Earhart looks quite different—softer, fuller, more feminine. The jacket, scarf, and bracelet are recognizable from other photographs, but she never wore a full skirt like that when she flew.

bined feminine allure and pep. (The actress Clara Bow best embodied "It.") In the 1930s the most alluring actresses possessed, according to *Photoplay,* something called the "X" quality. The four actresses who best embodied "X" were Marlene Dietrich, Greta Garbo, Katharine Hepburn, and Joan Crawford. True, they shared a certain body type ("broad shoulders, slender torso, long limbs almost like a boy's"), but there was also something that made these women different from all others, out of the ordinary, mysterious, intriguing.[60]

In Hollywood parlance, Amelia Earhart was "box office."[61] Like Hepburn or Dietrich, she was not a traditional beauty, but she had a strongly defined personal style. She conveyed intelligence, self-respect, and courage. The public was interested in knowing about her and seeing pictures of her. She was not a conventional sex symbol. Instead, her very representation had the potential to make audiences think about gender roles in dramatically new and open-ended ways.

Amelia Earhart offered the public a highly individualistic yet compelling new way to be a woman. This "slender figure in brown jodhpurs, orange silk blouse, and a brown bandana" slyly undercut the status quo of gender roles. Her image challenged received notions of femininity and women's identification with home and family but without abandoning womanliness entirely. What a film historian said of Katharine Hepburn applies equally well to Amelia Earhart: "She offers an intriguing demonstration of an acceptance of sexual difference combined with a refusal of sexist inequalities."[62] Here was a woman in public, acting, doing things, surrounded by props and symbols that left no doubt that she had left the kitchen and entered the public realm. More to the point, the very confidence and poise which she displayed in her public roles suggested that women had a right to such freedoms, that it was perfectly natural for women to be doing nontraditional things.

No messages in the media or popular culture are gender-free. In Earhart's case her widely distributed iconographic image served to challenge and potentially to subvert traditional notions of women's subordination. She claimed the public space not just as an individual but as a woman. And she claimed it not just for herself but for womankind as a whole.

According to art historian T. J. Clark, "Society is a battlefield of representations, on which the limits and coherence of any given set are constantly being fought for and regularly spoilt."[63] Amelia Earhart found many ways to get across her message of feminist liberation and independence: in interviews, on the lecture circuit, over the radio, in articles and newspaper columns. Sometimes she did not even need to open her mouth.

Popular Heroines /
Popular Culture

Page through old issues from the 1930s of *Mid-Week Pictorial,* a
forerunner of modern picture magazines like *People,* and you are
immediately struck by the number of pictures of women. Amelia
Earhart is not the only woman represented in these pages. Women
athletes, other women fliers, Hollywood actresses, career women,
women with offbeat accomplishments or interests—there they are,
page after page, coexisting with, almost overshadowing the images
of men. In the 1920s and 1930s it was not unusual for women to
win public acclaim or to be in the public spotlight. Like Amelia
Earhart, popular heroines such as Dorothy Thompson, Babe
Didrikson, Eleanor Roosevelt, Katharine Hepburn, Georgia
O'Keeffe, and Margaret Bourke-White served as role models and
examples of what women could accomplish in the modern world.
Like Earhart, they worked hard at their careers and consciously
sought out the media to keep their names before the public. Many

of them thrived on publicity. After all, it made their careers possible, if not more satisfying.

In the course of her career Amelia Earhart met many of these female trendsetters and newsmakers or had her name linked with theirs.[1] These were the kind of women Earhart admired and with whom she felt comfortable, and they returned the compliment. More important, many of them shared Earhart's individualistic approach to women's advancement. They may not have called themselves feminists or consciously identified with the cause of women, but by the very fact of their gender, they drew attention to women's ever-widening roles in modern life. If they could do it, so could other women, a message that was especially important in a period lacking an active feminist movement.

Why were the 1920s and 1930s so chock-full of popular heroines? It was still an era of women "firsts"—the first to cross the Atlantic, the first to hold an important federal job, the first to win two gold medals in the Olympics. The granting of the vote to women in 1920 symbolized the dramatic changes in modern women's lives, changes which stood in stark contrast with the far more restricted world of their grandmothers, even their mothers. The interwar years seemed to provide openings and cultural spaces for individual women to achieve and win approval on a par with men. Precisely because women had not done these things before, they were interesting to the general public. Photographer Margaret Bourke-White noted that while it was harder for a woman to begin, "once she gets started she has an easier time because her accomplishments attract more attention than a man's would."[2] In a news-hungry age, these women were news.

It is this hunger for news that holds a clue to the large number of women in the public eye in the 1920s and 1930s. Americans had more time for leisure, and they avidly followed developments in fields like sports, aviation, entertainment, and the movies, all areas where women had toeholds or, in the case of the Hollywood screen, practically dominated. Instruments of mass culture, such as newsreels, radio, high-circulation magazines, and the movies, brought these images within easy access of the broader public. The Great

Depression did not dim this fascination and may in fact have enhanced it.

Between 1928 and 1937 Amelia Earhart worked tirelessly before the public to encourage women to seize the new opportunities now open to them. The force of her message of autonomy, independence, and individualism was magnified and enhanced precisely because Earhart was not the only woman who embodied and promoted those traits. Models of individual female achievement and accomplishment were threaded throughout the popular culture. The messages were not uniform, but in general they reinforced and complemented the liberal feminist vision of individualism that was at the core of Amelia Earhart's philosophy. These messages served to keep feminism alive in the interwar period and beyond.

Hollywood is the place to start a discussion of women and popular culture in the 1920s and 1930s. The interwar years represented the height of the film industry's impact on American culture, and the California community of Hollywood symbolized the allure of the new medium. Hollywood was a young community, just a few decades old, and its denizens were young, too, drawn to what was perhaps America's last frontier. It was a one-industry town; people lived, died, and gossiped movies twenty-four hours a day. Even though only a tiny fraction of the film industry ever achieved the monumental wealth and fame of its top stars and movie moguls, Hollywood stood for leisure, opulence, personal fulfillment, and celebrity.[3]

Hollywood as a film industry was dominated in these years by the studio system. Studios had styles so distinctive that a moviegoer could begin watching a film after the credits had run and instantly tell whether it came from Paramount or Fox. But individual film style and a director's artistic vision often took a backseat to the dedication to make money, as studios, like factories, cranked out a feature or more a week. The Hollywood movie moguls identified with particular studios—Sam Goldwyn at Metro-Goldwyn-Mayer, Adolph Zukor at Paramount, David O. Selznick at RKO and then MGM, Darryl Zanuck at 20th Century-Fox—were not heavily involved in the actual making of the films. Instead they excelled at the business aspects, such as marketing, distribution, and audience research, skills crucial to this large, growing, and very profitable entertainment industry. Ultimate authority belonged to the owners and corporate officers located on the East Coast, mainly in New York, which was also George Palmer Putnam's base when he served on the editorial board of Paramount in the mid-1930s.[4]

In many ways, especially in the opportunities for women it offered, the film industry had parallels to aviation in its early years. In such a new industry anything went, and if women had something to contribute, they were in. Later, as the industry became more bureaucratized and hierarchical, opportunities for women declined and prejudice increased, a pattern found in other industries and corporate organizations. But in the 1920s and 1930s Hollywood offered women a great range of jobs and openings, with women well represented behind the scenes as technical workers, makeup artists, and costume designers. Women were especially valued as screenwriters (Anita Loos and Frances Marion are two examples),[5] production assistants, personnel managers, executives in studio management, and even occasionally directors, like Dorothy Arzner. Top management of the major studios, however, remained firmly in male hands.[6]

But like that of pilots in aviation, the most glamorous role for women in Hollywood was that of actress. Acting was one of the few professions in which a woman's opportunities were as great as a man's. Indeed, the 1920s and the 1930s represented a golden age for women in film. Viewers at the time, and film historians ever since, have been attracted to the "vibrant strength of character" personified by these fast-talking and autonomous screen heroines. These women were independent, they made choices, they took responsibility for their actions, and they were successful, both on-screen and off. Even if the plots did not always promote positive roles for women in the end, the allure of these actresses created new expectations for women. The liberated personae of the successful

Hollywood actresses bore striking similarities to the image projected by aviators like Amelia Earhart.[7]

Women's dominance of the screen was apparent during the silent
era, when Mary Pickford, Clara Bow, and Theda Bara rivaled
Rudolph Valentino and Charlie Chaplin for the loyalty of fans and
moviegoers. The introduction of sound in 1927 had a major impact
on the film industry in general and on the careers of silent screen
stars. Clara Bow and Mary Pickford did not survive the transition
to talkies. But other actresses, generally younger and new to the
screen, did. They included the enigmatic and hauntingly beautiful
Greta Garbo. So eagerly awaited was Garbo's first picture with
sound (in which she uttered the line "Give me a whiskey with ginger ale on the side—and don't be stingy, baby") that the studios
advertised it simply as "GARBO TALKS."

The films made between 1927 and 1933 exhibited an undeniable
openness, a willingness to challenge or flout traditional gender roles,
and an acceptance of overt sexuality on the screen that was unique
to the early years of sound. Garbo took advantage of this, as did
Marlene Dietrich. But the actress who best embodied women's equal
right to enjoy sex, indeed perhaps even exploit men for her own
sexual pleasure, was Mae West. The double entendres that slyly
escaped from West's lips ("It's not the men in my life," she said
deadpan, "it's the life in my men") titillated her audiences but proved
too much for nervous Hollywood censors. One result was a Production Code in 1934 that severely limited alternative representations of sexuality and morality with a stringent lists of dos and
don'ts for plots and themes.[8]

The Production Code had mixed results for the representation of
women on the screen. On the one hand, it cut off the openness and
fluidity that had characterized such films as *Design for Living* (1933),
Queen Christina (1933), *Blonde Venus* (1932), and *Susan Lenox—Her
Rise and Fall* (1931). On the other hand, by banning boudoir roles
as too seductive or amoral, it forced female characters out into the
real world, where they took on roles as working women, secretaries, journalists, and other independent heroines in the genre of

screwball or romantic comedies. It is primarily these post-Production Code heroines that give the decade of the 1930s its reputation for liberated roles for women.

In this age of fascination with both the on-screen roles of stars and their off-screen personae, two actresses stood out for their ability to convey independence and autonomy. One was Bette Davis. Davis was outspoken, direct, and totally concentrated on her career; she was a shrewd businessperson who expected good scripts and demanded the best in production support and working conditions. She was one of the few actresses able to take on unsympathetic roles, such as Mildred in *Of Human Bondage* (1934) and Julie Marsden in *Jezebel* (1938). Though not conventionally beautiful, she commanded attention. She once joked that her epitaph should read, "Here lies Ruth Elizabeth Davis—She did it the hard way." [9]

The second was Katharine Hepburn. The screen had never seen anything like "La Hepburn" when she moved from Bryn Mawr to the New York stage to Hollywood as a young actress in her twenties. From a privileged background (her father was a Hartford surgeon, and her mother a noted suffragist and birth control activist), she had fallen in love with the screen when she saw her first film. "If I could do that, I'd die of joy," she exclaimed. No matter what characters she played, her strong-willed personality came through, and she was one of the few actresses allowed to sacrifice love for career, at least temporarily. Even when she was labeled "box-office poison" in the late 1930s, she fought back with hits such as *The Philadelphia Story* (1940) and *Woman of the Year* (1942). Even more so than Davis, she personified female competence, intelligence, and individualism. To this day she is remembered as a model of independence and getting one's own way. [10]

Both Katharine Hepburn and Bette Davis exemplify what has been called the star system. In this formulation the audience's knowledge of the actor's or actress's private life or personal qualities informs and affects the reaction of viewers to whatever role is being played. In other words, the image of the star is filtered through not only the script but the accumulation of prior information about the star from magazines, gossip columns, articles, interviews, and

Katharine Hepburn was one of the few female figures to be widely photographed in slacks in the 1930s. This photograph is from the 1939 stage version of *The Philadelphia Story;* the next year the film version, featuring Hepburn, Cary Grant, and James Stewart, won two Oscars.

earlier roles. For both Hepburn and Davis, their star personalities were constructed along the lines of the Independent Woman. A similar star persona, of course, was constructed in the public mind for Amelia Earhart.[11]

Actresses like Hepburn and Davis occupied center stage in the popular culture of Hollywood's Golden Years. By extension they also acted as role models for the aspirations of young women. Acting was one of the few professions in which women could be assertive and independent without being penalized. Because actors generally did not come from the privileged class, acting could be a significant avenue of upward social mobility. It was also one of the few professions in which women and men were well paid. No wonder youth, especially young women, flocked to Hollywood or reached out to their favorite movie idols. According to Leo Rosten's analysis of fan mail received by a major studio in January 1939, between 85 and 90 percent of it came from girls, primarily between the ages of thirteen and twenty-one years old. The gender dynamics of this fan mail—that it was not just girls with crushes on male stars but women writing to female stars—suggests new ways of thinking about identification, role models, and identity.[12]

"Aside from film stars," notes historian Lois Banner, "the most prominent women in the United States in the 1920s and 1930s were sportswomen." These decades represented the Golden Age of Sports, a time when the country seemed to be on a "sports binge."[13] As the adulation extended to Gertrude Ederle for her 1926 Channel swim demonstrates, these heroic roles were open to both men and women athletes. In fact, sports figures joined Hollywood actresses, aviators, and other new popular figures on the "cutting edge of change" regarding women's roles.[14]

Women athletes emerged as popular heroines in the interwar years in part because of new ideologies and assumptions that challenged older notions of women's physical inferiority. But women athletes had a harder time winning legitimacy and respect than men; they trod a fine line between approval for their athletic prowess and a feared loss of femininity for their adoption of male competitive traits or, even worse, masculine physical appearances. Listen to Eleanor Holm, who had just won a medal at the 1932 Olympics in Los Angeles: "It's great fun to swim and a great thrill to compete in the Olympics, but the moment I find swimming is making me athletic looking, giving me big, bulky muscles, making me look like an Amazon rather than a woman, I'll toss it to one side." [15]

The most gifted female athlete of the period was Babe Didrikson. A natural athlete who excelled at a variety of sports (when asked her favorite, she replied, "The one I'm playing"), she came to popular attention by winning three medals in track and field at the 1932 Olympics held at Los Angeles. Amelia Earhart flew out to Los Angeles for the Olympics with her husband and his son, so perhaps she was in the crowd cheering "the Babe" on. Didrikson later visited Amelia and George at their home in Rye. [16]

Seeming not to care about her amateur status and also needing to earn her living during the worst of the depression, Babe Didrikson turned professional after the Olympics, touring with a men's exhibition basketball team. (There were no women's pro teams then.) By mid-decade she had decided to take up golf, the sport with which her name is most associated. In 1938 she married wrestler George Zaharias, who eventually gave up his career to become her manager. Besides getting an excellent manager (shades of Amelia Earhart and George Palmer Putnam, or the film combination of Katharine Hepburn and Spencer Tracy in the movie *Pat and Mike*), the marriage also removed doubts about her being a "normal" woman by providing her with heterosexual credentials. Combined with the switch to golf, a far more acceptable sport for women than track and field or basketball, Babe Didrikson Zaharias was on her way to the star status she enjoyed until cancer prematurely ended her career, and her life, in 1956. [17]

In the 1930s Babe Didrikson was certainly well known (she was heavily promoted), but she was perhaps not as congenial a role model as the Hollywood stars or aviators like Amelia Earhart. She disdained traditional female adornments, leading sportswriter Paul Gallico to note, "She was the muscle moll to end all muscle molls,

Babe Didrikson was probably the 1930s' most gifted athlete. Early in the decade she excelled at track and field; later she took up golf.

the complete girl athlete." It was not meant as a compliment.[18] She was arrogant, supremely sure of herself, and not necessarily a friend to other women. She wanted to be known as the best athlete of all time, not just the best female athlete. Her professional activities advanced her own career, not women's sports in general. What she said to the Ladies Professional Golf Association in the 1940s summed up her attitude: "Well, *I'm* the star and all of you are in the chorus." She rarely spoke out on issues of politics or feminism, a reticence that characterized most athletes, male and female, then and now. But at the same time she symbolized new opportunities opening to women in sports, mainly at the amateur level but also in the tentative beginnings of women's professional sports.[19]

More than any other sport, tennis was the athletic endeavor in which women received the most popular approbation in the 1920s and 1930s. Alongside activities like croquet, golf, figure skating, bicycling, and even swimming, tennis was seen as "ladylike," a sport that women could engage in without damaging their femininity or working up too much of a sweat. Tennis also enjoyed connotations of being an upper-class sport or amusement and was often associated with sun-drenched California, where people played year-round. Amelia Earhart, an occasional tennis player, had first learned to play there in the 1920s, and she continued to enjoy the opportunities the California climate offered for athletic endeavors for the rest of her life.

The two greatest female tennis figures of the 1920s were Frenchwoman Suzanne Lenglen and Californian Helen Wills, dubbed by a recent biographer "the goddess and the American Girl." Their single face-to-face meeting, a 1926 exhibition match on the French Riviera won by Lenglen, was promoted as "the Match of the Century" and received the kind of attention devoted to the World Series, championship boxing matches, and transatlantic flights. Helen Wills, called Little Poker Face for her composure during matches, did not lose a singles match (in fact, not even a set) from 1927 to 1933, confirming her domination of the game of women's tennis. She finally lost to Helen Hull Jacobs, another Californian noted for playing in shorts. This shocking innovation (by contrast, Helen Wills played in a middy blouse and full skirt) was a fashion hit that soon became the norm.[20]

Helen Hull Jacobs and fellow Californian Alice Marble were popular tennis players in the 1930s, but neither approached the celebrity of Helen Wills. Probably more so than Babe Didrikson, Wills was the best-known female athlete of the interwar years. She was lionized for qualities similar to those attributed to Charles Lindbergh and Amelia Earhart: her old-fashioned values, her abstinence from cigarettes and alcohol, and her cultivation of a conservative, nonflapper appearance. Even when she bobbed her hair, Wills still projected a demure, almost matronly demeanor, with her

Tennis player Helen Wills Moody confirmed that female athletes were also attractive modern women. After winning the French Open for the third straight year in 1930, she sampled the latest French fashions in Paris.

full figure and staturesque build. She effectively presented her tennis career as a mere hobby and on the side pursued semiprofessional work as an artist and as a journalist covering major sporting and other events. In the latter capacity she once secured an exclusive interview with Amelia Earhart, who was in Paris being honored by the French government after her 1932 transatlantic solo. To Helen Wills's great surprise, Earhart answered the telephone herself and graciously agreed to a telephone rather than an in-person interview since the tennis player's feet were blistered from a recent match at the French Open.[21]

In many ways these popular sports figures seemed like natural candidates for careers in Hollywood, just as Amelia Earhart had been mentioned for a possible screen career. But just as Earhart decided to stick with aviation, the athletes by and large stayed out of the movies, although not for lack of trying. Channel swimmer Gertrude Ederle was one of the first to find out that the public was interested in Ederle the swimmer, not Ederle the actress. Helen Wills did a screen test in the 1920s, only to be told that her build was too athletic for the screen. It was not just women athletes who failed to make the transition, however: neither did Babe Ruth, Bill Tilden, or Red Grange, all of whom attempted unsuccessfully to translate their athletic prowess into Hollywood stardom. One of the few to make it was figure skater Sonja Henie, followed later by swimmer Esther Williams.[22]

Backstroker Eleanor Holm also gave Hollywood a try after she won her gold medal at the 1932 Olympics. But when the studio wanted her to swim in movies, compromising her amateur status for the upcoming 1936 games, she quit. Ironically she was kicked off the 1936 Olympic team for training violations. "I train on champagne and cigarettes," she told a reporter, in only slight hyperbole. Instead of trying Hollywood again, she turned professional and became the star of Billy Rose's *Aquacade,* which was featured at the 1937 Great Lakes Exposition and later at the 1939 World's Fair in New York. Soon after Holm married producer Billy Rose, yet another client-producer alliance, and retired from professional swimming and performing.[23]

The general lack of opportunities for women athletes in Hollywood is significant because it cut off one of the few avenues for women to support themselves through sports if they needed to earn a living. Even if tennis players maintained their amateur status by taking money under the table or securing endorsement deals, only someone from a fairly well-to-do background could get by without a regular salary. The difficulties that Babe Didrikson had in turning her athletic talents into a viable career confirm how tough it was. Popular celebrity and fame were one thing; paying the bills was another, as Amelia Earhart could attest.

In addition to film stars and athletes, several figures from the worlds of journalism and the arts were emblematic of the way that female achievement was elevated into iconographic status in the 1930s. The first was Dorothy Thompson, the epitome of the woman journalist. Sometimes linked in the public mind with the other outspoken Dorothy, the playwright and wit Dorothy Parker,[24] Thompson is often recalled as one of the most powerful female role models of her time. She developed such an uncanny knack for being in the midst of breaking news that this exchange was attributed to two newspapermen: "Have you heard? Dorothy Thompson got into town at noon." "Good God, what happened at one o'clock?" When she was banned from Germany by Adolf Hitler in 1934, she promptly went on a lecture tour in the United States, bringing the story of nazism to audiences across the country. She also spoke widely on the radio.[25]

But Thompson's real fame came when she began her column "On the Record" for the *New York Herald Tribune* in 1936. By the end of the decade she had emerged as the preeminent American voice in the struggle to preserve democracy from the threat of fascism. Although she was to leave the *Herald Tribune* in 1940, she continued her thrice-weekly column until 1958, part of the elite corps of journalists like Walter Lippmann, Heywood Broun, Walter Winchell, Arthur Krock, Westbrook Pegler, and Eleanor Roosevelt who had nationally syndicated columns. (*New York Times* commentator Anne O'Hare McCormick, the first woman journalist to win a Pulitzer Prize, also wrote on world affairs, but her column was not syndicated.[26]) The column brought Thompson wealth (her personal income was estimated at one hundred thousand dollars in 1939) and fame; after Eleanor Roosevelt, she was the second most influential woman in the United States.

Almost as famous as Dorothy Thompson, as both a reporter and a photographer, was Margaret Bourke-White, whose name, face, and photographs were known to millions. Her picture of the Fort Peck Dam graced the first cover of *Life* magazine in 1936. Bourke-White got her real breakthrough in the early 1930s with *Fortune* magazine, in which she developed a reputation as a skilled and daring photographer. Like Amelia Earhart and Dorothy Thompson, she hit the lecture circuit, talking to audiences about her experiences in photography. Her endorsement of products (including Camel cigarettes, which she chain-smoked) further increased her familiarity to the public at large. With the calculated attention she paid to the promotion of her career—"My life and career was not an accident. It was thoroughly thought out"—she bore many similarities to Amelia Earhart, although she lacked a promoter husband to manage her career. Two other similarities: she wore slacks in public, and she loved aviation. "Airplanes to me were always a religion," confessed Bourke-White, a statement with which Amelia could heartily concur.[27]

By the late 1930s this well-known woman with her outsize career became practically synonymous in the public mind with the image of the woman photographer. Soon Hollywood was drawing on her real-life exploits and those of her colleagues for inspiration on the screen. The character played by Tallulah Bankhead in Alfred Hitchcock's *Lifeboat* (1944) was based loosely on Margaret Bourke-White's experience as a wartime correspondent when her ship was sunk by German submarines and the crew and passengers huddled in lifeboats until rescued several days later. Similarly, the character Tess Harding in the Katharine Hepburn–Spencer Tracy movie *Woman of the Year* (1942) was popularly assumed to have been modeled on columnist Dorothy Thompson. Hollywood's fascination with the woman journalist dovetailed with expanding opportunities for women in this profession in the 1920s and 1930s.[28]

Margaret Bourke-White's studio was on the sixty-first floor of the
Chrysler Building in Manhattan, and this 1931 photograph taken by
Oscar Grauber shows how she took advantage of her prime New York
location. The large building in the background is the Empire State
Building, nearing completion.

Just as Amelia Earhart became the iconographic representation of the woman aviator and Dorothy Thompson and Margaret Bourke-White stood for the woman journalist, so painter Georgia O'Keeffe embodied the woman artist in the 1930s. When gallery owner and photographer Alfred Stieglitz first saw O'Keeffe's paintings in 1915, he exclaimed, "Finally, a woman on paper!" Her paintings, so different from everything else being produced at the time, came to be seen as an expression of feminine sensibility, an interpretation she disdained. Her own public persona (or, in Hollywood parlance, star system) represented independence and intense personal autonomy, an image enhanced by her highly distinctive style of always dressing in black. Her life was intertwined with that of Stieglitz, twenty-three years her senior, whom she married in 1924; she was the subject of many of his most compelling, and sensual, photographic series. Starting in 1929, she began to spend part of each year in New Mexico, which had a profound effect on her painting. She was essentially a solitary person, and her sense of aloneness suffused her work and life.[29]

Also achieving mythic female status in the arts in the 1930s was dancer and choreographer Martha Graham. Paralleling Katharine Hepburn's first reaction to movies, Graham had exclaimed, "I will dance like that," when she saw a Kandinsky painting of a slash of red against blue. Martha Graham used movement to express inner feelings, including a frank recognition of sexuality. Like so many of the other popular heroines of the 1930s, she cultivated a distinctive personal style—in her case, black, slicked-back hair, simple dark clothes.

Graham's messages had special power and resonance for women. Most of her choreography was developed from the point of view of the woman, and her dance embodied an essential core of feminist principles, especially with its emphasis on the heroine. She encouraged the female dancers in her company to project freedom, strength, integrity, and power as they danced, just as she herself did onstage and in her choreography. Graham gave everything to her work, never realizing the level of financial comfort or affluence achieved by other female public figures and artists at the time. But in the process she revolutionized dance, in effect making modern dance an American art form.[30]

Finally, in a category all her own, was Eleanor Roosevelt, probably the preeminent female role model of the 1930s. Roosevelt was unusual in this pantheon of prominent women in that she was older and more associated with the world of politics than with the fields of sports, entertainment, or the professions which supplied most popular heroines in the interwar years. By contrast, political reformers like birth control activist Margaret Sanger, Secretary of Labor Frances Perkins, or New Deal politician Molly Dewson, while well known, were hardly such popular figures as Dorothy Thompson, Amelia Earhart, or Babe Didrikson. And towering figures from an earlier era, such as settlement leader Jane Addams or writer Charlotte Perkins Gilman, both of whom died in 1935, no longer had much of a popular following.

More than any other person in the 1930s Eleanor Roosevelt represented courage and integrity, a woman who stood up for her convictions, no matter how unpopular they were. Many people made fun of her for her appearance, her prominent teeth, and her squeaky voice, and many people disagreed vehemently with her views. But they respected her right to have them, and in 1938 *Life* magazine called her the greatest American woman alive. The next year the American public gave Eleanor Roosevelt an approval rating higher than that of the president. Like so many of the other popular heroines, Eleanor Roosevelt touched individual lives through the media—through newsreels, her newspaper column, "My Day," lecture tours, and extensive public appearances. She was a role model for countless women and no doubt a few men. She remains the decade's most widely known, and probably its most greatly admired, woman.[31]

These women in Hollywood, athletics, journalism, the arts, and politics are well known to history. They achieved public recognition in their own lifetimes and have continued to hold a fascination for later generations. Individually, and collectively, these women acquainted the general public with new models of womanhood. They did not usually think of themselves as part of a movement or a larger cause; their accomplishments were theirs, and theirs alone. But there were important connections among them, linked in large part by this very quality of individualism. To get to where they got, these women often displayed characteristics similar to those of Amelia Earhart, traits that bear on the larger story of postsuffrage liberal feminism.

What would a collective profile of popular heroines from this period look like? While it is impossible to fit this sampling of such diverse and highly individualistic women into neat categories, there are suggestive parallels in life choices, attitudes, and career paths. The most obvious is homogeneity in terms of race, class, and religious background. In terms of racial composition, the sample is totally white. Not only were all the popular heroines of the interwar period white, but they generally came from Protestant backgrounds. Like Amelia Earhart, they may not have come from prosperous middle-class families, but with the possible exception of Babe Didrikson, none was really poor. As their lives unfolded, they benefited from privileges and opportunities not available to large segments of the American population, male or female.

The absence of black women is especially arresting since the same world of music and entertainment that supported the Hollywood stars also fostered the heyday of jazz, a uniquely American art form. The careers of such jazz women as Bessie Smith, Ma Rainey, Ethel Waters, and Billie Holiday peaked in the 1920s and 1930s. Like white heroines, these spunky, independent jazzwomen and blues singers were pioneering in new areas of expression and personal freedom, especially in the realm of sexuality. Their lyrics expressed female sexual autonomy in direct and provocative language. Hazel Carby notes how women blues singers occupied a "privileged space": "They had broken out of the boundaries of the home and taken their sensuality and sexuality out of the private into the public sphere."[32] But these entertainers and performers from the world of jazz were largely unknown to the white press and white public, as were most prominent figures in the African-American community as a whole.[33] One of the few exceptions was the concert singer Marian Anderson, who, with Eleanor Roosevelt's intervention, performed a free concert at the Lincoln Memorial in 1939, after the Daughters of the American Revolution had denied her permission to use Constitution Hall.[34]

Another similarity among the white popular heroines in the 1930s was their age. They were mainly in their thirties and early forties; that meant they had been born in the 1890s and early 1900s. The range of dates of birth corresponded roughly to the nature of the occupations and activities that brought them fame by the 1930s, with the professional women being a bit older and the Hollywood stars and athletes younger. Eleanor Roosevelt, born in 1884, was the oldest of the group, followed by Georgia O'Keeffe (1887). Several of the birth dates are bunched in the 1890s—Dorothy Thompson (1893), Martha Graham (1894), and Amelia Earhart (1897)—with Margaret Bourke-White (born in 1904) being a comparative youngster. The Hollywood stars were on the younger side as well: Greta Garbo (1905), Katharine Hepburn (1907), and Bette Davis (1908). Then came the sports figures and athletes, ranging from Helen Wills (1905) and Gertrude Ederle (1906) to Babe Didrikson (1911) and Alice Marble (1913).

The ages of these popular heroines are significant in two ways: they confirm that heroines, like heroes, tend to be young, a trend consistent with the general emphasis on youth in modern culture. More important in terms of women's history, the dates of birth situated them well in terms of their future roles; no longer bound by the traditions of nineteenth-century Victorian America, they could take advantage of the opportunities opening up to modern women in the twentieth.

These new roles often began in childhood. Like Amelia Earhart, many of them were tomboys. Katharine Hepburn for a while cropped her hair and called herself Jimmy, thinking that perhaps she was the wrong sex. Helen Wills only reluctantly gave up wearing Indian feathers and running through the Berkeley hills for the more sedate game of tennis, and Alice Marble cried all night when she was told to take up tennis as a way to stop being tomboy. Babe Didrikson noted, "Well, with almost any woman athlete, you seem to get the tomboy talk," but that was fine by her: "The way I look at it a girl that wants to become an athlete and do some winning should get that kind of start by being a tomboy. Get toughened by boys' games, but don't get tough." For the rest of their lives these former tom-boys remained free spirits, restless adventurers, and risk takers. [35]

In the nineteenth century most women of achievement would have found it difficult to combine marriage and career and would likely have remained single. This twentieth-century cohort of achievers, on the other hand, was much more likely to marry; even if not married, they were usually publicly identified as heterosex-ual, unlike their predecessors, who were associated with a more predominantly female-affiliated world. When these women mar-ried, however, they did it on their own terms, and they often kept their own names. Most movie stars did this as a matter of course, but so did women professionals from other fields. Amelia Earhart was what was known at the time as a Lucy Stoner, as were Georgia O'Keeffe, Dorothy Thompson, and Margaret Bourke-White. Helen Wills took Frederick Moody's name when they married in 1929, but she resumed her given name after they were divorced several years later. Eleanor Roosevelt had the most original solution. She married her distant cousin and did not have to change her name at all. [36]

The issues of marriage and children offer clues to the priorities and life choices of these women, especially the difficulty of com-bining the two. They were not opposed to traditional roles for women—just not for them. Margaret Bourke-White captured this stance well: "Mine is a life into which marriage doesn't fit well. If I had had children, I would have charted a widely different life, drawn inspiration from them, and shaped my work to them. . . . But a woman who lives a roving life must be able to stand alone." Any regrets? "I have always been glad I cast the die on the side I did." Bette Davis, who eventually did have children, once jested that if babies could be born at age thirteen, she would not mind having one. [37] Georgia O'Keeffe very much wanted to have chil-dren, but the combination of husband Alfred Stieglitz's opposition and her own doubts about whether she would be able to continue her creative work meant that she never did. In general, many of these women remained childless, like Amelia Earhart, or at most had one or two children.[38] And a majority of these marriages ended in divorce, suggesting perhaps that independent lives and marital commitments were not so easy to balance after all.[39]

Few women were as outspoken about issues of marriage and career as Katharine Hepburn. She was briefly married in the early 1930s, but the public learned of her marriage to Ludlow Ogden Smith only when she divorced him in 1932. In her autobiography she describes her conduct as that of a "terrible pig," interested only in "ME ME ME." Apparently she never seriously considered having children. As she later remarked, "It was a matter of becoming the best actress I could be or becoming a mother. But not both; I don't think I could do justice to both." Rather than make a husband and children victims of her career, she was to avoid the conflict entirely, and with no regrets. "But I didn't have it both ways. I didn't have a career and family. Being a housewife and a mother is the biggest job in the world, but if it doesn't interest you, don't do it. It didn't interest me, so I didn't do it. Anyway, I would have made a terrible parent."[40]

Hepburn's use of phrases such as "living like a man" was in many ways the closest her generation could come to a description of their life choices. When she said, "I put on pants so many years ago and declared a sort of middle road," she was talking literally and symbolically. "I have not lived as a woman. I have lived as a man. I've just done what I damned well wanted to and I've made enough money to support myself and I ain't afraid of being alone." To her, assuming "a masculine role" meant that she earned her own living without expecting anyone to take care of her. She did not think of herself as a traditional woman, and she did not want to be a man, so she styled herself as a sort of third sex somewhere in between. Here Hepburn echoed nineteenth-century feminist Margaret Fuller, who said, "I love best to be a woman, but womanhood is . . . too straitly-bound to give me scope." As a commentator once observed of Hepburn, it was almost a case of being female without the inconvenience.[41]

More than any other factor, what bound together the group of women achievers in the 1930s was their commitment to work over domesticity. Some might have seen this choice as selfish or self-centered, but for many of these women it was the essence of their identity. This prioritizing of work certainly characterized Amelia Earhart's attitude toward aviation and her career, and this emphasis was shared by all the other female achievers in public life. Bette Davis was forthright about her choices and their rewards: "It is only work that truly satisfies. I think I've known this all my life. . . . No one has ever understood the sweetness of my joy at the end of a good day's work. I guess I threw everything else down the drain." Margaret Bourke-White called work "a religion to me, the only religion I have. Work is something you can count on, a trusted, life-long friend who never deserts you."[42]

Most of this cohort of popular heroines were far too bound up in their individual careers to be very involved in organized political movements, including feminism, but several joined Amelia Earhart in speaking out in favor of the Equal Rights Amendment. In fact, women who operated on the principle of a deeply felt individualism were more likely to support the ERA than were social reformers like Eleanor Roosevelt, who feared the impact of the amendment on protective legislation for working women. Georgia O'Keeffe had first been involved in women's issues as a suffragist, as had Dorothy Thompson. Said O'Keeffe to sculptor Malvina Hoffman of feminism: "It is the only cause I get much interested in outside my own work." In part because of her lifelong friendship with National Woman's Party leader Anita Pollitzer, O'Keeffe wrote to Eleanor Roosevelt in 1944 to ask her to change her stance against the ERA. "Equal Rights and Responsibilities is a basic idea that would have very important psychological effects on women and men from the time they are born," O'Keeffe argued. "It could very much change the girl child's idea of her place in the world. I would like each child to feel responsible for the country and that no door for any activity they may choose is closed on account of sex." At base was O'Keeffe's belief that "all men and women stand equal under the sky." Eleanor Roosevelt withdrew her opposition to the ERA soon after,[43] but O'Keeffe's entreaty was only one of many influences that led E.R. to change her mind.

Katharine Hepburn endorsed the idea of complete equality between men and women as well. Her link to the ERA was through her mother, who was a member of the National Woman's Party, and especially her aunt Edith Houghton Hooker, a prominent NWP official. "In the theatre there is complete equality between men and women," Hepburn argued. "If that has worked well for the theatre, why not for all other walks of life?"[44] In both these statements the women affirm in remarkably similar language their belief in the essential equality of men and women. It was the individual, not the sex of the individual, that counted. That principle was the essence of their lives.

They embraced this principle not so much in spoken ideology as in how they lived. In order to be taken as seriously as men in their chosen fields, these women operated de facto within Eleanor Roosevelt's definition of feminism, which stressed "equal opportunity and Equal Rights" with any other citizens.[45] They were committed to breaking down barriers and debunking women's inferiority, and they believed that women, like men, could pull themselves up by the bootstraps if given a fair chance. Even if they did not specifically call themselves feminists, they acted on the core principles of feminism (especially those of liberal feminism) by expecting to be treated exactly as men's equals. The struggles of women aviators, and by extension those of many prominent interwar women in their respective fields, were emblematic of the rewards and the setbacks that women faced as they tried to make their way as ungendered individuals in a world where gender did, alas, still count.

When we survey the popular heroines and cultural figures of the 1930s, it is clear what a talented, unusual, spirited, and truly exceptional group they were. The appeal of Amelia Earhart makes more sense when placed in this broader context. This constellation of popular heroines collectively functioned as role models for wider and more fulfilling lives for women than the society usually allowed. "I'm like the Statue of Liberty to a lot of people," Katharine Hepburn wrote in her appropriately titled autobiography, *Me*. "When you've been around so long, people identify their whole lives with you."[46] Therein lies their enduring appeal: even if a woman could not realistically expect to fly the Atlantic, meet with Hitler, or win an Oscar, at least she could identify with someone who had.

There exists scattered and fragmentary, but intriguing, evidence that individual women (and an occasional man) in fact did identify with Amelia Earhart along these lines. Few of the undoubtedly thousands of letters written to Earhart survive, lost in fires that damaged various Earhart and Putnam residences or simply never systematically kept. Thus it is hard to discern from the limited available sources why her fans specifically selected Amelia Earhart as an object for admiration and idolization rather than or alongside, say, a Hollywood actress, a sports figure, or a male hero, such as explorer Richard Byrd or aviator Charles Lindbergh.[47]

Gender clearly was part of the story, however. A vast majority of her followers were women, even as early as the 1928 flight. As she wrote in *20 Hrs. 40 Min.*, "Best of all the letters are those from average people about the country—mostly women—who have found some measure of satisfaction, or perhaps a vicarious thrill, in the experiment of which I happened to be a small part." Although teenagers often wrote to Earhart, her fan club was not made up just of adolescent girls; mature women and married women followed her career, too. There were hardly any letters from men or boys.[48]

Some of these letters fell under the category of schoolgirl crushes—those fans who knew "that if I could be just like Amelia Earhart I would be the happiest person alive."[49] Another common refrain was "Although I never met her, it's just as if we were old friends." One young girl so totally identified with her idol that their lives practically merged in the retelling: "When Miss Earhart was a little girl she was just like I am. I am always playing football, or basketball or baseball. I never did go much for dolls. I like to do things the boys do. I am interested in Mechanic work. I don't like dresses. I would rather wear slacks anytime, they feel comfortable. Some people ask me if I won't wear dresses when I fly. I said, 'No Amelia Earhart doesn't so I am following her footsteps so I will do what she does regardless.' "[50]

But the admiration that Earhart engendered went far beyond just schoolgirl crushes. Many admirers seemed to derive a real sense of inspiration from her example, and a spur to personal (if not political) change. Wrote one admirer: "For I am one of those girls who has been aloft and doesn't want to come down to earth any more." On finishing *Last Flight,* a student at a Connecticut boarding school wrote to George Putnam, "There are many times when I am ashamed or impatient with my sex, predatory parasitic females; but today I am proud." Or as a teacher said to Amelia's mother after she was lost, "She is an ideal of so many women who dream but do not dare to do the pioneering." The teacher added tellingly, "Quite a few of my little girls in school have Amelia Earhart books and scrapbooks. She was our favorite 'big person.' " Many of those scrapbooks are no doubt gathering dust in attics, unless, of course, they were passed along to future generations. Louise Bode promised to do just that: "If I grow up and have a little girl of my own, I am going to give her my book and have her hand it on to her little girl and so on. So you can see it 'will live on.' "[51]

Why are these scrapbooks important? Because identifying with a popular heroine could represent the first step in a process of self-awareness and discovery, the feeling that perhaps a woman could make her life different or at least dream about such change. Writes literary critic Rachel Brownstein: "Young women like to read about heroines in fiction so as to rehearse possible lives and to imagine a woman's life as important—because they want to be attractive and powerful and significant, someone whose life is worth writing about, whose world revolves around her and makes being the way she is make sense." Many of Brownstein's conclusions about novel reading are relevant to the reasons why women identified with popular heroines in the 1920s and 1930s. "To want to become a heroine, to have a sense of the possibility of being one, is to develop the beginnings of what feminists call a 'raised' consciousness: it liberates a woman from feeling (and therefore perhaps from being) a victim or a dependent or a drudge, someone of no account."[52] The domestic novel could strengthen and shape a female reader's aspirations; so, too, could images from movies, newsreels, and other forms of popular culture. Given the range of twentieth-century popular heroines, the possibilities seemed vivid, indeed limitless.

The prominent and widely publicized female figures who dotted the landscape of the first half of the twentieth century suggested alternative, and exciting, ways of being women. Popular heroines like Amelia Earhart, Dorothy Thompson, and Katharine Hepburn personified the ideal of individual success and personal autonomy that was the essense of liberal feminism in the 1920s and 1930s. These public figures varied widely in how consciously they identified themselves with women's concerns, but none of them could ever escape being perceived through the lens of gender: each was always seen as a *woman* writer rather than a writer; an actress, not an actor; an aviatrix, not a pilot; and so forth. When the media presented their individual accomplishments as breakthroughs for women or as symbols of women's new roles in the modern world, these women played a part in the survival of a feminist impulse without their even having to swear allegiance to the cause.

This open-ended message forms a critical part of the history of twentieth-century feminism. The model of female independence drawn from popular culture served as a substitute for a more overtly political vision in the decades between the two waves of organized American feminism. As sociologist George Lipsitz has argued, popular culture can under certain circumstances become "a rehearsal for politics, trying out values and beliefs permissible in art but forbidden in social life."[53] This connection between the representations of women in popular culture and the ideology of feminism in twentieth-century America gives liberal feminist messages of equal rights and equal opportunity a central position in the history of feminism, especially in periods without mass feminist movements. The dispersal of images of women's accomplishments through popular culture spread and reinforced the essence of individual female achievement that is pivotal to understanding modern feminism.

A few women were more forthright in their support. Amelia

Earhart consciously identified herself as a feminist and proudly served as a role model for individual women who wanted to break free of earthbound conventions. Her philosophy of trying things out, accepting challenges, breaking down barriers, and never taking no for an answer could be profoundly liberating, indeed revolutionary if someone decided to "rehearse" Earhart's life. If feminism was her message, then popular culture was her medium. She was in good company.

The Last Flight

A year after Amelia Earhart's disappearance in 1937, Hilton Railey, who had been part of the 1928 *Friendship* promotion team that launched a young Boston social worker on her very public career, concluded that Amelia Earhart had become "caught up in the hero racket." This racket "compelled her to strive for increasingly dramatic records, bigger and braver feats that automatically insured the publicity necessary to the maintenance of her position as the foremost woman pilot in the world." According to Railey, who himself had promoted many of these explorers and adventurers, "she was a victim of the era of 'hot aeronautics' which began with Colonel Charles Lindbergh and Admiral Byrd and which shot 'scientific' expeditions across continents, oceans, and polar regions by dint of individual exploration." It was Earhart's tragedy, he concluded, that "the very qualities which brought her fame in the late 1920's are no longer needed by the late 1930's."[1] Or as *Aviation* magazine put it in a 1937 editorial, "The real tragedy of Amelia Earhart is that hers was the psychology of the Age of Vikings applied at a time when aviation had already passed over into the Age of the Clipper."[2]

Had Amelia Earhart become an anachronism by the end of her career? Was her round-the-world flight merely a "stunt without constructive benefit to the aeronautical industry"? She would have answered no on both counts, but she did understand that the winds of aviation were changing, and so, too, of necessity would her career change. Before she left on her last flight, she confided to several friends and her husband that this was to be her last spectacular expedition and that she planned to settle down to more routine phases of aviation after she returned. "I have a feeling that there is just about one more good flight left in my system," she said, "and I hope this trip around the world is it. Anyway, when I have finished this job, I mean to give up long distance stunt flying." She mentioned her interest in returning to Purdue to carry out an intensive flight research program, as well as her realization "that I'm getting old and want to make way for the younger generation before I'm feeble too."[3]

Although George Putnam certainly could have orchestrated an enthusiastic reception when she returned from her 1937 world flight (lecture dates at five hundred dollars a shot were already under contract before she left), it is hard to imagine Amelia Earhart receiving the kind of heroine's welcome she had gotten after her 1928 or 1932 flights. She was now thirty-nine years old, hardly the girl flier anymore, and she had been in the public eye for almost a decade. The publicity value of a successful monthlong, leisurely circumnavigation of the earth at the equator in 1937 remained unclear. Despite Putnam's promotional talents, this one might have been very hard to pull off.[4]

An *unsuccessful* round-the-world flight, however, was a different matter, especially when the plane and its occupants were never found. Without doubt, the mystery of Amelia Earhart's disappearance brought the aviator far more publicity than any stunt the intrepid promoter G. P. Putnam could have dreamed up. Ironically, the unresolved circumstances surrounding her death have kept her before the public to a far greater extent than if she had returned home safely. As she approaches what would have been her centenary in 1997, Amelia Earhart is as much in the news as, perhaps more so than, before she disappeared in 1937.

Yet this posthumous cult, which is quite distinct from the celebrity she enjoyed during her lifetime, threatens to obscure her legacy. While she was alive, she was celebrated for what she accomplished and for what her example meant to women and aviation. Once she was presumed missing, Amelia Earhart the role model for women was increasingly replaced by Amelia Earhart the lost aviator, and attention shifted away from her strongly articulated feminism to speculation about the circumstances of her fateful last flight. Yet Amelia Earhart the role model and inspiration for women has never really died. In fact, her appeal will probably outlast all attempts to mine the vast expanses of the Pacific Ocean for clues to her final fate.

Up until 1935 Amelia Earhart's public career had been remarkably free of criticism or controversy. To be sure, an occasional editorial or cartoon suggested that women had no place in aviation,[5] but such jabs were fairly infrequent. Earhart's charmed life regarding publicity ended in 1935. Her two major flights that year—the solo from Hawaii to the mainland in January and trips to and from Mexico in the spring—both received the combination of negative publicity and public approval that foreshadowed the ambiguities of her round-the-world flight in 1937. Perhaps not coincidentally, these two flights were the only ones of Earhart's that actually paid their way.[6]

Criticism of her impending solo from Hawaii to California began to surface as Earhart prepared for the flight in December 1934. Following her customary procedure, she did not announce her plans for the flight in advance, but in order to fly back from Hawaii, she had to ship her plane from California, which was a bit of a tip-off. (It was lashed to the ocean liner's tennis court.) A local editorial

intoned, "If Amelia intends to fly solo from Hawaii to the mainland, responsible authorities should stop her from doing it." Even
though no aviator, male or female, had made the trip, the writer
believed the flight would add nothing to aviation, pose too many
risks in a single-engine plane not equipped for a water landing, and
set in motion an expensive and costly sea search if aborted en route.
Earhart suspected that she was being singled out because she was a
woman, noting, "Women always have a burden of criticism in any
undertaking of the kind, anyway." Acting as her spokesperson, her
husband said, "Go ahead and say what you like. We will go ahead
in our quiet way."[7]

The flight was a stunning success. After just over seventeen fog-
bound hours in the air, she landed in Oakland, where she was
mobbed by more than five thousand well-wishers. Her record-setting flight received front-page coverage in all the country's newspapers, won her another invitation to address the National
Geographic Society, and elicited a congratulatory letter from President Franklin Roosevelt, which said in part, "You have shown
even 'doubting Thomases' that aviation is a science which cannot
be limited to men alone." The only one who missed out on the
celebration in Oakland was husband George Putnam, who was
somewhere "on the high seas bound for San Francisco, vastly irri-
tated at my having taken a short cut, leaving him to travel the long
way."[8]

The success of the flight silenced the naysayers, who had said
things like "She is 36 years of age and so ought to know better"
(actually, she was thirty-seven), but did not entirely squelch the
negatives. The real issue was not gender but the public's suspicion
of a paid stunt. Earhart was criticized for accepting a dubious ten-
thousand-dollar promotional fee from the Hawaii Sugar Planters'
Association to promote goodwill between the islands and the mainland. G.P.'s statement that "I have no idea how many people bought
cans of pineapple as a result of AE's flight of the Pacific, or how
many people got their first urge to see Hawaii . . ." was a bit dis-
ingenuous since he arranged the deal for precisely that purpose.
And Amelia delivered, not just by successfully making the flight

but by repeatedly plugging the island in her interviews and syndicated columns after the event.[9]

The *Nation* was the most vociferous in its criticism. Calling it "sticky business," the editors thought that the reputation of "our foremost woman flier" had been "badly tarnished." "We are more than willing to believe that Miss Earhart, whose passion for flying is perhaps matched only by her desire to demonstrate that women are the equals of men in the air or out of it, would rather fly the Pacific than have $10,000 if the choice were necessary," they wrote, but that she would be privately paid that amount as a fee to promote Hawaiian interests rather than receive it as a prize struck them as unseemly. Amelia Earhart's postflight comments about the trip itself confirmed that "the greatest hazard I had to overcome was the criticism heaped on my head for even contemplating the flight." Even though she felt it was entirely unwarranted, it "manifested itself in a physical strain more difficult than fatigue" and made the Pacific flight harder than either of her Atlantic crossings.[10]

Criticism of a different sort surfaced over her flights to and from Mexico in April and May 1935. These truly were moneymaking ventures, conceived and executed by George Putnam with the goal of visiting Mexico as guests of the government and financing the jaunt through the sale of stamp covers and other promotional schemes.[11] Earhart carried a batch of limited-issue stamp covers with "Flight of Amelia Earhart to Mexico 1935" superimposed, which dramatically increased their value. Soon Gimbel's was advertising them for the hefty price of $175. Stamp collectors were a major source of funds for expeditions and flights, as promoter G. P. Putnam well knew. But he offended many of them by announcing that he personally would keep 240 of the stamps to resell at any price he could get to defray the expenses of her flight. Coming just months after criticism of the $10,000 fee from the sugar planters' association, this episode blatantly revealed to the public what was usually a behind-the-scenes process of paying for and profiting from record-breaking flights. Soon people were saying that Amelia Earhart "did the things she did for the sake of money."[12]

What had changed? The Pacific solo was as dangerous and daring a flight as any of her other exploits. No pilot, male or female, had ever made the twenty-four-hundred-mile trip alone, so she had garnered a true world's first. Similarly, the record-breaking return from Mexico City to Newark in May 1935 was comparable to her transcontinental records in 1932 and 1933. But she had done flights like these before, many times, and it was getting a bit too routine. And never before had the moneymaking aspects been quite so visible. Such commercialism did not sit well with a public that liked its heroes and heroines to be above money, no matter how impractical such a stance was in the expensive business of aviation record setting and exploration.

The 1935 flights also seemed to lack the outpouring of women's identification with the accomplishment that had characterized her flights in 1928 and especially in 1932. The Hawaiian solo and the Mexico–Newark record hop were described more as progress for general aviation than as symbolic breakthroughs for women. Uncharacteristically Earhart herself failed to plug women in any of her postflight interviews or columns. Perhaps she thought that the moneymaking aspects of these flights made them unlikely candidates for presentation as feminist breakthroughs or that she no longer always needed to make her point. For the world flight the "woman's angle" was more prominent, but hardly as dominant as it had been earlier.

The year 1935 was one of transitions for Amelia Earhart. The first was geographical. When she and George were first married, they lived mainly on the East Coast, in George's spacious house in Rye or in New York City hotel suites. During the mid-1930s they spent increasing amounts of time on the West Coast. Because of Putnam's association with Paramount Pictures, he needed to make frequent trips out to Hollywood. Many times Amelia gave him a ride, making them one of the first bicoastal commuting couples and probably the only one where the wife flew the plane. Renting a house in the Toluca Lake district, they dabbled in the Hollywood scene as well as made friends with the many aviators who made Southern California their base.

When fire damaged the Rye house in late 1934, destroying many mementos and most of Earhart's papers, the couple relocated to Southern California, which was a perfect base for Amelia's flying. In 1935 they purchased a house in North Hollywood and began extensive remodeling. The renovations included a guest suite for Amelia's mother, who was spending increasing amounts of time in California with her older daughter.[13]

After their marriage Amelia and George had settled into what one biographer calls the "high-profile lifestyle" of a celebrity couple. The Putnams were not independently wealthy, but they were certainly well-off. Since both worked enormously hard, they earned, and spent, large sums of money. Their residences were always fully staffed with household help, gardeners, and secretaries for Amelia's voluminous correspondence. In keeping with Amelia's domestic feminism, she and George kept scrupulous accounts to ensure that each paid half the household expenses. Whatever was left over went into a common savings account. Considering the lavishness with which they lived and entertained, the lingering effects of the Great Depression, and Amelia's very expensive hobby of aviation, there usually was not much left over.[14]

During this period of relocating to California Amelia Earhart took up her position as an aviation adviser and career counselor for women at Purdue University. At a salary of two thousand dollars for the academic year, Earhart was not a regular member of the faculty. She spent several weeks in residence each term in 1935–1936, meeting individually with students, giving lectures, and working to improve the climate for women on the campus. One of the first things she noticed was the condescending attitude of the Purdue men toward the women undergraduates. This lack of understanding was encouraged by the fact that the two sexes rarely took classes together, with the men gravitating toward science and engineering and the women concentrating in home economics. "Today, it is almost as if the subjects themselves had sex so firm is the line drawn between what girls should study, and boys," she noted.[15]

Just observing in person the fascinating and subtly charismatic Miss Earhart, who lived in the women's residence hall when she was on campus, no doubt had an effect more profound on the Pur-

Amelia Earhart learned a lot from her stint as a career counselor at Indiana's Purdue University. Here she poses with undergraduates at the college airstrip in her brand-new Lockheed Electra, which Purdue alumni helped finance.

due undergraduates than whatever speeches and public appearances she made. Even though she was more than fifteen years older than any of them and a married woman at that, she fitted in quite well, although one observed, "She's terribly busy. I often hear her typewriter clear up to midnight." When George visited the campus, this high-powered couple provided an intriguing real-life example of Earhart's oft-preached message of combining marriage and career. (In response to a lighthearted news piece wondering if this was the first night he had ever spent in a women's dormitory, G.P. quickly put out a press release asserting that it was.) Earhart's independence, shown when she put her elbows on the table at dinner or once showed up for a meal in flying clothes instead of the required skirt, did cause a few ripples, however. When the students tried to use Earhart's example to loosen the rules, the housemother solemnly replied, "As soon as you fly the Atlantic, you may!"[16]

Helen Schleman, the dean of women at Purdue, confirmed the deep influence that the aviator had on the female students. Often after dinner students followed her into the housemother's den to continue their conversations. Amelia sat on the floor like everybody else, and they all talked and talked. "The conversations invariably centered around Miss Earhart's belief that women should have and really did have choices about what they could do with their lives. . . . There was no question that she, through her own achievements and persuasiveness, was an effective catalyst to heretofore unthinkable thoughts for all of us." These late-night "milk and cookies" confidences shaped Amelia's ideas about the rising generation of women, too, and what awaited them once they left college. As she wrote her mother, "The work has been very interesting and has served to crystallize some of my ideas which were rather formless before."[17]

In December 1935 Earhart gave a speech that presaged the last chapter of her career. Her trusty single-engine Lockheed Vega, in which she had flown both the Atlantic and the Pacific, was being overtaken by faster and more technologically advanced aircraft. "I'm looking for a tree on which new and better airplanes grow, and I'm looking for a shiny new one to shake down." At the time of that speech negotiations were already well under way among her husband, President Elliott of Purdue, and a group of Purdue alumni to provide Earhart not only with her shiny new machine but with the financial backing to pursue the long-distance flights she dreamed of. "It is not often that we of the feminine persuasion are given such opportunities to pioneer in our chosen fields," said a grateful Amelia as she took possession of her $80,000 ($1.5 million in current dollars) twin-engine customized Lockheed Electra in July 1936. G.P. promptly dubbed it "the flying laboratory," borrowing the term from the description of Lindbergh's plane in 1930. Soon George and Amelia were both deeply immersed in plans for a round-the-world flight.[18]

The world flight was just the latest in a string of sensational aviation feats that Putnam, with the help and support of his wife, had been orchestrating for nearly a decade. As Amelia told a reporter, "Mr. Putnam has had much experience in expedition organization. I think he has had a lot of fun—and some grief!—in working out the arrangements." They used the same fund-raising techniques— lecture trips, private backers, commercial sponsors, syndication and book rights, stamp sales—that they had used before to raise money for each of her major flights. This was demanding, time-consuming work, all with the goal of getting Earhart into the air for this one last long flight and then getting her safely back in order to reap the rewards.[19]

Starting in early 1936, George threw himself into the very complicated arrangements for this flight. By now he had quit his publishing and Hollywood jobs and was managing his wife on a full-time basis. He made the contacts with Purdue University and the private donors who supplied the Lockheed Electra; he dealt with governmental bodies, such as the State Department and the navy, whose cooperation was necessary for the global itinerary; he cajoled contributions in kind from aeronautical supply companies; he negotiated a syndication deal with the *New York Herald Tribune* and a book contract with Harcourt, Brace; he arranged for another lucrative stamp cover deal to be handled by Gimbel's in New York; he booked seventy lectures for after Earhart's return. He called in his favors, gave a few in return,[20] put in most of their savings, and, in essence, mortgaged their future. No insurance company would insure the Lockheed Electra on such a risky undertaking. When Amelia disappeared, the estate was practically flat broke.

Although Amelia Earhart was only marginally involved in the business end of the planning, she took the lead in dealing with President Roosevelt, who had become a friend of the Putnams' through Eleanor. Less than a week after FDR's successful reelection in November 1936 Amelia enlisted his help for the logistics of the flight. The key problem was the wide expanse of the Pacific Ocean. At first Earhart inquired about the possibility of a refueling in the air over Midway Island;[21] then she switched to the possibility of landing on an uninhabited atoll called Howland Island, one of the few islands in flying range of both New Guinea and Hawaii. "Please forgive troublesome female flyer for whom this Howland Island project is key to world flight attempt," ran one telegram to the president. FDR did all he could to facilitate her plans, including putting in a good word for the Putnams at the navy, authorizing extensive naval and air backup in the region, and even supporting a congressional appropriation of WPA funds to build a small airstrip on Howland. Without such governmental (indeed, presidential) support, the flight would have been impossible.[22]

Amelia had her promotional chores, too, which she undertook with the usual good humor. By the spring of 1936 she had asked for and been granted a leave of absence from Purdue to involve herself fully in flight preparations. That year she gave 150 money-raising lectures in addition to the time she spent training for the world flight. And she autographed five thousand stamp covers to be carried on the flight. To be sold at five dollars each through Gimbel's, the revenue would have defrayed a significant portion of the expenses of the expedition.[23] Signing these stamp covers (her "philatelic homework") became a game with George as referee: ten autographs before her morning orange juice, fifteen before her bacon and eggs, twenty-five before bed. In order to have her flight, she was willing to jump through the hoops one more time.[24]

It was harder work to pull off this 1937 flight than the 1928 and 1932 Atlantic crossings. As early as 1932 an article in the *Literary Digest* noted that the public was "sick and tired of ocean flights." While not mentioning Earhart specifically, it pointed out that the novelty had worn off, the commercial backers and endorsers had disappeared, and the syndication deals were drying up.[25] All the major routes had been spanned, and many were now serviced by regularly scheduled air transport. The only thing left was to find new routes or to do old ones faster or with another twist or gimmick. That was 1932. By 1937 it was even harder. Moreover, by the late 1930s such stunts increasingly competed for public attention with international developments, most notably the rise of fascism and the growing threat of war in Europe and the Far East.

Another problem was that flying around the world was not really

How many more before dinner, G.P.? When it came to raising money for her flying, Amelia Earhart was willing to do whatever it took, including signing five thousand stamp covers before the round-the-world flight.

newsworthy anymore, despite G.P.'s sometimes frenetic attempts to make it so. For one thing, it was not all that novel. Between 1924 and 1933 six expeditions had circled the globe, including two by Wiley Post in his Lockheed Vega *Winnie Mae*. Once Pan American started its Clipper service to China in 1935, it was possible to

traverse the Pacific by commercial air routes. Earhart's only novelty was flying around the globe close to the equator, a distance of
twenty-seven thousand miles, which was ten thousand more than
Wiley Post's solo trip in 1933. And, of course, being a woman.[26]

Although rumors about her plans had been circulating ever since
she took possession of the Lockheed Electra, the flight was not officially announced to the public until February 12, 1937. Putnam and
Earhart continued to stress the flying laboratory pitch of the summer before, as well as the supposed scientific benefits of studying
long-distance flight. "The human reaction of pilots flying over long
periods of time and distance is still an unknown quantity with respect
to safety in air transport," the aviator explained to the assembled
reporters. "Problems of fatigue, food, efficiency, and the norm of
alertness still confuse both airplane designers and pilots alike." She
said the main object of her flight was to establish the feasibility of
circling the globe by commercial air transport. Putnam's elabo-
rately staged announcement was buried on page 25 of the *New York
Times*.[27]

Soon Earhart found herself subjected to the same kind of personal criticism of her motives that had surfaced after the 1935 Hawaii
and Mexico flights. In a widely distributed column aviation writer
Al Williams penned a scathing attack on the whole idea behind
transoceanic flights and on Earhart personally. "[T]he personal profit
angle in dollars and cents, and the struggle for personal fame, have
been carefully camouflaged and presented under the banner of 'scientific progress,' " Williams claimed. What possible scientific or
technological information could be gained from Earhart's flight, he
wondered, when there was "nothing in that 'Flying Laboratory'
beyond duplicates of the instruments and apparatus to be found on
board every major airline transport"? He was especially critical of
the thousands of dollars that Earhart and her "manager-husband"
would make on the stamp cachets, which belied the labeling of the
flight as "purely scientific" for public consumption. He ended by
calling on the Bureau of Air Commerce not to grant "Mr. and Mrs.
Amelia Earhart" permission for their next "out-of-the-cockpit and

on-to-Broadway flights." Amelia Earhart's response was short and pained: "I'm glad a woman didn't write it."[28]

Al Williams's view that the world flight was just a useless stunt to hoodwink a gullible public was too extreme. Earhart was genuinely intrigued by the chance to fly around the world in a fancy big plane, testing her skills as a pilot while she did some exotic global sight-seeing at the same time. For his part George hoped that he could promote the flight in a way that, at the least, paid for itself and that, if it succeeded, set them up financially for the rest of their lives.

Amelia also had more deeply rooted motivations for undertaking the trip. Uppermost again was promotion of her liberal feminist agenda: "Like previous flights I am undertaking this one solely because I want to, and because I feel that women now and then have to do things to show what women can do." (A little time away from George's schemes and promotions was probably also welcome.) But mainly she repeated the refrain that had animated all her previous adventures: "I am going for the trip. I am going for the fun. Can you think of a better reason?" She put it another way to her close friend Louise Thaden: "I've worked hard and I deserve *one* fling during my life time."[29]

After the months of hard work and preparation, the headline on March 18, 1937, finally read MISS EARHART OFF ON WORLD FLIGHT as she and three passengers (navigators Harry Manning and Fred Noonan and technical adviser Paul Mantz, who was hitchhiking to Hawaii to see his fiancée) flew from Oakland to Honolulu, a reverse of her 1935 flight. The departure was delayed several times because of weather, and the switchboard at the airport was flooded with hundreds of calls inquiring when she would take off. At least 75 percent of the calls came from women, reported the *New York Herald Tribune,* "who seem to feel Miss Earhart is a champion of their sex's ability to accomplish feats of flying equaling those of any man." Once she was finally in the air, one of the San Francisco papers caught a striking aerial shot of the Electra framed against the Golden Gate Bridge as the plane headed out to the Pacific.[30]

Three days later she was back on the front pages after she crashed

Amelia Earhart's Lockheed Electra takes off from Oakland, heading west toward Hawaii on the first leg of her round-the-world trip in March 1937. The Golden Gate Bridge was officially opened that same year.

on takeoff from Hawaii on March 20. Picking up speed down the runway at Luke Field, the plane ground-looped—that is, made a sharp, uncontrollable turn while still on the ground. She compared it with driving an automobile at seventy miles an hour and having the front tire blow out. As the plane lurched, its landing gear collapsed, badly injuring the underbelly. Luckily it did not catch on fire. "Something must have gone wrong," said a grim-faced Amelia. A few hours later she was sailing back to Los Angeles, her damaged ship ("a poor battered bird with broken wings") to follow for extensive repairs at the Lockheed factory.[31]

This accident was devastating news. "Whether you want to call it a day or keep going later is equally jake with me," wired G.P.

from California, but he must have known the outcome. "Amelia has a habit of finishing what she starts," and she made it clear she wanted to try again as soon as possible. The enormousness of the task quickly became apparent. Putnam estimated the cost of repairs to the plane alone at twenty thousand dollars, a vast sum in depression America, especially after he had already helped raise approximately eighty thousand dollars for the expedition. But once again he came through, raising the extra cash from corporate sources and from wealthy individuals like Floyd Odlum (whose wife was aviator Jacqueline Cochran), Vincent Bendix, and Bernard Baruch. Here is yet another case where George made an enormous difference to Amelia's career.[32]

Time was a critical factor. If the crew did not get off within a few months, global weather patterns would force an even longer delay, which everyone wanted to avoid. They figured if they were under way by the end of May and changed the direction of the flight to a west to east direction, they could still go. All the arrangements that Putnam had orchestrated—getting visas and permissions, spotting oil and gasoline at remote airstrips along the equator, coordinating plans with the navy in the Pacific—had to be redone to reflect these changes in the direction of the itinerary, and redone quickly. Many of the costs associated with the original route could never be recovered.

What was the rush? one wonders. One biographer attributes it to a "vortex of two converging currents": pride and money. Amelia had invested so much in this flight. Her future earnings were at stake, and so was her reputation. If she did not go forward, she feared she would always be remembered as the woman who tried and failed. This she could not accept.[33]

There also seems to be a combination of arrogance, fatalism, and sheer stubbornness on the part of both Amelia and George to forge ahead. Bradford Washburn, who had been approached about becoming a navigator on the original flight, later recalled a conversation about installing radio equipment on Howland Island in which he was rebuffed by Putnam's terse "If we have to get radio equipment all the way out there, there wouldn't be any chance of getting your book out for the Christmas sale." Washburn is not the first or the last to think that Putnam's commercial instincts got the better of him and that he sent Amelia off on a flight for which she was inadequately prepared. But she was just as stubborn about flying around the world as he was focused on promotion, and if she wanted to go ahead, go ahead she would. When the flight finally got under way, Amelia was exhausted, having worked nonstop for two months to patch her dream back together. "Well, I'm mortgaging the future," she told G.P., "but then, what are futures for?"[34]

Temperamentally, of course, Amelia would have preferred doing the whole thing alone, just she and her plane. But because her equatorial route contained vast expanses of ocean flying, she needed help with the navigating. Captain Harry Manning and Fred Noonan both originally signed on, but when the crash in Hawaii postponed the trip for two months, Manning dropped out, and Noonan took on sole responsibility as navigator. Noonan had extensive experience with Pan American Airways, but a drinking problem had made it hard for him to keep a steady job. Recently married, he hoped that his part in a successful Earhart mission would get him back on track professionally.[35]

What a relief it must have been to be off; finally her great adventure was to begin. With little fanfare the "second attempt" (as the hastily changed stamp covers were reprinted) began from Miami on June 1. Actually the flight had really begun in Oakland several days before, but the crew wanted to use the flight across the United States as a shakedown out of publicity's eye for the recently refurbished Lockheed Electra. Everything checked out just fine for this new attempt.

The world flight itinerary called for Earhart and Noonan to fly by day and then stop at designated airports or landing strips for refueling, repairs, and maintenance each night. From Miami, their first stop was San Juan, where a nervous G.P. telephoned just to make sure things were going well. Their next ports of call were Venezuela, Dutch Guiana, and Brazil, where they hopped the South Atlantic to Africa at about its shortest distance. Making landfall in Senegal instead of Dakar ("What put us north?" penciled Amelia to her navigator),[36] they flew all the way across equatorial Africa, over Eritrea and the Red Sea to Pakistan and India, down toward Singapore and Java, and then on to Australia. They kept in touch with the real world by telegram and an occasional phone conversation. (A.E. talked to George only twice en route. In the days before global telecommunications, Fred and Amelia were out of touch for most of the trip.) After Australia it was on to Lae, New Guinea, and then the hardest leg of the journey: to the tiny Howland island. After Howland would have come Hawaii and then the official end point of the trip in Oakland, the last stretch being a replay of her 1935 solo. She was due back in early July, although delays en route meant that she would have just missed a Fourth of July arrival, no doubt to her husband's promotional chagrin.

In addition to piloting the plane on this twenty-seven-thousand-mile journey, Amelia Earhart played reporter and scribe. She quickly realized that it was easier to talk to reporters and let them write the stories than to do it all herself, especially after flying all day. Earhart had never enjoyed writing under deadline pressure, but she realized the trip would not be possible without the syndication money paid for her dispatches and the projected royalties from the book to follow, so she gamely complied. The thirty thousand words she sent back, written in odd moments at night, during meals, or in hangars as she waited for the Electra to be serviced or refueled, were part of the price she paid for doing what she loved best.[37]

The dispatches were written in the usual Earhart style: straightforward, lacking personal emotion, informative but dry. (Putnam embellished these dispatches substantially when he published them as *Last Flight*.) Until the dramatic finish, which, of course, she never wrote about, the aviation part of the flight was fairly routine, making her articles as much travelogues as aviation adventure. Her sheer joy at seeing parts of the world that she had never visited before came through clearly. Whenever she had a chance, she tried to do some sight-seeing, which she described for the readers back home— riding camels in Calcutta, visiting the Shwe Dagon Pagoda in Rangoon, often dragging an unenthusiastic Noonan along as company.

She relished describing the food, the clothes, and the local customs. As always, Amelia the feminist made sociological observations about the status of women in the countries which she visited. But she had to resist the temptation of shopping, since the extra weight of souvenirs would have disrupted the Electra's aerodynamics.[38]

Despite the strain of keeping her plane in good running order, the fatigue of flying almost every day while writing her columns, and keeping an eye on her alcoholic navigator, she was having the time of her life. "Just to fly and fly and fly"—that had been her fondest wish when she set off. From her dispatches and communications back to her husband in the States, it is clear that if Amelia had had her druthers, she would have lingered much longer in almost every spot rather than always (in her phrase) "pushing through." Regrets at sticking to her schedule and "trying to get to some other place instead of enjoying the place we'd already got to" recur throughout, testimony to the inherent conflict between the two sides of her life: the record-setting aviator on a publicized round-the-world trip and the indefatigible traveler and recreational flier who was having a wonderful time just vagabonding around, like the carefree days after the 1928 flight. She was determined someday to retrace the steps of her round-the-world flight, revisiting its exotic locales in a more liesurely manner. Said Amelia with a sigh: "Some time I hope to stay somewhere as long as I like."[39]

Earhart's and Noonan's disappearance on the last leg of the flight from New Guinea to Howland Island on July 2, 1937, put them on the front page of every newspaper in the country for the next two weeks. But until that point America had not exactly been following the world flight with fervid anticipation. The papers carrying the dispatches usually gave them either front-page or page 3 coverage (after all, they had paid for the syndication rights), so readers could follow the story fairly easily. But if your regular newspaper did not carry it, you were out of luck.

Because of the syndication deal, major sectors of the national market were not covered. For example, a paper like the *New York Times,* which lost out on the rights to the rival *New York Herald*

Tribune, ran only small wire service blurbs, just several inches of column buried in the middle of the newspaper, about where she was and where she was going next. It is doubtful that newspaper readers would have switched their subscriptions (and loyalty) to a rival paper just to get the Earhart story. Since the aviator was under strict orders not to jeopardize her news value by talking to reporters along the way ("Bottled up tight" was how *New York Herald Tribune* publisher Helen Rogers Reid described what she demanded as part of the contract[40]), there were no anecdotes, human-interest angles, or other tidbits to form even the nucleus of an independent news story. Readers in large chunks of the national market had to search carefully to keep track of her whereabouts, and while most Americans who followed the news probably knew she was on the trip, many were unaware of the day-to-day progress of her flight until she was lost.

However, readers who were closely following Earhart's progress knew that the 2,556-mile leg from Lae, New Guinea, to Howland Island was the most difficult challenge of the entire flight. Just a month earlier, A.E. had stood on the other shore of the Pacific, looking westward. Now having completed most of her circumnavigation, she gazed eastward across the same ocean with trepidation. I shall be glad when we have the hazards of its navigation behind us." Perhaps Earhart's followers watched for the news dispatches and listened to their radios a little more anxiously than usual that day.[41]

Noonan and Earhart took off from Lae, New Guinea, at midmorning on July 2. (It was July 1 in the United States, east of the International Date Line.) Their destination was a small and exceptionally remote island only a mile and a half long and barely twenty-five feet above sea level, and they hoped to reach it by early the next morning after approximately eighteen hours in the air. During the day they planned to get their bearings by using islands that dotted the Pacific along their route. When darkness fell, they planned to rely on celestial navigation and dead reckoning. Needless to say, finding the speck of an island in the vast Pacific expanse was incredibly difficult under the best of circumstances, and only the slightest miscalculation could throw them miles off their course.

As the fliers came within radio range of Howland Island, the coast guard cutter *Itasca* began to send radio homing signals to the Lockheed to bring them into the island's newly constructed airstrip. Radio contact was made at 2:45 A.M., but because of Earhart's and Noonan's unfamiliarity with standard radio procedures, they never stayed on the correct frequency long enough for the *Itasca* to get a proper bearing on the plane's location. These ill-fated attempts at establishing communication continued for the next six hours, with the *Itasca* receiving increasingly ominous messages from Earhart and Noonan that they were running low on fuel and confused about where they were. The final one came in at 8:44 A.M., with Earhart reporting in an obviously strained voice that they were running north and south to try to find out their location.[42]

Within an hour the captain of the *Itasca* had concluded that they were out of fuel (they had been in the air for almost twenty-four hours at that point) and began a search. The search lasted for a week, at a cost of four million dollars. Despite covering approximately 250,000 miles at sea, the most extensive sea search in U.S. history found no trace of the fliers or their plane.[43]

The news stunned America and the world. Newspapers printed full-page banner headlines saying simply, AMELIA LOST, and she remained on the front pages for ten days while the search continued. People stayed glued to their radios, grasping for news and remembering their feelings from two years earlier, when news came that Will Rogers and Wiley Post had crashed in Alaska. Newsreels supplied updates on the story, showing stock footage of the aviator, her Lockheed Electra, and the expanses of the Pacific Ocean where the search was being conducted. Perhaps newsreel viewers connected the Earhart search in the Pacific with another air tragedy—the crash of the *Hindenburg* dirigible in Lakehurst, New Jersey, which had been captured in riveting newsreel film just two months before.[44]

Especially devastated were the devoted fans of Amelia Earhart, who had followed the career of their heroine with such fervor and identification. Letters came in to Amy Otis Earhart, Muriel Morrissey, and George Palmer Putnam expressing a sense of grief coupled with hope that somehow she might be found. One fifteen-year-old California girl referred to July 2, 1937, as "that tragic day" and said, "I want to choke the Navy for not finding her. . . . I feel she is alive and I know she needs us." A young Kentucky woman was so distraught during the search that she could not eat or sleep and lost six pounds; another wrote Mrs. Earhart, "I got up at seven every morning so I wouldn't miss any of the news broadcasts. I hardly went outdoors because I didn't want to miss anything." One aspiring aviatrix from Oakland was also glued to the radio for news, and she shared her feelings with Amelia's husband: "I have had people tell me I was crazy to stay up all night listening to the radio about Amelia and they say Miss Earhart was nothing to me, but I loved Miss Earhart as if she were my own sister, because I know she is a kind and wonderful woman. There isn't another woman that I worship more than her." The carefully kept scrapbooks of Amelia's career now became chronicles of the increasingly bleak news coming back from the Pacific.[45]

As the days went by and no trace of the fliers was found, the newspapers kept reporting every bit of possible news, including a fair number of hoaxes from those who claimed to have been in radio or even psychic communication with the downed fliers. Amelia's sister, Muriel, still maintained hope for a rescue but admitted, "If it should be God's will that Amelia does not come back to us and that this is her last flight, I know that she would rather meet death this way—with wings outstretched—the end of a gallant flier."[46] George Putnam, grim and distraught, kept a vigil for news of his lost wife, although after a while he, too, seemed to accept that she would not be found. Newspapers, never quite sure when to print an obituary, began to run editorials eulogizing the lost flier. Many prominently mentioned her meaning to women,[47] as did the letters that continued to come to Amelia's family.[48]

But it is wrong to think that the obsession with the circumstances of Amelia Earhart's fate began the day she hit the front page on July 2, 1937, and has snowballed ever since. Despite her undisputed status as the world's best-known female aviator, public interest lagged in the immediate aftermath of her disappearance and presumed death. Once the search was called off in mid-July, the attention of the nation returned to more ordinary pursuits. Earhart was knocked off the front page of New York's tabloid *Daily News* by a heat wave. Since no wreckage was immediately found, there was still room for hope that the two fliers were stranded on a desert island, awaiting rescue. "If they are not found I will always think of them as Queen Amelia and King Frederick of some island," wrote one of Earhart's loyal followers. But by the fall, except for the diehard believers (including Amelia's mother, who never really accepted that she was dead), Amelia Earhart was yesterday's news.[49]

In November 1937 her husband published his much-enhanced version of *Last Flight,* and while sales were strong, it was scarcely a runaway best seller. When he published a biography of his wife entitled *Soaring Wings* in 1939, sales were also modest. The Amelia Earhart Foundation had trouble raising money for projects to memorialize the aviator, and the National Woman's Party got a surprisingly disappointing response to a major fund-raising drive named for her.[50] And the plans for a film of the aviator's life (Katharine Hepburn was prominently mentioned for the leading role) fell through. As the United States entered World War II, the memory of Amelia Earhart and all that she represented seemed to be fast receding.[51]

Although there were always rumors about certain unexplained aspects of the disappearance, the real beginnings of the Amelia Earhart cult date to 1943.[52] The major source for the widely held view that she was on a secret spy mission for the U.S. government at the time of her disappearance was an RKO movie called *Flight for Freedom* (1943), which starred Rosalind Russell as a famous aviator named Tonie Carter and Fred MacMurray as the navigator she falls in love with while on a round-the-world flight. They deliberately plan to get lost over the Pacific in order to provide the rationale for an extensive search which will yield important military information about Japanese military fortifications in the area. When the

Japanese learn of the scheme in advance and plan to foil it, the aviator takes off alone. She patriotically chooses death by ditching her plane somewhere else so that the search can go on anyway. The film was advertised as "The Story Hollywood Didn't Dare Tell before Pearl Harbor" and was complete with a Lockheed Electra as the main prop. It didn't take much for moviegoers to link Tonie Carter to Amelia Earhart.[53]

Ever since then the suspicion that Earhart was on a secret mission for President Franklin Roosevelt has flourished in popular culture, although no conclusive evidence has been found in any government archives or military records to confirm that theory. President Roosevelt died without ever discussing it, but Eleanor Roosevelt stated repeatedly that she never had any evidence of such a plot. The former first lady personally assured Muriel Morrissey and Amy Otis Earhart, "Franklin and I loved Amelia too much to send her to her death." George Putnam never put any credence in the spy stories, to which he would certainly have been privy, given his role in the flight preparations. It is hard to imagine such a publicity seeker "sitting" on such a story for the rest of his life if it had been true. Putnam did believe, however, that the massive air and naval search for Amelia was used after the fact to gather information about the Japanese presence in the Pacific, an entirely plausible supposition.[54]

Flight for Freedom was shown to American troops stationed overseas, many of whom participated in the extensive U.S. military engagements against Japanese forces throughout the Pacific area near where she disappeared. Quite a few GIs reported conversations with local inhabitants who remembered, usually on the basis of second- or thirdhand information, stories of a plane wreck involving a white woman and man several years before. This event, especially the presence of a white "bird-woman," was so unusual that it had not been forgotten. These memory fragments inflamed rumors that Amelia Earhart might be alive after all.[55]

According to military intelligence sources, GIs also linked Amelia Earhart to Tokyo Rose, the Japanese-American disc jockey who broadcast to U.S. troops in the Pacific starting in early 1943. The soldiers were not accusing Amelia of going over to the enemy; they assumed that she had been brainwashed by her Japanese captors to make the broadcasts. Even after George Putnam, who served in the Pacific during the war, had positively stated that Tokyo Rose's voice could not be Amelia's, the rumors continued. [56]

What if Earhart and Noonan had ditched the Electra in the ocean and managed to survive in the lifeboat stowed aboard? When Colonel Eddie Rickenbacker and seven castaways survived for twenty-four days in a lifeboat at sea after their B-17 plane went down in the Pacific near Samoa in 1942, the popular imagination linked the survival tale to the possibility that Fred and Amelia might have done the same. One person who always thought that A.E. might have landed on a desert island, and perhaps stayed put, was her friend Eugene Vidal. "Wouldn't it be wonderful to just go off and live on a desert island?" she had said to him once, and then proceeded to discuss in great detail how one could survive. [57]

Among the many scenarios proposed since the 1940s, by far the most popular have Earhart and Noonan landing off course on some remote Pacific atoll or being picked up by fishing boats in the vicinity before being captured by the Japanese. Any American found in Japanese waters in the late 1930s would certainly have been viewed as a hostile interloper and immediately been taken prisoner and probably executed. In 1960 Paul Briand suggested in *Daughter of the Sky* that Amelia and Fred had landed on Saipan, where they presumably later died at the hands of the Japanese. (Saipan is nowhere near the projected flight plan from New Guinea to Howland or, necessarily, within the fuel capacity of the Lockheed.) In 1966 Fred Goerner's best seller *The Search for Amelia Earhart* concluded that Earhart and Noonan made a forced landing on the Japanese-controlled Marshall Islands while on an informal spying mission, were taken prisoners by the Japanese, and died in captivity after being removed to Saipan. One of the most farfetched theories has the Japanese releasing former prisoner of war Amelia in 1945, after which she, weary of publicity, assumes an alias and settles in New Jersey! [58]

New theories continue to surface in the 1990s. According to historic aircraft researcher Richard Gillespie, Earhart and Noonan landed at Nikumaroro, an uninhabited atoll in the Phoenix group 350 miles southeast of Howland. The investigation team points as evidence to a piece of fuselage found on Nikumaroro which could have come from the Electra and a size nine Cat's Paw shoe heel which matched A.E.'s size and the kind of shoe she was photographed wearing before she disappeared. Nikumaroro offered food, but no fresh-water, and if the aviators had not been too badly injured by their forced landing, they would presumably have died of thirst when they failed to be rescued.[59] Such a slow, lingering death would have been totally at odds with how Amelia Earhart lived her life and how she contemplated her death. "When I go," she once told her husband, "I'd like best to go in my plane. Quickly."[60] Let us hope she got her wish.

Whether Amelia Earhart died when her plane ran out of fuel and sank somewhere near Howland Island (as most experts believe) or whether her life had a different ending may never be known. There are enough discrepancies and gaps in the story to support unlim-ited, even contradictory theories. As long as the public stays tuned, the search will go on.[61]

Perhaps just as intriguing, and rarely asked, is the question of what would have happened to Amelia Earhart if she had returned safely and slipped into a postflight career. Of course, the immediate aftermath would have been hectic and full: reunions with friends and family; public appearances and homecoming parades; writing a book about the trip, maybe even making it into a movie. The weeks and months after completing the flight would have been the time to "cash in" while public interest was high, as it certainly would have been. Amelia had gone through precisely the same routine in 1928 and 1932, so she was a practiced hand.

Those postflight chores would have occupied her for a while, but what next? In many interviews before she left, she expressed a strong desire to continue working with the Purdue Research Laboratory on scientific projects concerning aviation and long-distance flight. As George explained to Purdue's president, "The target we are shooting at is to find some other properly scientific activities which such an expedition could undertake and which could be tied up closely with Purdue." George already had such an expedition involving financier Bernard Baruch on the back burner before Amelia left on the world flight.[62]

Of course, whether she would have stayed married to George had she returned (and vice versa) is an open question. There are many who think that the marriage was on shaky grounds before her departure[63] and that she might have decided to go her own way on her return, exercising the escape clause included in their marriage contract six years earlier. Temperamentally and financially she was quite capable of living on her own. And if she was no longer involved in "hot aeronautics," then one of the main rationales for the personal and professional partnership with G.P. would have disappeared. Putnam married twice more, both times to women very different from his independent second wife. He died in 1950.[64]

If Amelia had returned from her world flight, where would she have fitted into the next stage of aviation? She could have pursued business deals with Paul Mantz, her technical adviser on the last flight, or with her former partner and friend Eugene Vidal. Perhaps she would have used her earnings from the world flight to start her own airline or flight-training school. Yet since aviation was soon to be changed so dramatically by World War II, even the immediate future was hard to predict. Considering her long-standing pacifism, however, it is hard to imagine her playing a large role in the military during World War II; remember she had joked that she and Caroline O'Day would be locked up in a federal prison as war resisters if hostilities ever broke out. Perhaps she would have been involved in humanitarian work. But in any event she would have had her Lockheed Electra since the plane was hers to keep outright as part of the Purdue deal. Many of those vintage Electras are still in the air today, and she could have looked forward to many years of happy flight time from her trusty machine.

Amelia might have surprised us. Remember, this was the woman who said in 1932 that she had had 28 jobs and hoped to have 228 more. Her experience as a career counselor at Purdue had been so stimulating that perhaps she would have returned to the field of higher education: Dean of Women, maybe even President Earhart, especially of a women's college. Being head, at least for a while, of a settlement house like Denison House in Boston or Greenwich House in New York City would no doubt have appealed. Given her love of fast cars, she might have become the first female professional race car driver. Of course, she would have had to forfeit her 1963 commemorative airmail stamp, since the Post Office so honors only those who have been dead for ten years.

Amelia Earhart certainly would have continued her activism for feminism and women's professional causes. No doubt each year she would have been the featured speaker at college commencements and other ceremonial events. If she were still alive in 1961, her dear friend Eleanor Roosevelt would have made certain that President John Kennedy appointed her to the Presidential Commission on the Status of Women. Amelia would have been delighted at the revival of feminism in the 1960s and 1970s and probably would have been a charter member of the National Organization for Women, the bastion of liberal feminism. Who knows? She might have lived to celebrate her hundredth birthday in 1997. After all, her mother lived until she was ninety-five, and Muriel lived well into her nineties.

This fanciful last chapter in Amelia's life ("The Later Years, 1937 to the Present") is a reminder that her death on the world flight was not preordained, that there could have been many other outcomes. The intent here is to rescue Amelia from the clutches of the cult of her disappearance and to refocus attention on her life itself, especially its sense of enthusiasm and endless possibility where women are concerned. She would have hated for her disappearance to make her a cult figure like Marilyn Monroe, Elvis Presley, or James Dean, all of whom added to their popular mystiques by dying young. She most certainly would not want to be turning up on the cover of supermarket tabloids ("Amelia Earhart found Alive! She's 95 years old and living on tiny island in South Pacific!")[65] nearly sixty years after her disappearance.

Amelia Earhart was not afraid of death; she said so many times. She would have faced death with the same unflinching courage and honesty with which she lived her life. But even she, who loved life

What if Amelia Earhart had come back? Perhaps she would have just nonchalantly walked in from the tarmac at some airport in an obscure part of the world, wondering what all the fuss was about. Whatever her fate, she would have had no regrets.

so much, could never really envision herself growing old. The words Amelia Earhart had bravely written to her husband before another dangerous flight now became a prophetic epitaph: "Please know I am quite aware of the hazards. I want to do it because I want to do it. Women must try to do things as men have tried. When they fail, their failure must be but a challenge to others." Her friend and great admirer Eleanor Roosevelt was certain that Amelia Earhart's last words were "I have no regrets."[66]

Where Did They All Go?

In her 1963 classic *The Feminine Mystique,* Betty Friedan bemoaned the lack of role models in the 1950s in comparison with the independent heroines she remembered from the 1930s. Leafing through back volumes of women's magazines at the New York Public Library, Friedan believed she had discovered a change in the image of the American woman. In 1939 "New Women" proudly had careers and conveyed an aura of "moving into a future that was going to be different from the past," a description that could have applied to Amelia Earhart or any of the numerous popular heroines at that time. These heroines "reflected the dreams, mirrored the yearning for identity and the sense of possibility that existed for women then." But suddenly, according to Friedan, the image blurred. "The New Woman, soaring free, hesitates in midflight, shivers in all that blue sunlight and rushes back to the cozy walls of the home." The feminine mystique—the postwar emphasis on domesticity and traditional gender roles—now gripped America, and women's aspirations plummeted or were nipped in the bud.[1]

Betty Friedan identified an important characteristic of postwar popular culture. People today have trouble thinking of popular heroines from the 1950s and 1960s who have anything like the appeal and charisma of those of earlier decades. To be sure, individual women continued to excel after World War II, and they received recognition for their contributions to such fields as literature, the arts, the professions, and politics. But it is much harder to point to the kind of larger-than-life role models like Amelia Earhart who inspired such strong loyalty and identification, then and now. The absence of popular heroines after the 1940s was especially unfortunate, since women trapped in the era of the feminine mystique probably needed role models more than ever.

Yet in other ways Betty Friedan's contrast of postwar popular culture with the interwar period was too starkly drawn: the 1930s were neither so liberated nor the 1950s so claustrophobically domestic as she claimed. Historian Joanne Meyerowitz's survey of women's magazines from 1946 to 1958 found that in fact, they continued to promote and celebrate individual female achievement in ways similar to those of the interwar period. Arguing that the postwar discourse was more diverse than simply a harsh insistence that women return home, Meyerowitz found an openness to public roles for women, a celebration of individual success, and even a critique of certain kinds of domesticity. As in the 1930s, popular culture was "riddled" with multiple messages, which could be read as supporting or undermining traditional gender roles, or both.[2]

What seems to be missing in the 1950s are not examples of individual female achievement, which abound,[3] but a climate that validated, nurtured, and rewarded such accomplishment. In the 1920s and 1930s young women like Amelia Earhart, Dorothy Thompson, Katharine Hepburn, and Margaret Bourke-White represented the rising generation of women, entering public life alongside the now-aging suffragists and Progressive reformers who were finishing their careers. By the 1950s women like Thompson, Hepburn, and Bourke-White (but not, alas, Earhart) were nearing the peak of their careers and influence. Where was the next generation of women coming along to provide role models for the future? Although women like Rachel Carson and Hannah Arendt first made their marks in this decade, as did other individual women of achievement, the collective impact of their accomplishments was diminished, if not lost, in a postwar climate unsupportive of women's aspirations. A whole generation of popular heroines is missing.[4]

Other factors also help explain why the supply of role models and popular heroines dried up. Hollywood had been popular culture's driving force in providing liberating and exciting roles for women on-screen and off in the 1920s and 1930s, but Hollywood, and especially the star system, were changing. The trade magazine *Variety* noted that audiences in the 1950s were much slower to "make" a star. Newcomers had a hard time competing for fan loyalty with old-timers, who managed to maintain their popularity.[5] (Maybe a similar process was at work with popular heroines, many of whom seem just as popular today as they were in the 1930s.)[6] Stars like Katharine Hepburn and Bette Davis continued to be box office for the rest of their careers, but Hollywood was no longer providing many models of female independence on the screen. Buxom Marilyn Monroe and Jane Russell, the elfish Audrey Hepburn and the wholesome Doris Day became the decade's new female stars. But few would interpret the roles they were allowed to play or their star personas as a significant step forward for female independence and autonomy. Teenager Gloria Steinem left a movie theater in embarrassment after watching the "whispering, simpering, big-breasted . . . vulnerability" of Marilyn Monroe in *Gentlemen Prefer Blondes* (1953).[7]

By the late 1940s Hollywood also faced stiff competition from the new and fast-expanding medium of television. There never was a golden age for women on the tube, unlike films. Television programming fully endorsed the subordination of women to domesticity and family. Of course, viewers may have constructed their own alternative meanings to the texts offered, but they would have been hard pressed to interpret what they saw on television as an agent of change for women in the 1950s or, with a few exceptions, even today.

America's experience of fighting a world war and then plunging into new global responsibilities in the postwar period may also have hastened the decline of the type of popular heroine associated with the 1920s and 1930s. As the United States established economic and political hegemony over the postwar world order, women's leadership and expertise were rarely utilized. Many of the designated heroes of the 1940s and 1950s were men linked to World War II or the ensuing cold war struggle against communism. Dwight Eisenhower, Douglas MacArthur, George Kennan, even a young John Kennedy made their reputations in areas of diplomacy, national elective office, and the military, areas from which women were effectively barred. Other postwar heroes such as Dr. Jonas Salk, the discoverer of the polio vaccine, came from the field of science and research, another area where women found it hard to succeed. When the Mercury astronauts were chosen in the late 1950s from the eligible pool of test pilots, women candidates were deliberately excluded, confirmation of how women's earlier contributions to aviation had been effectively erased.[8]

But perhaps the real "culprit" for the decline in popular heroines was less the glorification of domesticity in the 1950s, the cold war, or Hollywood's eclipse by television than the changes in the whole notion of hero worship and celebrity. In an increasingly bureaucratized mass culture, there was less room for individual exploits of explorers, adventurers, and pathbreakers like Charles Lindbergh and Amelia Earhart. The world's oceans, mountains, and continents had seemingly been conquered, and there were few new frontiers to tame besides outer space; this perhaps explains why the original Mercury astronauts came the closest to receiving the frenzied hero worship that had greeted explorers earlier in the century. It was just too hard to do something that had not been done before. This shift had already occurred by the 1930s and would have had wide-ranging implications on the course of Amelia Earhart's career if she had returned from her world flight.

Women were also in part victims of their own, and liberal feminism's, call for individual achievement and success. When Earhart first crossed the Atlantic in 1928, a good part of the hoopla could be traced to the pattern that anything untried or unusual a woman did was news, big news. By the postwar period women's accomplishments were no longer so unusual or so noteworthy, precisely because they had become relatively more common. The first woman to do something gets big play; far less newsworthy is the second, or the third, or the hundredth. Unfortunately this lack of interest in the cumulative nature of women's accomplishments, which was potentially far more significant than token individual breakthroughs, robbed women of one of their major sources of information about their sex's ongoing progress in the modern world.

By the time that the social movements of the 1960s challenged the postwar liberal consensus of affluence at home and cold war superiority abroad, individual heroes and heroines seemed even more anachronistic. Movie stars continued to serve as cultural icons, but Hollywood no longer held the cultural sway it did at its height in the 1930s. The closest models for hero status were the highly visible, and highly paid, figures from the world of professional sports, who were predominantly male, although a few women (mainly tennis players) crept in after 1970. The truly self-made hero or heroine who won public acclaim for achieving something noteworthy was increasingly replaced by the celebrity, a creation of the media who, in Daniel Boorstin's witty definition, "is well-known for his well-knownness."[9]

At the same time, the social protest movements of the 1960s and 1970s, especially the civil rights revolution, opened opportunities for a far wider cast of Americans to participate in the political system. Women enthusiastically and forcefully seized the chance to present demands specifically addressed to their newly recognized needs as women. Barriers fell quickly—in sports, in higher education, in the professions, in the media. For many women, not just Betty Friedan, the women's movement "changed their lives," offering them the tools, the political consciousness, and the mass support to take the feminist revolution many steps beyond the limited demands of the suffrage movement or interwar liberal feminism.

Once the women's movement offered so many choices and options to redefine what it meant to be a woman, there was less need to live vicariously (as Frances Perkins had done in 1928 with Amelia Earhart's first Atlantic crossing) through the lives of exceptional figures from popular culture. Women could do it themselves. Or could they? Perhaps one key to the ongoing fascination with Amelia Earhart as a popular heroine is that her message of aspiration, individual fulfillment, and breaking down barriers still inspires women today.

Amelia Earhart would have been one hundred years old in 1997. She remains the center of one of the greatest unsolved mysteries of all time, and the cult surrounding her disappearance shows no sign of waning. But that is not the only reason she should be remembered. Amelia Earhart was very much of her times yet also ahead of her times; her feminist message, even with its obvious limitations, seems fresh and compelling today. Women are the equals of men, and both should have equal opportunities. There are no limits to what women can accomplish if given the chance. Women and men must learn to live together as equal partners. Despite all the changes in women's lives over the last several decades, women have yet to find the true equality in the air or on the ground that Amelia Earhart championed as women's due.

Notes

Abbreviations used in notes

AE   Amelia Earhart
AOE   Amy Otis Earhart
COHC   Oral History Collection, Columbia University
GPP   George Palmer Putnam
LC   Library of Congress
MEM   Muriel Earhart Morrissey
NYHT   *New York Herald Tribune*
NYT   *New York Times*
SL   Schlesinger Library, Radcliffe College

PROLOGUE: "LADY LINDY"

1. The best place to start for the Lindbergh phenomenon is John William
   Ward, "The Meaning of Lindbergh's Flight," *American Quarterly* 10
   (Spring 1958), pp. 3–16. See also Orrin Klapp, "Hero Worship in
   America," *American Sociological Review* XIV (February 1949), pp. 53–
   62, and Leo Braudy, *The Frenzy of Renown: Fame and Its History* (New

York: Oxford University Press, 1986). For general material on Lindbergh, see Perry D. Luckett, *Charles A. Lindbergh: A Bio-Bibliography* (Westport, Conn.: Greenwood Press, 1986). For photographic images, see Francis Trevelyan Miller, *Lindbergh: His Story in Pictures* (New York: G. P. Putnam's Sons, 1929).

2. Dorothy Binney Putnam (Mrs. George Palmer Putnam) quoted in NYT, June 19, 1928, p. 3.

3. In another lovely phrase, Vidal said that as her fame increased, Earhart "took her place in the heavens as yin to Lindbergh's yang." Gore Vidal, "Love of Flying," *New York Review of Books* (January 17, 1985), pp. 14, 15, and 16.

4. Clippings from 1928 found in Denison House papers, SL; NYT, June 4, 1928, p. 4; Strandenaes quoted in Doris L. Rich, *Amelia Earhart: A Biography* (Washington, D.C.: Smithsonian Institution Press, 1989), pp. 57–58. One newspaper even went so far as to claim that there was a conscious stunt to make Earhart into a feminine Lindbergh, that she had been "in training, coached by promoters, to emulate Lindbergh in every respect, in attitude, pictures, and behaviour." *Lantern* editorial (July–August 1928), quoted in Mary S. Lovell, *The Sound of Wings: The Life of Amelia Earhart* (New York: St. Martin's Press, 1989), p. 111. But promoter George Palmer Putnam said the phenomenon "had to be treated simply as a gift with which the gods had surprised us." GPP, *Soaring Wings: A Biography of Amelia Earhart* (New York: Harcourt, Brace and Company, 1939), p. 178. The truth is somewhere in between those two statements.

5. *Daily Mirror* editorial, June 19, 1928, found in Purdue Special Collections.

6. Lady Astor quoted in NYT, June 28, 1928, p. 16.

7. Ibid.

8. AE, *20 Hrs. 40 Min.: Our Flight in the Friendship* (New York: G. P. Putnam's Sons, 1928), p. 202; AE quoted in Leonard Mosley, *Lindbergh: A Biography* (Garden City, N.Y.: Doubleday, 1976), p. 149; AE to Anne Morrow Lindbergh, May 1929, quoted in GPP, *Soaring Wings,* pp. 179–80. How much of a resemblance there really was in many ways depends on the eye of the beholder. True, they were of similar build and coloring, and both had short hair. The flying togs that all aviators, male or female, wore also invited such comparisons. On the other hand, no other female aviator was ever compared in looks with Lindbergh, so there is more than a passing resemblance. See Chapter Five on iconography and representation.

9. Telegram from Amy Guest to AE, 1932, Purdue Special Collections; NYT, June 5, 1932, p. 20; NYT, May 23, 1932, p. 3; Mayor Walker quoted in *Chicago Tribune,* June 21, 1932, p. 9.

10. Anne Morrow Lindbergh, *Hour of Gold, Hour of Lead: Diaries and Letters, 1929–1932* (New York: Harcourt Brace Jovanovich, 1973), p. 121.

11. Luckily, the caption gave women the last word: "Capt. William H.

(Skeptical Bill) Winkle has had certain women in the town half crazy."
Cartoon by Fontaine Fox, "Toonerville Folks," 1932, found in Purdue
Special Collections.

12. Harry Bruno, *Wings over America: The Inside Story of American Aviation*
(New York: Robert M. McBridge and Company, 1942), pp. 186–87.

13. See Mosley, *Lindbergh,* for the rest of Lindbergh's career. See also
Lindbergh's posthumously published *Autobiography of Values* (New
York: Harcourt Brace Jovanovich, 1977).

14. Bess Furman, *Washington By-Line: The Personal History of a Newspaperwoman* (New York: Alfred A. Knopf, 1949), p. 95.

15. Eleanor Roosevelt quoted in Shirley Dobson Gilroy, *Amelia: Pilot in
Pearls* (McLean, Va.: Link Press, 1985), p. 53.

16. Ederle quoted in "How a Girl Beat Leander at Hero Game," *Literary
Digest* 90 (August 21, 1926), p. 52.

CHAPTER I: A MODERN WOMAN MAKES HISTORY

1. Universal Service clipping, May 9, 1935, found in Clarence Strong
Williams papers, SL; NYT editorial, July 20, 1937, p. 22.

2. AE, "Flying the Atlantic," *American Magazine* 114 (August 1932), p.
72; "The Reminiscences of Muriel Earhart Morrissey" (1960), COHC,
p. 18; GPP, *Soaring Wings: A Biography of Amelia Earhart* (New York:
Harcourt, Brace and Company, 1939), p. 24.

3. Helen Ferris, ed., *Five Girls Who Dared* (New York: Macmillan, 1938),
p. 5.

4. AE, *The Fun of It: Random Records of My Own Flying and of Women in
Aviation* (New York: Harcourt, Brace and Company, 1932), p. 18.

5. Ibid., p. 6; AE, "Flying the Atlantic," p. 17.

6. AE, *The Fun of It,* pp. 8, 11; AE, "Flying the Atlantic," p. 72.

7. AE, "Flying the Atlantic," p. 72.

8. AE, *The Fun of It,* p. 3; MEM quoted in the *Boston Globe,* 1989.

9. For example, on the eve of her 1928 transatlantic flight she told her
mother in one of her "popping off" letters, "Our family life tends to
be too secure." GPP, *Soaring Wings,* p. 57. This letter was not found
until after Earhart's death.

10. AE, "Flying the Atlantic," p. 72.

11. AE, *20 Hrs. 40 Min.: Our Flight in the Friendship* (New York: G. P.
Putnam's Sons, 1928), p. 34.

12. Ibid., p. 31.

13. AE quoted in Mary S. Lovell, *The Sound of Wings: The Life of Amelia
Earhart* (New York: St. Martin's Press, 1989), p. 30.

14. AE, *20 Hrs. 40 Min.,* p. 44.

15. AE, *The Fun of It,* pp. 48, 26.

16. Ibid., p. 51; Marian Stabler quoted in Doris L. Rich, *Amelia Earhart:
A Biography* (Washington, D.C.: Smithsonian Institution Press, 1989),
p. 41. For material on women and automobiles, see Virginia Scharff,

Taking the Wheel: Women and the Coming of the Motor Age (New York: Free Press, 1991).

17. AE, *The Fun of It*, p. 52.
18. Scrapbook entitled "Activities of Women" (1920s), in AE papers, SL.
19. For a general introduction to feminism and women's voluntary associations in the 1920s, see Nancy F. Cott, *The Grounding of Modern Feminism* (New Haven: Yale University Press, 1987). See also Chapter Four.
20. For a new perspective on the Women's Educational and Industrial Union, see Sarah Deutsch, "Learning to Talk More like a Man: Boston Women's Class-Bridging Organizations, 1870–1940," *American Historical Review* 97, No. 2 (April 1992), pp. 379–404.
21. The application, dated August 18, 1926, is found in the WEIU papers, SL.
22. Marion Perkins, "Who Is Amelia Earhart?," *Survey* 60 (July 1, 1928), p. 393. See also the 1928 clipping from a Boston newspaper, Denison House papers, SL.
23. Perkins, "Who Is Amelia Earhart?," p. 393; AE, *The Fun of It*, p. 51; MEM and Carol L. Osborne, *Amelia, My Courageous Sister* (Santa Clara, Calif.: Osborne Publisher, 1987), p. 32.
24. AE, *The Fun of It*, p. 53; undated (1927–1928) questionnaire circulated at Boston Conference of National Federation of Settlements, done by younger workers after a discussion about "flaming youth." Found in Eva Whiting White papers, SL.
25. AE, "My Lucky Turning Point," NYHT, no date (1934–1935), found in Denison House papers, SL; GPP, *Soaring Wings*, p. 53; AE quoted in Ruth Nichols, *Wings for Life* (Philadelphia: J. B. Lippincott Company, 1957), pp. 93–94. The letter was to explore the possibility of an organization of women who were fliers, and it continues: "I cannot claim to be a feminist, but do rather enjoy seeing women tackling all kinds of new problems—new for them, that is." See Chapter Four.
26. AE, *Last Flight* (New York: Harcourt, Brace and World, 1937), p. 9; AE, *20 Hrs. 40 Min.*, pp. 99–100. In fact, Marion Perkins claimed that many in Boston noted AE's resemblance to Lindbergh even before they knew she was a flier. See 1928 clippings found in Denison House papers, SL.
27. Perkins, "Who Is Amelia Earhart?," p. 393; AE quoted in NYT, June 5, 1928, p. 3; GPP, *Soaring Wings*, p. 55. Note how fairly intimate family contacts, like letters to her sister and mother, were released to the press and widely publicized as part of Earhart's developing celebrity.
28. AE remarks reprinted in *National Geographic* 62 (September 1932), p. 363; AE, *The Fun of It*, pp. 86–87.
29. AE, *20 Hrs. 40 Min.*, pp. 144, 201; syndicated AE article, NYT, June 21, 1928, p. 1.
30. Syndicated AE article, NYT, June 19, 1928, p. 1; syndicated AE arti-

cle, NYT, June 20, 1928, p. 1; AE, *The Fun of It,* p. 84.

31. Men responded to her model, although despite a few obligatory marriage proposals that seem to greet all new celebrities, she never became a major sex symbol like some of the Hollywood stars or a maternal "girl next door you want your son to marry" type such as tennis star Helen Wills. See Chapter Five.

32. Frances Perkins quoted in NYT, July 8, 1928, p. 16, at the reception at the Women's City Club in AE's honor.

33. Carrie Chapman Catt quoted in NYT, July 8, 1928, p. 16; Lillian Wald quoted in NYT, July 9, 1928, p. 3.

34. AE, "Try Flying Yourself," *Cosmopolitan* (November 1928), p. 32; AE, *The Fun of It,* p. 85.

35. Syndicated AE article, NYT, June 21, 1928, p. 1; AE, "My Lucky Turning Point," Denison House papers, SL.

36. Quoted in GPP, *Soaring Wings,* p. 49.

37. AE, *The Fun of It,* p. 88.

38. GPP, *Soaring Wings,* p. 77; MEM, COHC, p. 9. One exception is the introductory speech by President Herbert Hoover when Earhart received the National Geographic Society medal after her 1932 flight. After noting that she belonged "in spirit with the great pioneering women to whom every generation of Americans has looked up," he noted, "It is significant that she found the first outlet for her energies in social settlement work, and that through all her succession of triumphs in aviation, her transcontinental and transoceanic flights, she has continued active in this warmly human labor." Quoted in *National Geographic* 62 (September 1932), p. 363.

39. Syndicated AE article, NYT, June 20, 1928, p. 1.

40. When I began my research, I looked first in *Readers' Guide to Periodical Literature* and was surprised at how relatively few articles there were on her. Newspaper coverage turned out to be more extensive but mainly centered on specific exploits and record-breaking flights.

41. GPP, *Soaring Wings,* p. 98.

42. AE, "Flying the Atlantic," p. 72; NYT, September 1, 1928, p. 1.

43. AE quoted in NYT, September 15, 1928, p. 9.

44. NYT, September 1, 1928, p. 1; Rich, *Amelia Earhart,* p. 84. The first three were to Phoebe Omlie, Ruth Nichols, and Lady Mary Heath.

45. MEM, *Amelia, My Courageous Sister,* p. 74. See also NYT, November 23, 1928, p. 22.

46. NYT, November 23, 1928, p. 22; coverage of divorce in NYT, December 19, 1929, p. 22, and December 20, 1929, p. 22; AE-GPP marriage announcement, NYT, February 8, 1931, p. 1; NYT, November 10, 1930, p. 11; NYT, November 11, 1930, p. 25.

47. For example, Earhart was quoted on a 1932 trip to Chicago: "Not that I'm rabid about it, at all, nor a Lucy Stoner. But I think women in aviation should have the same privileges as women who write—and my husband doesn't mind. For social purposes, I think Putnam's a

grand name, though." Quoted in *Chicago Tribune*, June 25, 1932, p. 1.

48. AE to AOE, February 22, 1931, AOE papers, SL.

49. AE quoted in Jean L. Backus, *Letters from Amelia, 1901–1937* (Boston: Beacon Press, 1982), p. 83; AE quoted in GPP, *Soaring Wings*, p. 74.

50. I am using the most complete version cited in Lovell, *Sound of Wings*, pp. 165–66, which is slightly fuller than the one that Putnam himself included in *Soaring Wings*, p. 76. The original is found in the Amelia Earhart collection at the Seaver Center for Western History Research, Los Angeles County Museum of Natural History, Los Angeles, California.

51. I am referring primarily to paid employment. Married middle-class women often found fulfillment in benevolent and charitable activities in their communities, and this political activity greatly lessened their isolation in their homes. See Anne Firor Scott, *Natural Allies: Women's Associations in American History* (Urbana: University of Illinois Press, 1991) and Lori D. Ginzberg, *Women and the Work of Benevolence* (New Haven: Yale University Press, 1990).

52. The best introduction to the marriage and career question is found in Cott, *The Grounding of Modern Feminism*, Chapters 5 and 7. See also Joyce Antler, *Lucy Sprague Mitchell: The Making of a Modern Woman* (New Haven: Yale University Press, 1987). For an example of a professional woman who lived her life with another woman, see Susan Ware, *Partner and I: Molly Dewson, Feminism, and New Deal Politics* (New Haven: Yale University Press, 1987).

53. In Earhart's case, she might have succumbed to what historians have called the compulsory heterosexual imperatives of the consumer culture of the 1920s and 1930s. In the late nineteenth century professional women, Earhart's forerunners, often chose not to marry and instead established households with other women that approximated the commitments of a marriage. (These were sometimes called Boston marriages.) This option was an accepted and respectable choice for women of upper-middle-class backgrounds who were either unwilling or unable to marry. Since women were not seen as having much sexual passion, there were few hints of the possibility of sexual expression in such relationships, although clearly such feelings were there.

   But increasingly, especially by the time Amelia Earhart was entering adulthood, such female friendships were becoming suspect. With the wider dissemination of the works of Freud and Havelock Ellis, doctors and the lay public began to reinterpret such friendships as abnormal, deviant, and stigmatized. From the other side, the consumer culture of the 1920s validated the heterosexual choices of dating, drinking, and selected sexual experimentation, especially if it was pointed toward marriage. Amelia Earhart was such a loner that she had few good friends of either sex, so it is hard to know if she ever felt attracted to other women. But just to put her choices in a social rather than a sexual context, if Earhart had been making a similar decision in 1891 rather than in 1931, she might have more likely stayed single or chosen to share her life with another woman. By the 1930s the trend was toward heterosexuality. For an introductory overview, see John D'Emilio and Estelle B. Freedman, *Intimate Matters: A History of Sexuality in America* (New York: Harper & Row, 1988).

54. AE quoted in Lovell, *Sound of Wings,* pp. 153–54.
55. Rich, *Amelia Earhart,* p. 116; AE, *Last Flight,* p. 11.
56. Barbara Miller Solomon, *In the Company of Educated Women: A History of Women and Higher Education in America* (New Haven: Yale University Press, 1985), p. 177.
57. AE quoted in Backus, *Letters from Amelia,* p. 115; MEM, *Amelia, My Courageous Sister,* p. 141; MEM, COHC, p. 18; AE interview in the *Chicago Tribune,* June 25, 1932, p. 1; GPP, "The Forgotten Husband," *Pictorial Review* 34 (December, 1932), pp. 12–13. See Chapter Four for a fuller discussion of her attitudes on birth control.
58. Here is how Earhart responded in one interview: "Some people seem to think Mr. Putnam said he wanted me to have a baby, and he has been writing letters ever since reiterating what he really did say and that he is not a frustrated husband." NYT, March 5, 1935, p. 21. For George's reaction, see GPP, "A Flyer's Husband," *Forum* 93 (June 1935), pp. 330–32. Muriel's quote comes from MEM, COHC, p. 18.
59. AE, "Flying the Atlantic," p. 17.
60. Descriptions of the flight by AE are found in *National Geographic* (September 1932) and the NYT, May 22 and May 23, 1932. See also Associated Press clipping from London, May 23, 1932, found in MEM papers, SL.
61. When she was in Paris, she charmed the French Senate by saying, "It is much more difficult to make a good law than a good Atlantic flight." One French legislator replied, "Madame, what you did imperiled only yourself, whereas what we do carries danger to many others." Quoted in NYT, June 8, 1932, p. 6.
62. *National Geographic,* pp. 358–59; Rich, *Amelia Earhart,* p. 143.
63. NYT, May 23, 1932, p. 3; AE, "Flying the Atlantic," pp. 15, 16; NYT, May 22, 1932, p. 26.
64. AE, "Flying the Atlantic," p. 17; AE, *The Fun of It,* p. 210; NYHT, May 22, 1932, p. 1; NYT, June 22, 1932, p. 3.
65. Telegrams from Hurst to AE, no date (May 22, 1932), and Carrie Chapman Catt to AE, June 19, 1932, in Purdue Special Collections. Folder III.c contains many other telegrams from well-known figures down to obscure organizations like the San Antonio Women's Club. All felt moved to send their greetings to the American flier in Londonderry.
66. Lou Henry Hoover quoted in Backus, *Letters from Amelia,* p. 132.
67. Herbert Hoover quoted in NYT, May 22, 1932, p. 1.

CHAPTER 2: GENDER AND AVIATION

1. AE, "My Flight from Hawaii," *National Geographic* 65 (May 1935), p. 605; AE, *Last Flight* (New York: Harcourt, Brace and World, 1937), p. 29.
2. Joseph J. Corn, *The Winged Gospel: America's Romance with Aviation, 1900–1950* (New York: Oxford University Press, 1983), pp. 15–16.
3. AE, *20 Hrs. 40 Min.: Our Flight in the Friendship* (New York: G. P. Putnam's Sons, 1928), pp. 310; 1935 radio speech quoted in Shirley Dobson Gilroy, *Amelia: Pilot in Pearls* (McLean, Va.: Link Press, 1985), p. 19.
4. Louise Thaden, *High, Wide and Frightened* (New York: Stackpole Sons, 1938), p. 258.
5. Corn, *Winged Gospel,* p. 12; Lady Heath quoted in *Equal Rights* (December 8, 1928), p. 349.
6. AE quoted in *Chicago Tribune,* July 22, 1928, p. 21; AE, *The Fun of It: Random Records of My Own Flying and of Women in Aviation* (New York: Harcourt, Brace and Company, 1932), p. 103; AE, "Try Flying Yourself," *Cosmopolitan* (November 1928), p. 32; AE, "Shall You Let Your Daughter Fly?," *Cosmopolitan* (March 1929), pp. 88–89; Dorothy Verill, *The Sky Girl* (New York: Century Company, 1930), p. 210.
7. Margery Brown, "Flying Is Changing Women," *Pictorial Review* 31 (June 1930), pp. 30, 109; Thaden, *High, Wide and Frightened,* p. 138.
8. See the epilogue to Corn, *Winged Gospel,* pp. 135–47.
9. Henry Ladd Smith, *Airways: The History of Commercial Aviation in the United States* (New York: Alfred A. Knopf, 1942), p. 49. For more general information on the growth of the industry in the interwar period, see Corn, *Winged Gospel;* John Frederick, *Commercial Air Transportation* (Chicago: Richard D. Irwin, 1942); and Walter Boyne, *Smithsonian Book of Flight* (Washington, D.C.: Smithsonian Books, 1987).
10. Quoted in undated clipping (c. 1934), "Flyer Designs Sports Clothes," found in AOE papers, SL.
11. General information on TAT is found in Smith, *Airways; Sportsman Pilot* (August 1929), p. 48; and NYT, July 2, 1929, p. 2. Earhart first met Anne and Charles Lindbergh through TAT, specifically on the inaugural flight of the airline, when AE and Anne were passengers and Charles piloted one of the planes partway.
12. Flyer found in Purdue Special Collections. See also AE, "The Most Traveled Road" (November 1930) in the American Institute of Aeronautics and Astronautics Collection, LC.
13. Information contained in *Boston and Maine Employees Magazine* (July 1933), found in Purdue Special Collections. In this case Earhart invested twenty-five hundred dollars of her own money. Along with similar amounts from her three partners, Eugene Vidal, Paul Collins, and Sam Solomon, that represented the entire capitalization of the airline—enough to buy two used airlines and to cover the operating expenses of the

corporation for a few months. Doris L. Rich, *Amelia Earhart: A Biography* (Washington, D.C.: Smithsonian Institution Press, 1989), pp. 171–74.

14. AE, *The Fun of It,* p. 106.
15. Ibid, pp. 111, 106.
16. AE quoted in *Literary Digest* (October 26, 1929), p. 57; AE quoted in Florence Yoder Wilson, "What Women Can Do for Aviation," *Needlecraft: The Magazine of Home Arts* (May 1930), p. 16.
17. AE, "Are Women Holding Aviation Back?," p. 14; NYT, April 2, 1933, p. 12. Here is the opening line of Bess Furman's Associated Press story: "The first lady of the land and the first woman to fly the ocean went skylarking together last night in a big Condor plane. . . ." (Copy reprinted in MEM and Carol L. Osborne, *Amelia, My Courageous Sister* [Santa Clara, Calif.: Osborne Publisher, 1987], p. 175.) For more on the Roosevelt connection, see Susan Ware, "Amelia Earhart and the Roosevelts," *The View from Hyde Park: The Franklin and Eleanor Roosevelt Institute Newsletter* (Fall 1990).
18. AE, "Women's Influence on Air Transport Luxury," *Aeronautical Review* (March 1930), p. 32; AE, "Are American Women Holding Aviation Back?," p. 14.
19. AE, "Mother Reads as We Fly," *Cosmopolitan* (January 1931).
20. There are further interesting parallels between the development of the automobile and that of the airplane with regard to gender. Automobiles had been a male domain which women invaded, and taking the wheel represented "a conspicuous cultural statement about female assertiveness." To brave the rigors of the road, women discarded traditional female clothing in favor of male garb such as heavy coats, breeches, and leather goggles. Once behind the wheel of a car, women drivers were stereotyped for their "emotional instability, physical weakness, and intellectual deficiencies." As historian Virginia Scharff noted, "The enduring figure of the woman driver continues to embody fears about what women might do with plenty of money, big powerful machines, and relatively unrestricted freedom of movement [p. 172.]" All those images applied to women in aviation as well.

Even though the parallels between the airplane and the automobile regarding gender are striking, the differences are just as salient. When automobiles were in their early stages of acceptance, women's emancipation was a much more hotly debated topic than it was by the 1920s and 1930s, the golden age of aviation. Despite hopes for an airplane in every garage, the plane never developed into the means for personal transportation that the automobile did. It never became a consumer toy and certainly was never associated with "fun, sex, and sin" the way the automobile was by the 1920s, especially by young people. And because it cost so much more to take lessons or to own your own plane, the liberatory aspects of flight were never as widespread as the early days of motoring for women. On the other hand, the airplane was never harnessed to domesticity as the automobile eventually was, becoming not a tool of women's liberation but an instrument for women to fulfill their domestic and familial duties. See Virginia Scharff, *Taking the Wheel: Women and the Coming of the Motor Age* (New York: Free Press, 1991).

21. AE, "What Flying Is Teaching Women," *Home Magazine,* found in American Institute of Aeronautics and Astronautics Collection, LC; AE, "Women's Influence on Air Transport Luxury," *Aeronautic Review* (March 1930), p. 32.

22. Only once in 1929 did she let herself deviate from this approach publicly by suggesting, hesitantly at the very end of an article, "How would it do for advertisers to admit the wings which bear aloft precious human freight have Department of Commerce licences? Would the mention of steel tube fuselages in the headlines be a breach of etiquette? Yes, I believe that women may be waiting for this sterner stuff, and I think they can bear it." See AE, "Shall Hard Facts Give Way to Gentle Blandishments?" *Sportsman Pilot* (July 1929), p. 30.

23. Louise Thaden quoted in Corn, *Winged Gospel,* p. 75.

24. AE, "Why Are Women Afraid to Fly?," *Cosmopolitan* (July 1929), p. 138; AE to Miss Mintern, February 28, 1929, AE General File, National Air and Space Museum Archives, Washington, D.C.

25. AE, "Dropping In on England," *McCall's* (October 1928), p. 21. See Chapter Four for a discussion of the term "feminism."

26. The experiences of African-Americans in aviation hold many parallels to those of women, with black women experiencing the discriminations of both groups. Like feminists, African-Americans were determined to use the success of individual black aviators, both male and female, as a way of showing white America what blacks were capable of. Success in the sky would translate into increased opportunities, respect, and racial harmony on the ground. This did not happen, just as it did not happen with women. Also like women, blacks faced discrimination and prejudice when seeking training, with some early aviators like Bessie Coleman (who was killed in an accident in 1926) being forced to go to France in order to learn to fly. Blacks of both sexes made no headway in commercial aviation until the civil rights movement of the postwar era finally opened the informally segregated cockpits just about the time women were also entering the field. The one difference was the roles as pilots available to black men in the military starting in World War II and continuing in the postwar era. For them the military provided a clear career path.

 For brief mention, see Corn, *Winged Gospel,* pp. 35–36, 59–60. Elizabeth Hadley Freydberg of Northeastern University is writing a biography of Bessie Coleman that deals more broadly with issues of race and aviation in the 1920s. See Ken Gornstein, "No Flight of Fancy," *Northeastern University Magazine* 16 (March 1991), pp. 19–21.

27. "The Reminiscences of Muriel Earhart Morrissey" (1960), COHC, pp. 7–8.

28. See Susan Ware, *Beyond Suffrage: Women in the New Deal* (Cambridge, Mass.: Harvard University Press, 1981). For women in Hollywood, see Wendy Holliday, "Hollywood's Modern Women: Work, Culture, and Politics, 1915–1940," dissertation in progress, New York University.

29. Ruth Elder letter, November 13, 1927, quoted in Paul C. Richards catalog (November 1982), in AE Biography file, SL; AE, "Are You Air-Minded?," *Independent Woman* (October 1933), p. 359.

30. AE Purdue speech, quoted in GPP, *Soaring Wings: A Biography of Amelia Earhart* (New York: Harcourt, Brace and Company, 1939), p. 245.

31. See Ruth Milkman, *Gender at Work: The Dynamics of Job Segregation by Sex during World War II* (Urbana: University of Illinois Press, 1987) for the best discussion of this phenomenon.

32. Radio talk by AE for the National Woman's Party, November 1931, found in Alliance for Guidance of Rural Youth Records, Duke University Archives.

33. See Corn, *Winged Gospel,* pp. 89–90. To get the flavor of the coverage at the time, see also W. B. Courtney, "High-Flying Ladies," *Collier's* 90 (August 20, 1932), pp. 29f.; Ethelda Bedford, "Hostess of the Air," *Independent Woman* (February 1932), pp. 52, 77; Marjorie Shuler, "Their Home Is in the Troposphere," *Christian Science Monitor Magazine* (June 17, 1936), p. 5; and "Stewardess on an Air-liner," *Literary Digest* 115 (February 18, 1933), pp. 35–36.

34. "Flying Supermen and Superwomen," pp. 22–23; Bedford, "Hostess of the Air," p. 52; Courtney, "High-Flying Ladies," p. 30. The number of stewardesses who married and left their jobs was a major problem, according to the airlines. But they were more likely to marry passengers they met in the course of their duties than pilots. The policy of dismissing women who married was in line with general discrimination against married women workers in the 1930s. See Lois Scharf, *To Work and to Wed: Female Employment, Feminism, and the Great Depression* (Westport, Conn.: Greenwood Press, 1980).

35. AE radio talk for the National Woman's Party, November 1931; AE, "Women's Status in Aviation," *Sportsman Pilot* 1 (March 1929), p. 9; AE speech reprinted in *Changing Standards: Proceedings of the Fourth Annual New York Herald Tribune Women's Conference on Current Problems* (September 26–27, 1934), p. 135; AE quoted in *Literary Digest* (October 26, 1929), p. 57. For evidence that things were changing, approximately 25 percent of all model-airplane builders in the 1930s were women or girls, a far higher percentage than later. Corn, *Winged Gospel,* p. 114.

36. Newspaper clipping, Boston, 1932, MEM papers, SL. See also *Equal Rights* (June 4, 1932), p. 140; AE, "Women's Status in Aviation"; and

AE, "The Feminine Touch," *Aero News and Mechanics* 2 (April–May 1930), p. 35. She quotes figures of fewer than one hundred women pilots and approximately eight thousand men.

37. Ruth Nichols quoted in Vera L. Connolly, "Daughters of the Sky," *Delineator* 115 (August 1929), p. 83.

38. W. B. Courtney, "Ladybird," *Collier's* 95 (March 30, 1935), p. 16. For more on Richey, see Glenn Kerfoot, *Propellor Annie* (Lexington, Ky.: Kentucky Aviation History Roundtable, 1988).

39. AE, "Why Are Women Afraid to Fly?," p. 138. This language sounds remarkably prescient of the modern justifications of the affirmative action programs introduced in the 1970s.

40. AE quoted in Corn, *Winged Gospel*, p. 78; Margery Brown, "What Men Flyers Think of Women Pilots," *Popular Aviation* (1929), quoted in Wendy Boase, *The Sky's the Limit* (London: Macmillan, 1979), p. 14; AE, "Why Are Women Afraid to Fly?," p. 138.

41. AE quoted in Frances Drewry McMullen, "The First Women's Air Derby," *Woman's Journal* 14 (October 1929), p. 11; Corn, *Winged Gospel,* pp. 79–80; "The Reminiscences of Ruth Nichols" (1961), COHC, p. 38.

42. Nichols and Allen quoted in *Newsweek* 6 (November 16, 1935), p. 22; AE quoted in GPP, *Soaring Wings,* p. 156; AE quoted in Universal Service Clipping, May 9, 1935, found in Clarence Strong Williams papers, SL.

43. The representations of gender in aviation magazine ads further reinforced stereotypes of flying. *Aviation* magazine (from which all these examples are drawn) advertised itself as "edited by men who fly, for men interested in air transport" (September 1934), and many of its ads were also geared exclusively to them: "BOYS—Build a Stinson 'Reliant' Model" (August 1933), "A New World for Ambitious Men at the Parks Air College" (July 1933), and so forth. Ads pitched to women as potential consumers were rare. Instead a company like Douglas Amphibion used a picture of a woman passenger with the head "COMFORT is always important" (March 1933), and Texaco pictured a Braniff hostess in a modified Mexican outfit for its new Texaco airplane oil (November 1935). Bellanca Aircraft pitched an ad, "Just a word to the WIVES and SWEETHEARTS," assuring them, "You'll appreciate the Bellanca ideal in airplane design and construction much more than that head-strong, lovable, grown-up boy of yours," with the assumption that she might influence the man when the "subject of a new plane is discussed" (March 1934). And Beech Aircraft followed the custom of testimonials from women fliers such as Arlene Davis and Charlotte Frye in a January 1936 ad under the head ". . . and so Easy to Fly!" In fact, what is most noticeable when you look through the advertisements and endorsements in major aviation magazines, considering women's individual prominence in the 1930s, is how rarely women appear at all.

44. In fact, these women of the 1930s were the second generation to try to make this point. Here is pioneer aviator Ruth Law speaking right after World War I: "There is the world-old controversy that crops up again whenever women attempt to enter a new field. Is woman fitted for this or that work? It would seem that a woman's success in any particular line would prove her fitness for that work without regard to theories to the contrary." Ruth Law quoted in Claudia M. Oakes, *United States Women in Aviation through World War I* (Washington, D.C.: Smithsonian Institution Press, 1978), p. 1.

45. AE to Beatrice Pugsley, September 26, 1936, in MEM papers, SL; AE, *The Fun of It,* p. 95; NYT editorial, March 19, 1937, p. 22.

46. AE radio speech for National Woman's Party, November 1931; AE, *The Fun of It,* p. 179; AE, "The Feminine Touch," p. 35.

47. AE, *The Fun of It,* p. 162; Corn, *Winged Gospel,* p. 72. Although marriage was compatible with flying, motherhood was chancier. The woman who taught Amelia Earhart to fly, Neta Snook, stopped flying entirely when her first child was born. Some of the strains that women with children experienced are captured in this quotation from Louise Thaden's autobiography: "To a psychoanalyst, a woman pilot, particularly a married one with children, must prove an interesting as well as inexhaustible subject. Torn between two loves, emotionally confused, the desire to fly an incurable disease eating out your life in the slow torture of frustration—she cannot be a simple, natural personality." Thaden, *High, Wide and Frightened,* p. 139.

48. AE quoted in NYT, June 12, 1929, p. 3; AE, *The Fun of It,* p. 152. Rich, *Amelia Earhart,* pp. 88–94, provides a good summary of the race, as does AE, *The Fun of It,* pp. 152–54.

49. McMullen, "The First Women's Air Derby," p. 10; Thaden, *High, Wide and Frightened,* p. 76; AE, *The Fun of It,* p. 138. Earhart spoke in similar terms: "Marvel Crosson left a challenge to the women of the Derby and there is certainly no aftermath of fear among us." Quoted in Thaden, *High, Wide and Frightened,* p. 76.

50. AE, *The Fun of It,* p. 157. This has shades of Alaska's Iditarod race, which for several years in a row in the 1980s was won by women, prompting the slogan "Alaska—where men are men, and women win the Iditarod." The women's victories in the Bendix in the 1930s did not produce similar fears perhaps because they were seen as so unusual or perhaps because the women's tactic of being taken seriously as individuals actually worked.

51. AE, "Why Are Women Afraid to Fly?," p. 138; AE, "Women's Status in Aviation," p. 9; AE, *The Fun of It,* p. 161.

52. Charles E. Planck, *Women with Wings* (New York: Harper and Brothers, 1942), pp. 307–26, contains a useful chronological summary of women's records, awards, and other accomplishments for the 1930s.

53. Journalist Margery Brown observed in 1930, "There is something in the very nature of aviation that tends to unite individuals as well as

nations, and it is creating a bond among women, knitting womankind into a better understanding of their common problems—first on the field, then in the business world and in the home. It is fostering sympathy and sex-consciousness (a consciousness of one's own sex) and is arousing a sincere desire to submerge the personal in the ideal." Margery Brown, "Flying Is Changing Women," *Pictorial Review* 31 (June 1930), p. 108.

54. The 1931 constitution quoted in letter from AE to "Dear Ninety-Niner," January 19, 1932, found in AOE papers, SL; form letter from Neva Paris and AE, November 16, 1929, found in AE papers, SL. Other names suggested included Breezy Girls, Climbing Vines, Noisy Birdmen, Homing Pigeons, Gad Flies, and Queens High. See Corn, *Winged Gospel,* p. 86; *History of the Ninety-Nines* (Oklahoma City: Ninety-Nines, Inc., 1979), p. 10, copy found in the National Air and Space Museum Archives. As Corn points out, there was always a tension between the professional and feminist agenda and the purely social one, a split which was well demonstrated in the diverse stories in the newsletters and other publications.

55. See NYT, April 26, 1931, p. 26, for her election, and May 8, 1933, p. 17, for her resignation.

56. See Nancy Cott, *The Grounding of Modern Feminism* (New Haven: Yale University Press, 1987), for this trend. See also Chapter Four.

57. Corn, *Winged Gospel,* pp. 87–88. See also the 1979 *History of the Ninety-Nines.*

58. Blanche Noyes quoted in Gilroy, *Amelia: Pilot in Pearls,* p. 53; Phoebe Fairgrave Omlie, "Amelia—Our 'Trail Blazer,' " undated clipping from *National Aeronautic Magazine,* found in the American Institute of Aeronautics and Astronautics Collection, LC.

59. "The Reminiscences of Blanche Noyes" (1960), in COHC, p. 10; Cochran quoted in Planck, *Women with Wings,* p. 220; Ruth Nichols, *Wings for Life* (Philadelphia: J. B. Lippincott Company, 1957), pp. 99–100; Elinor Smith, *Aviatrix* (New York: Harcourt Brace Jovanovich, 1981), p. 94.

60. Planck, *Women with Wings,* p. 215; Mrs. Hazel Colson to AOE, January 21, 1939, AOE papers, SL.

61. William L. Riordon, *Plunkitt of Tammany Hall* (New York: E. P. Dutton, 1963), p. 4.

62. The original women were Louise Thaden, Nancy Harkness, and Helen McCloskey, later supplemented by Helen Richey and Blanche Noyes. Phoebe Omlie, an important New Deal Democrat and a member of the Aeronautical Advisory Board of the Department of Commerce, helped get them hired with funds from the WPA. See *Aviation* (November 1935), p. 63; and *Time* 28 (August 24, 1936), p. 48.

63. Probably the career of Jacqueline Cochran comes the closest. Married to a wealthy man and the head of her own very successful cosmetics company, she helped win roles for women aviators in World War II

and in the postwar period was the first woman to break the sound barrier. See Jacqueline Cochran and Maryann Bucknum Brinley, *Jackie Cochran: An Autobiography* (New York: Bantam Books, 1987), as well as the earlier Jacqueline Cochran, *The Stars at Noon* (Boston: Little, Brown, 1954.) Whether Amelia Earhart, a committed pacifist, would have supported the war is far from certain. Also unclear is whether Earhart's marriage to George Palmer Putnam would have survived without her high-profile career for him to manage. See Chapter Seven.

64. Nichols, COHC, p. 7; Corn, *Winged Gospel*, pp. 81, 84.
65. Nichols quoted in Connolly, "Daughters of the Sky," p. 83.
66. Many of these themes are laid out in Sian Reynolds, " 'High Flyers': Women Aviators in Pre-War France," *History Today* 39 (April 1989), pp. 36–41.
67. Cochran and Brinley, *Jackie Cochran*, p. 12; Smith, *Aviatrix*, p. 70; Ruth Nichols quoted in NYT, September 6, 1936, p. 3; AE quoted in NYT, August 22, 1932, p. 3; AE quoted in NYT, June 12, 1929, p. 3.
68. Thaden, *High, Wide and Frightened*, pp. 258, 259.

CHAPTER 3: IT'S HARD WORK BEING
A POPULAR HEROINE

1. Ederle quoted in NYT, August 7, 1926, p. 1; AE, "Questions I Have Met," *Aeronautic Review* (February 1929), p. 7.
2. Orrin E. Klapp, "Hero Worship in America," *American Sociological Review* 14 (February 1949), pp. 53–62. The quote is from pp. 61–62.
3. Ederle returned home to a tumultuous New York ticker tape parade and received commercial offers totaling close to a million dollars, but she was unable to cash in on them. She toured vaudeville houses with a swimming act but had no success converting her athletic prowess into a Hollywood career. Never bitter, she became a swimming instructor in New York and never married. For more on Ederle, see "How a Girl Beat Leander at the Hero Game," *Literary Digest* 90 (August 21, 1926), pp. 52–67.
   Ruth Elder was also treated as a heroine, honored by the National Woman's Party and offered a chance for a screen test in Hollywood. She made several silent movies, went on tour, and made a lot of money. But she spent it just as quickly. Even though she continued to fly for sport (she competed in the 1929 Powder Puff Derby and was a charter member of the Ninety-Nines), she dropped out of sight in the 1930s. Married six times, including to the New York socialite Walter Camp, Jr., she died in 1978. For more, see Judy Lomax, *Woman of the Air* (New York: Dodd, Mead and Company, 1987), pp. 65–66, and Kathleen Brooks-Pazmany, *United States Women in Aviation, 1919–1929* (Washington, D.C.: Smithsonian Institution Press, 1991), pp. 21–22.
4. GPP, *Soaring Wings: A Biography of Amelia Earhart* (New York: Harcourt, Brace and Company, 1939), p. 190. Or, as he said on the same

page, "In itself, being a celebrity is very hard work indeed."

5. AE quoted in Universal Service clipping, May 9, 1935, found in Clarence Strong Williams papers, SL.

6. *Newsweek* (January 19, 1935), quoted in Doris L. Rich, *Amelia Earhart: A Biography* (Washington, D.C.: Smithsonian Institution Press, 1989), p. 196; AE to Bert Kinner, February 1933, quoted ibid., p. 155; Universal Service clipping, May 9, 1935, found in Clarence Strong Williams papers, SL.

7. Bobbie Trout quoted in Rich, *Amelia Earhart,* p. 119; Mary S. Lovell, *The Sound of Wings: The Life of Amelia Earhart* (New York: St. Martin's Press, 1989), p. xvii; Elinor Smith, *Aviatrix* (New York: Harcourt Brace Jovanovich, 1981), pp. 73–74.

8. Lovell, *Sound of Wings,* p. 81; Anne Morrow Lindbergh, *Locked Rooms and Open Doors: Diaries and Letters, 1933–1935* (New York: Harcourt Brace Jovanovich, 1974), p. 5.

9. Jacqueline Cochran and Maryann Bucknum Brinley, *Jackie Cochran: An Autobiography* (New York: Bantam Books, 1987), p. 137; Pancho Barnes quoted in Grover Ted Tate, *The Lady Who Tamed Pegasus: The Story of Pancho Barnes* (Los Angeles: Maverick Publishing, 1984), p. 47. She continued: "Whenever she fucked up he would scold her as a child. He kept this up until she almost lost confidence in herself so then he backed off." While few had kind words to say about Putnam personally, Barnes's assessment seems too stark. Many others, including woman fliers who knew the couple, found the relationship symbiotic and mutually satisfying.

10. AE quoted in NYT, March 14, 1937, p. 34; NYHT, June 21, 1934, p. 1; Fay Gillis Wells at Amelia Earhart Symposium, Smithsonian Institution, reprinted in *Aviation Journal* (June 1983), p. 5.

11. GPP, *Wide Margins: A Publisher's Autobiography* (New York: Harcourt, Brace and Company, 1942), p. 3. The best biographical information about Putnam is found in Lovell, *Sound of Wings,* which presents a very sympathetic assessment of the man and his importance to AE.

12. GPP, *Wide Margins,* p. 252; Lovell, *Sound of Wings,* pp. 83–84.

13. Bradford Washburn, "Amelia Earhart's Last Flight," *Boston Museum of Science Newsletter* 33 (January–February 1984), p. 2.

14. Lovell, *Sound of Wings,* covers GPP's later career. In all the Hollywood books I have read about the studio system in the 1930s, Putnam is never mentioned; this suggests that he was not a major player.

15. Edward Bernays defined public relations as "(1) information given to the public; (2) persuasion directed at the public to modify attitudes and actions; and (3) efforts to integrate attitudes and actions of an institution with its publics and of publics with that institution." Bernays, *Public Relations* (Norman: University of Oklahoma Press, 1952), p. 3. See also Edward Bernays, *Crystallizing Public Opinion* (New York: Boni and Liveright, 1923); Eric F. Goldman, *Two-Way Street: The Emergence of the Public Relations Counsel* (Boston: Bellman Publishing, 1948); and

Daniel Boorstin, *The Image* (New York: Atheneum, 1961).

    Sometimes Putnam went too far, like his transparent attempt to capitalize on Eleanor Roosevelt's popularity by dubbing Earhart "The First Lady of the Air." (The name did not stick.) Quoted in Lovell, *Sound of Wings*, p. 215. Or his 1935 press release stating, "Amelia Earhart is now a grandmother," when his son David Binney Putnam and wife had a child. Quoted in Rich, *Amelia Earhart*, p. 208.

16. GPP, *Soaring Wings*, p. 209.

17. Ibid., p. 88; Rich, *Amelia Earhart*, pp. 178, 202. When a researcher does a lot of newspaper research on microfilm, you notice things like this because the Sunday papers take much longer to scan.

18. AE quoted in *Newsweek* 5 (May 18, 1935), p. 35; Putnam quoted in Rich, *Amelia Earhart*, p. 199; clipping, June 22, 1932, cited ibid., p. 146; Ruth Nichols quoted in NYHT, May 22, 1932, p. 3; GPP, *Wide Margins*, p. 282.

19. AE, *20 Hrs. 40 Min.: Our Flight in the Friendship* (New York: G. P. Putnam's Sons, 1928), pp. 282–83. Hollywood celebrities like Jean Harlow and Carole Lombard often endorsed cigarettes, especially Lucky Strike. For more on smoking in Hollywood, see Cal York, "What Do They Smoke?," *Photoplay* (September 1931). Other products that prominent women endorsed in *Photoplay* included Pond's cream (socialite Anne Morgan), Auburn cars (Marlene Dietrich), and handbags (Carole Lombard and Ginger Rogers).

20. NYT, July 31, 1928, p. 8; Byrd to AE, July 30, 1928, Purdue Special Collections; AE, *20 Hrs. 40 Min.*, pp. 282–83; GPP, *Soaring Wings*, pp. 193–94.

21. A general introduction to endorsements is William M. Freeman, *The Big Name* (New York: Printers' Ink Book, 1957). See also Boorstin, *The Image*.

22. "I would try it again with WASP," the cable which AE sent back from Ireland after her flight, was no doubt part of an endorsement deal with the Pratt & Whitney aircraft company. See *Aviation* (July 1932).

23. Similarly, an ad for Stanavo aviation gasoline and engine oil includes a picture taken before the flight along with this text: "Great credit is due Miss Earhart and her associates for the careful preparation contributing to her brilliant flight. Careful preparation has characterized all successful transatlantic flights, the list of which includes every attempt made using Stanavo products." *Aviation* (July 1932).

24. Time Savers were notes, envelopes, and blotters from White and Wyckoff that were "thin-packed to slip into your bag or pocket so you may WRITE WHILE YOU WAIT at the restaurant, dressmakers', hairdressers', dentist's, doctor's, between appointments, and on boat, train, or airplane." They had a logo of Amelia Earhart's name, with a red plane and trail cutting across. Sample found in AE papers, SL.

25. Rich, *Amelia Earhart*, p. 238.

26. AOE manuscript (no date), AOE papers, SL; press release (no date),

found in American Institute of Aeronautics and Astronautics collection, LC.

27. Advertisement (c. 1933), found in AOE papers, SL.

28. Sigrid Arne, "Midstream with Modern Women," *Knickerbocker Press* (May 16, 1934), p. 7; "Amelia Earhart Turns from Flying to Designing" (1934), promotional brochure put out by the United States Rubber Company, found in Purdue Special Collections.

29. U.S. Rubber brochure, Purdue Special Collections; Janet Mabie, "A Bird's Eye View of Fashion," *Christian Science Monitor Magazine* (February 7, 1934), p. 3. Or as Earhart said on another occasion, "Aviation itself is, it seems to me, a great untapped source for fashion inspiration. . . . I am using this type of decorative detail both because it gives a fresh touch to sports clothes and because through it I perhaps can bring some of the beauty I have found in aviation closer to all women." U.S. Rubber brochure, Purdue Special Collections.

30. AOE manuscript; *Women's Wear Daily,* December 11, 1933, p. 19, and NYT, November 24, 1933, p. 30; "Photoplay Announces Macy's Cinema Shop," *Photoplay* (June 1934). A Macy's executive said thirty stores had accepted the franchise: "The idea behind the whole thing is to prevent pirating or reproduction. There is to be no attempt for volume." Quoted in *Women's Wear Daily,* December 11, 1933, p. 19.

31. An article in *Woman's Home Companion* 61 (August 1934), p. 33, also advertised Amelia Earhart patterns for the fashions, available for twenty-five cents from the Woman's Home Companion Service Bureau.

32. U.S. Rubber brochure, Purdue Special Collections.

33. GPP, *Soaring Wings,* p. 202; Rich, *Amelia Earhart,* p. 146; clippings found in Purdue Special Collections and AE General File, National Air and Space Museum Archives; NYT, May 16, 1931, p. 19; "Miss Earhart's Adventure on the Floor of the Sea," *Cosmopolitan* (November 1929); NYT, July 23, 1929, p. 18, and July 24, 1929, p. 3. AE was upset at the headline MISS EARHART BALKS, which implied she had lost her nerve. In fact, the suit she was wearing was too large and leaked.

34. GPP to President Edwin Elliott, June 10, 1935, Purdue Special Collections.

35. AE, "A Friendly Flight across the Country," *New York Times Magazine* (July 9, 1931), pp. 7, 23.

36. Louella Parsons rumor cited in Rich, *Amelia Earhart,* p. 159. Here is the full quote: "Some day, if it's a proper story—if they let me play my unromantic self, slacks, engine grease and all. If something comes along that will be useful in advancing women—if it will help flying—if-if-if-" Quoted in GPP, *Soaring Wings,* pp. 165–66.

37. Mortimer Franklin, "Amelia Earhart Looks at the Films!," *Screenland* (June 1933), p. 76. She had definite ideas about aviation and Hollywood: "I think it's too bad when aviation movies depend for their excitement upon plane wrecks, lost flyers, and all that sort of thing. Perhaps that's good drama, perhaps it isn't; but it certainly isn't mod-

ern aviation. . . . Aviation has grown up, you know. It isn't a play-thing anymore. It has become a serious and useful industry. . . ." She also spoke out against war. "As an individual I'm opposed to war, anyway, and naturally I think it's extremely unfortunate that war should be emphasized, and to some extent even glorified, in any kind of film." Ibid., p. 29.

38. Mark Lankin, "What Happens to Fan Mail?," *Photoplay* (August 1928), pp. 38–40.

39. AE, *20 Hrs. 40 Min.*, p. 281.

40. Quoted in GPP, *Soaring Wings*, pp. 85, 210.

41. Ibid., p. 86; AE to Harry Manning, February 19, 1934, quoted in Shirley Dobson Gilroy, *Amelia: Pilot in Pearls* (McLean, Va.: Link Press, 1985), p. 68. It remains true, however, that there really are not that many personal letters from AE extant. In part this is because many of her personal effects were burned in the fire at the Rye house in late 1934. Also her life-style was fairly peripatetic, so she was unlikely to save material when she was on the road. (There are no thorough correspondence files for George Putnam either.) The most extensive letters are those to her mother and sister excerpted in Jean L. Backus, *Letters from Amelia, 1901–1937* (Boston: Beacon Press, 1982), drawn from the collections at the Schlesinger Library.

42. After she lent Muriel money to purchase a house, she expected it to be a businesslike relationship: "I'm no scrooge to ask that some acknowledgment of a twenty-five hundred dollar loan be given me. I work hard for my money. Whether or not I shall exact repayment is my business nevertheless Pidge should feel some responsibility for protecting me against the loss of that sum." When she got involved in the summer vacation for the Morrissey family and Mrs. Earhart, she told them where to go and what kind of place to stay in: a nice rental, "not a cheap hole where there are things to put up with. For instance, I DO NOT WANT YOU AND PIDGE TO DO HOUSEWORK. IN FACT I FORBID THAT." AE to Mrs. Eho, April 27, 1931, and AE to Mother, June 25, 1931, AOE papers, SL.

43. AE to Mammy, December 26, 1928, and AE to Mother, June 2, 1935, AOE papers, SL.

44. AE to Maw, September 18, 1932, and AE to Mother, December 1, 1931, AOE papers, SL.

45. Roxana Robinson, *Georgia O'Keeffe: A Life* (New York: Harper & Row, 1989), p. 270.

46. See, for example, GPP to AOE, November 26, 1935, AOE papers, SL, in which George tries to explain why AE may not be available for some family function. "I guess we will have to leave the decision in all this up to Amelia. For self-protection she simply has to be hard-boiled about getting away from people. Realize, please, this is a problem repeated two or three times a day every day for the last few months."

47. AE, *The Fun of It: Random Records of My Own Flying and of Women in*

Aviation (New York: Harcourt, Brace and Company, 1932), p. 87; GPP, *Soaring Wings*, p. 174.

48. The *Lantern* (July–August 1928), cited in Lovell, *Sound of Wings*, p. 111; AE, "What Miss Earhart Thinks When She Is Flying," *Cosmopolitan* (December 1928), p. 28; AE, *20 Hrs. 40 Min.*, p. 280.

49. NYT, August 30, 1928, p. 2.

50. AE, *The Fun of It*, pp. 209–18. The Schlesinger Library has a copy of the 78 rpm record, which is about two minutes long.

51. For example, see *NYT Book Review*, September 16, 1928, p. 10; *Saturday Review of Literature* 5 (October 13, 1928), p. 240; *Books* (June 19, 1932), p. 5; *NYT Book Review*, June 26, 1932, p. 8.

52. MEM and Carol L. Osborne, *Amelia, My Courageous Sister* (Santa Clara, Calif.: Osborne Publisher, 1987), p. 101; AE and GPP, "My Husband/ My Wife," *Redbook* (October 1932), pp. 22–23; AE, "Flying and Fly-Fishing," *Outdoor Life* 62 (December 1934), pp. 16–17; AE, "My Flight from Hawaii," *National Geographic* 65 (May 1935), pp. 593–609.

53. The NYT had the rights to the 1928 and 1932 flights. The NYHT syndicate paid for exclusive rights for her California–Mexico and Mexico–Newark flights as well as for the round-the-world flight. The rights to the 1935 Hawaii–Oakland solo went to the North American Newspaper Alliance, Inc.

54. NYHT, May 9, 1935, p. 1. Ditto when she flew from Hawaii to California; the *Los Angeles Times*, January 13, 1935, p. 1, noted that she went directly into the Hotel Oakland, where she met with her husband's business representatives and wrote her exclusive story for the *Los Angeles Times* and other papers in the syndicate.

55. Telegram to AOE inviting her to attend, June 18, 1932, AOE papers, SL; NYT, July 4, 1928, p. 3, and July 12, 1928, p. 9; *National Geographic* (September 1932), p. 358; NYHT, May 23, 1932; NYT, December 1, 1928, p. 36; Rich, *Amelia Earhart*, p. 161; NYT, December 1, 1928, p. 36; clipping, "Today on the Radio," May 26, 1933, in AOE papers, SL; Rich, *Amelia Earhart*, p. 208.

56. GPP, *Soaring Wings*, p. 79; telegram from AE to GPP, April 18, 1936, Purdue Special Collections.

57. AE to Mother, September 6, 1932, AOE papers, SL; GPP to Mrs. Earhart, September 21, 1935, AOE papers, SL; AE, *20 Hrs. 40 Min.*, p. 281; AE to AOE (no date), and AE to Mother, January 18, 1936, AOE papers, SL.

58. Backus, *Letters from Amelia*, p. 149; Rich, *Amelia Earhart*, p. 210; AE itinerary found in AOE papers, SL. This was just one of several such trips that year. The schedule is truly mind-boggling, especially when one realizes that she is doing a fair bit of it by car.

59. On fees, see Lovell, *Sound of Wings*, p. 205, and Rich, *Amelia Earhart*, p. 159. At three hundred dollars a shot, that represents forty thousand dollars in income a year.

60. AOE manuscript (no date), AOE papers, SL; Rich, *Amelia Earhart,* p. 219.
61. GPP to F. C. Crawford, November 30, 1935, Purdue Special Collections; AE to Mother, March 8, 1935, and November 3, 1935, in AOE papers, SL; AE to Hiram Bingham, July 19, 1932, AE general file, National Air and Space Museum Archives; AE to Mother, February 14, 1933, AOE papers, SL.
62. "The Reminiscences of Muriel Earhart Morrissey" (1960), COHC, p. 11; Fay Gillis Wells at Amelia Earhart Symposium, Smithsonian Institution, reprinted in *Aviation Journal* (May 1983), p. 5.
63. Address to DAR, April 21, 1933, found in MEM papers, SL.
64. Mary Spencer to AOE, March 15, 1935, and Harriet Palmer to AOE, August 10, 1941, AOE papers, SL; Alice Kalousdian quoted in Gilroy, *Amelia: Pilot in Pearls,* p. 50; Jane Dow Bromberg, December 19, 1984, quoted in Rich, *Amelia Earhart,* p. 82.

CHAPTER 4: FEMINISM AND INDIVIDUALISM

1. Quoted in Doris L. Rich, *Amelia Earhart: A Biography* (Washington, D.C.: Smithsonian Institution Press, 1989), p. 200. The other women Eleanor Roosevelt cited were Nobel Peace Prize winner Jane Addams, suffrage leader Carrie Chapman Catt, Secretary of Labor Frances Perkins, and novelist Dorothy Canfield Fisher.
2. *Equal Rights* (December 1930), p. 6; NYT, December 10, 1935, p. 29. Similarly, writer Mary Roberts Rinehart compiled a list of Women of the Year which included Dr. Alice Hamilton, industrialist Josephine Roche, journalist Dorothy Thompson, Willa Cather, Jane Addams, and sculptor Malvina Hoffman. Rinehart's list also tried, perhaps consciously, to select a few younger women, such as painter Georgia O'Keeffe, actress Greta Garbo, and Amelia Earhart. Mary Roberts Rinehart, "Women of the Year," *Pictorial Review* 36 (January 1935), pp. 6–7.
3. Mrs. J. Borden Harriman to AE, no date (late 1934), found in Florence Rose papers, Sophia Smith Collection. Further documentation of Earhart's role in this dinner is found in the Margaret Sanger papers, LC. Thanks to Esther Katz and the staff of the Sanger papers at NYU for bringing this material to my attention.
4. This list was the result of a nationwide poll conducted jointly by the National Council of Women and the *Ladies' Home Journal.* A total of 128,882 ballots was cast by women (men were excluded from the voting). See the NYT, December 21, 1932, p. 21.
   In response to the *Ladies' Home Journal* poll, the *New York Daily News* came up with its own list on December 26, 1932. The only overlap was Mary Baker Eddy and Frances Willard. In general, the *Daily News* poll tended to cite contemporary women, especially in newer

fields of entertainment, such as Mary Pickford, Irene Castle, and Geraldine Farrar. Respondents also picked leaders of contemporary causes, such as birth control activist Margaret Sanger and antiprohibitionist Pauline Morton Sabin. Amelia Earhart was not included on this second list.

5. Nancy F. Cott, *The Grounding of Modern Feminism* (New Haven: Yale University Press, 1987), p. 281.

6. Eleanor Roosevelt quoted in Ruby A. Black, "Is Mrs. Roosevelt a Feminist?," *Equal Rights* (July 27, 1935), p. 163.

7. "Are women, we ask, to behave for ever like a little girl running behind her big brother and calling out, 'Me, too?' " asks Eleanor Rathbone in "Changes in Public Life," in *Our Freedom and Its Results,* ed. Ray Strachey (London: Hogarth Press, 1936), p. 57. Rathbone says the phrase was first coined by Kathleen Courtney. In general, there are many parallels between the history of interwar feminism in the United States and England. See Brian Harrison, *Prudent Revolutionaries: Portraits of British Feminists between the Wars* (Oxford, England: Clarendon Press, 1987).

8. For example, Earhart was distressed when, at a 1935 dinner at the Lotos Club in her honor, a club leader assailed the Roosevelt administration for its antibusiness leanings. Earhart went ahead with her speech about aviation but the next day released this statement: "I was unaware that politics was to be injected. It is fine for women to seek better government, but they should not be selfish about it. . . . I am sure that my host did not intend placing me in the position of identifying myself with a partisan meeting." See NYT, December 23, 1935, p. 13.

9. On GPP's politics, see Mary S. Lovell, *The Sound of Wings: The Life of Amelia Earhart* (New York: St. Martin's Press, 1989), pp. 198–99; on Amy Otis Earhart's Republicanism, see Jean L. Backus, *Letters from Amelia, 1901–1937* (Boston: Beacon Press, 1982), pp. 146–49. See also GPP to AOE, November 7, 1940, AOE papers, SL, which opens, "Too bad about Willkie."

10. Quoted in NYT, September 20, 1936, p. 7. On the only recorded campaign appearance for the candidate in upstate New York, Earhart found that her voice did not carry well from the window she was supposed to speak from, so a desk was hauled from the building and placed on the sidewalk so she would be closer to the crowd. For a woman who spent a good deal of her life on the lecture platform, this was ironic. See NYT, September 27, 1936, p. 2.

11. In a few of the surviving examples she suggested that her homecoming parade in 1932 be canceled and the money given to the unemployed, a suggestion not taken. (Rich, *Amelia Earhart,* pp. 140–41, suspected this was as much an attempt to evade the ceremony as to help the poor.) And in November 1932 she lent her name to an appeal for support for the Welfare and Relief Mobilization of 1932, an attempt to raise money and awareness about the needs of the unemployed. Speaking from Williamstown, Massachusetts, Earhart suggested that each listener give

up a meal to understand what it was like to be hungry. Support for established social services was crucial, she argued, not just to deal with the tragic consequences of unemployment but also to prevent such economic dislocations in the future. AE quoted in NYT, November 14, 1932, p. 2.

12. NYT, September 30, 1936, p. 17; GPP, *Soaring Wings: A Biography of Amelia Earhart* (New York: Harcourt, Brace and Company, 1939), p. 148; AE, "Draft Women for War!," *Home Magazine* (August 1935), p. 60.

13. AE quoted in Shirley Dobson Gilroy, *Amelia: Pilot in Pearls* (McLean, Va.: Link Press, 1985), p. 70; telegram from AE to Gerald Nye, September 11, 1934, Purdue Special Collections; AE address to DAR, April 21, 1933, *Conference Proceedings of the National Society, Daughters of the American Revolution*, pp. 655–61, found in MEM papers, SL. See also NYT, April 22, 1933, p. 11. The bulletin contains a transcription of Earhart's address which conveys very well her lecture style.

14. AE, "Draft Women for War!," p. 22. Earhart continued, "The trenches, combat service in the air, transport jobs in advanced positions, and a startlingly reduced number of other less brilliant arenas of activity are the last remaining strongholds of men; and I have a feeling men would rather vacate the arena of war altogether than share it with women. . . ." This veiled critique of male bonding and exclusion was similar to the stance developed by Virginia Woolf in *Three Guineas* (New York: Harcourt, Brace and World, 1938).

15. GPP, *Soaring Wings,* p. 160; Cott, *The Grounding of Modern Feminism,* p. 5.

16. *Bulletin of the Society of Woman Geographers* (June 1932), found in the National Air and Space Museum Archives, Washington, D.C.; telegram from Harriet Chambers Adams to Amelia Earhart, June 7, 1932, Purdue Special Collections.

17. She belonged to the Business and Professional Women (founded in 1919), although its journal, *Independent Woman,* carried news about her far less frequently than the National Woman's Party journal, *Equal Rights.* For membership in BPW, see NYT, July 24, 1937, p. 17, which mentions the tributes to her at the BPW convention.

18. NYT, November 6, 1938, p. 5. In 1932 Earhart had chaired a Zonta committee offering an annual award for outstanding achievement by a woman pilot. She explained the reasoning behind the award and behind supporting women in the professions in general as she unsuccessfully tried to enlist the Radcliffe president Ada Comstock to serve on the committee: "To me, the idea of a group of business women encouraging other women in a new industry seems laudable. Somehow aviation tends to reward those who do more or less spectacular things and leave unnoticed others whose every-day flying may be just as worthwhile with or without press hullabaloo. There will probably be more than six hundred women pilots by next year. Some of these

need to be let know that good work is appreciated." AE to Ada Comstock, October 22, 1932, Ada Comstock presidential files, SL. See also Comstock to AE, October 26, 1932, ibid., in which Comstock ends, "Please let me add how much I have admired the courage and skill which you have displayed in your achievements as a pilot."

19. Material on dinner found in Mary Ritter Beard papers, SL. This archive never got off the ground, but its materials formed part of the core for the Radcliffe Women's Archives (now known as the Schlesinger Library), which was founded in 1943.

20. Mary Beard to Marjorie White, December 2, 1937, Marjorie White papers, SL. Beard wrote, "I loathe the airplane myself as the worst menace to living men and women. In the New Year we can have some more intellectual aspects of archives when people at large are interested in their value." Beard had already stated this theme when she wrote to the activist and cosponsor of the archives Rosika Schwimmer in 1935 that she did not want Earhart at the first meeting because it was to have "as much semblance of the intellectual as possible." Beard bemoaned the fact that in her opinion, Earhart had not spoken out forcefully enough against war: "If she would only come out boldly against war, as an aviator, what a help that would be to the human spirit! But she suggests merely equality in the business of war promotion. It disgusts me." Mary R. Beard to Rosika Schwimmer, October 6, 1935, Schwimmer-Lloyd papers, New York Public Library. My thanks to Nancy Cott for bringing this to my attention.

21. *Changing Standards: Proceedings of the Fourth Annual New York Herald Tribune Women's Conference on Current Problems* (September 26–27, 1934), p. 132. Meloney closed with this statement: "I wish that all the youth of the land might feel the personal inspiration of contact with Amelia Earhart [p. 136]."

22. Anna Kelton Wiley to AE, February 7, 1935, National Woman's Party papers, LC; *Equal Rights* (January 15, 1938), p. 195, and (June 4, 1932), p. 138. For general background on the National Woman's Party, see Cott, *The Grounding of Modern Feminism,* Chapter 2; Susan D. Becker, *The Origins of the Equal Rights Amendment: American Feminism between the Wars* (Westport, Conn.: Greenwood Press, 1981); and Leila J. Rupp and Verta Taylor, *Survival in the Doldrums* (New York: Oxford University Press, 1987).

23. Editorial, "Amelia Earhart, Ardent Feminist," *Equal Rights* (June 15, 1937), p. 82; *Equal Rights* (June 4, 1932). The accompanying editorial entitled "She Showed Them" gushed, "The more we think of the stupendous and breath-taking achievement of Amelia Earhart and the way she took the thing, the more we are impressed with the innate power of the Feminist movement [p. 138]."

24. *Equal Rights* (September 5, 1931), p. 248. Further showing the NWP's single-mindedness for the cause, its telegram to Earhart after her 1932 Atlantic solo read in full, "Congratulations equality before the law for

men and women." Telegram, NWP to AE, May 24, 1932, Purdue Special Collections.

25. AE quoted in NYT, September 23, 1932, p. 1. See also *Equal Rights* (October 1, 1932), p. 275.

26. Telegram enclosed in letter from Anita Pollitzer to Alma Lutz, November 27, 1933, Alma Lutz papers, SL; *Equal Rights* (November 25, 1933), p. 335; quoted in NYT, December 20, 1933, p. 15; AE quoted in NYT, November 15, 1936, pp. 1–2.

27. AE interviewed by Marguerite Martyn, *St. Louis Post-Dispatch,* April 7, 1936, clipping found in AE papers, SL. For general background on the Equal Rights Amendment in the 1930s, see Susan Ware, *Holding Their Own* (Boston: Twayne Publishers, 1982), Chapter 4; Lois Scharf, *To Work and to Wed* (Westport, Conn.: Greenwood Press, 1981); and Becker, *The Origins of the Equal Rights Amendment.* See also Sybil Lipschultz's work in progress on the minimum wage for women and its meaning for American feminism. One of the few possible compromises might have built on the sentiment expressed by American suffragist Harriet Burton Laidlaw in 1912, as paraphrased by Nancy Cott: "insofar as women were like men they deserved the same rights, and insofar as they differed they ought to represent themselves." Quoted in Cott, "Feminist Theory and Feminist Movements: The Past before Us," *What Is Feminism?,* ed. Juliet Mitchell and Ann Oakley (New York: Pantheon, 1986), p. 52.

28. See Susan Ware, *Beyond Suffrage: Women in the New Deal* (Cambridge, Mass.: Harvard University Press, 1981) for the anti-ERA attitudes of social reformers in the 1930s.

29. Dorothy Dunbar Bromley, "Feminist—New Style," *Harper's* 155 (October 1927), pp. 552–60.

30. September 1927 letter quoted in GPP, *Soaring Wings,* p. 160; AE, "Women and Courage," *Cosmopolitan* (September 1931), p. 148. In his biography her husband followed the same line: "that while her work was aviation, her absorbing interest and concern, without being offensively feministic, was the place of women, both actually and ideally, in the world which she saw changing so rapidly." GPP, *Soaring Wings,* p. 137.

31. Quoted in Cott, *The Grounding of Modern Feminism,* p. 15.

32. Ibid., pp. 4–5, 267, 275–76.

33. Ibid., p. 283. In my definition, if a woman is advancing her personal and professional interests at the same time she hopes her achievements will benefit women as a group, she is a liberal feminist; if she is just out for herself, she is an individualist. On the other hand, if my argument about popular culture's sustaining feminism is correct, whether or not the popular heroines actually identify with women as a group is less central. See Chapter Six and the Epilogue.

34. As Cott says, "The trend toward individual accomplishment unrelated to womanhood as such or to gender identity might be read to measure

the success of feminism's aims—or the exhaustion of its spirit. Each reading has its truth." Cott, *The Grounding of Modern Feminism*, p. 239. The thrust of her argument suggests a generally negative reading of this shift, while my interpretation sees it in a more positive light. Specifically, when Cott argues (p. 281) that individualism's models of individual achievement cannot "engender a program for change in the position of women as a group," I argue that it can, through the coming together of liberal feminist messages and popular culture. See Chapter Six and Epilogue.

35. A good introduction to liberal feminism is Alison M. Jaggar, *Feminist Politics and Human Nature* (Totowa, N.J.: Rowman and Allanheld Publishers, 1983), especially Chapters 3 and 7; see also Zillah Eisenstein, *The Radical Future of Liberal Feminism* (New York: Longman, 1981).

36. AE, *Last Flight* (New York: Harcourt, Brace and Company, 1937), p. 34. The statement came from her trip to Mexico in 1935.

37. Ibid., pp. 48–49; quoted in GPP, *Soaring Wings*, pp. 248–49.

38. AE quoted in NYT, July 30, 1929, p. 18; quoted in GPP, *Soaring Wings*, p. 89; Fuller quoted in Alice S. Rossi, ed., *The Feminist Papers* (New York: Bantam Books, 1973), p. 150.

39. The Port Huron statements are found in Purdue Special Collections. See also Dobson, *Amelia: Pilot in Pearls*, pp. 20–23.

40. AE quoted in GPP, *Soaring Wings*, p. 139; AE quoted in Antoinette May, *Different Drummers* (Millbrae, Calif.: Les Femmes, 1976), p. 5.

41. Here is a statement from Earhart's *Last Flight:* "I think my husband has always found a sort of grim satisfaction—a species of modern martyrdom—in being, for once, the male left behind while the female fares forth adventure-bound, thus turning topsy-turvy the accepted way of the world in such matters [p. 65]." On the other hand, since Putnam so extensively rewrote and embellished the skeleton draft manuscript of *Last Flight*, it is hard to know whether these are her words or once again his rendition of what he knew she would say. See Chapter Three.

42. GPP quoted in Elizabeth Clark, "Lesser Halves of Famous Wives: George Palmer Putnam Isn't Henpecked by Amelia Earhart," *New York World-Telegram*, February 8, 1932, p. 14.

43. "Flyer Designs Sports Clothing," clipping (no date), found in AOE papers, SL. Describing her own situation, she noted, "Mr. Putnam tries not to interfere with my flying, and I try not to toss any monkey-wrenches in the way of his activities. Of course one or the other has to be inconvenienced, now and then; but the arrangement is actually and theoretically a pretty good basis for contented companionship." AE, "My Husband," *Redbook* (October 1932), p. 23.

44. AE quoted in GPP, *Soaring Wings*, p. 139; AE quoted in Donna Remillard, "Leading Feminist of Her Day," *Atchison Daily Globe*, July 20, 1976, p. 1a. See also AE, "My Husband," p. 97. Earhart and Putnam tried very hard to put into practice the shared financial responsibility of running their various households. They shared a bank account, into

which they each put every month a percentage of their earnings to pay for all their common living expenses. Beyond that, recalled her husband, "We each have our own funds, for personal investments, luxuries and idiosyncrasies, gifts and individual responsibilities." (Putnam could not decide whether a Lockheed Vega was a luxury or an idiosyncrasy.) GPP, "The Forgotten Husband," *Pictorial Review* (December 1932), p. 13.

45. Press release, June 2, 1935, Purdue Special Collections.
46. Figure cited in GPP, *Soaring Wings,* p. 247.
47. A copy of the Purdue questionnaire is found in AOE papers, SL.
48. Quoted in GPP, *Soaring Wings,* pp. 248–49.
49. AE, "My Husband," p. 97.
50. AE, "My Husband," p. 97; AE quoted in Sigrid Arne, "Midstream with Modern Women," *Knickerbocker Press,* May 16, 1934, p. 7; GPP, "My Wife," *Redbook* (October 1932), p. 22.
51. AE quoted in Remillard, "Leading Feminist of Her Day," p. 1a.
52. AE quoted in Rich, *Amelia Earhart,* p. 212. For single-sex friendships, see Lillian Faderman, *Surpassing the Love of Men: Romantic Friendships and Love between Women from the Renaissance to the Present* (New York: William Morrow and Company, 1981) and *Odd Girls and Twilight Lovers: A History of Lesbian Life in Twentieth-Century America* (New York: Columbia University Press, 1991).
53. Amelia had given her sister, Muriel, *The Doctor's Manual of Marriage* for birth control information; she later complained to her mother, "Surely if Pidge can't manage things it is important for him to do so. . . . I think he should share the mechanics of being a husband." Rich, *Amelia Earhart,* pp. 118, 125. From the tone of these comments, Earhart seemed to be recommending that her sister use a diaphragm and, if not that, that the husband use condoms. Such an arrangement was common among middle-class families in the 1930s and was likely the birth control strategy practiced in the Earhart-Putnam household. For general histories of the birth control movement, see Linda Gordon, *Woman's Body, Woman's Right* (New York: Penguin, 1976); James Reed, *The Birth Control Movement and American Society: From Private Vice to Public Virtue* (Princeton: Princeton University Press, 1978); and Ellen Chesler, *Woman of Valor: Margaret Sanger and the Birth Control Movement in America* (New York: Simon & Schuster, 1992).
54. Similarly, there was no mass working-class movement agitating for changes in the liberal capitalist system even in the midst of the gravest economic collapse the United States had ever faced. For a cogent discussion of the intersection of politics and mass culture in ordinary lives in the 1930s, see Lizabeth Cohen, *Making a New Deal: Industrial Workers in Chicago, 1919–1939* (New York: Cambridge University Press, 1990).
55. General historiography on the 1920s includes Cott, *The Grounding of Modern Feminism;* Dorothy M. Brown, *Setting a Course: American Women*

in the 1920s (Boston: Twayne Publishers, 1987); J. Stanley Lemons, *The Woman Citizen: Social Feminism in the 1920s* (Urbana: University of Illinois Press, 1973); and Elaine Showalter, ed., *These Modern Women: Autobiographical Essays from the Twenties* (Old Westbury, N.Y.: Feminist Press, 1978).

56. For the new emphasis on heterosexuality, see Estelle Freedman and John D'Emilio, *Intimate Matters: A History of Sexuality in America* (New York: Harper & Row, 1988); Kathy Peiss, *Cheap Amusements: Working Women and Leisure in Turn-of-the-Century New York* (Philadelphia: Temple University Press, 1986); and Carroll Smith-Rosenberg, "The New Woman as Androgyne: Social Disorder and Gender Crisis, 1870–1930," *Disorderly Conduct: Visions of Gender in Victorian America* (New York: Oxford University Press, 1985).

57. The phrase "to break into the human race" was used by feminists in the 1910s. A humorous play on this was the tombstone Chase Going Woodhouse joked she wished to be buried under: "Born a Woman, Died a Person." Quoted in Cott, *The Grounding of Modern Feminism*, p. 238.

58. Edein French to Harry Grob, May 9, 1976, MEM papers, SL. French wrote in response to Grob's request for information about Earhart in an issue of *Social Work*. While she noted that the episode was not exactly what he was looking for, she recalled it as "very formative" for her.

59. Quoted in Ruby A. Black, "Is Mrs. Roosevelt a Feminist?," *Equal Rights* (July 27, 1935), p. 164.

CHAPTER 5: ICONOGRAPHY
AND REPRESENTATION

1. Francis Trevelyan Miller, *Lindbergh: His Story in Pictures* (New York: G. P. Putnam's Sons, 1929), p. 11; AE quoted in NYT, April 21, 1935, p. 1.

2. Amelia Earhart, "The Fun of It," *House and Garden* (April 1933), pp. 62–63. This is a good example of the kind of disguised promotion that George Putnam sought, timed to promote Earhart's most recent book as well as build on the interest in her 1932 solo. The text and accompanying pictures, in a full two-page spread designed to look like an article, are really an ad for the Cine-Kodak Eastman Movie Camera. AE's copy ends: "However, standing behind my own Cine-Kodak directed at others is still a very real part of 'the fun of it'!"

3. Doris L. Rich, *Amelia Earhart: A Biography* (Washington, D.C.: Smithsonian Institution Press, 1989), p. 32.

4. See Stuart Hall, "Culture, Media, and the 'Ideological' Effect," *Mass Communication and Society*, ed. James Curran, Michael Gurevitch, and Janet Wollacott (Beverly Hills: Sage, 1979). As defined by Judith Williamson, "A sign is quite simply a thing—whether object, word, or picture—which has a particular meaning to a person or group of peo-

ple. It is neither the thing nor the meaning alone, but the two together."
A signifier is the material object or thing; the signified is its meaning
or idea. The space between the signifier and the signified is the individual subject. Judith Williamson, *Decoding Advertisements: Ideology and
Meaning in Advertising* (London: Marion Boyars, 1978, 1983), p. 17.

5. General sources on popular culture that have influenced my interpre-
tation include Lorraine Gamman and Margaret Marshment, eds., *The
Female Gaze: Women as Viewers of Popular Culture* (London: Women's
Press, 1989); Leslie G. Roman, Linda K. Christian-Smith, and Eliza-
beth Ellsworth, eds., *Becoming Feminine: The Politics of Popular Culture*
(London: Falmer Press, 1988); George Lipsitz, *Time Passages: Collective
Memory and American Popular Culture* (Minneapolis: University of
Minnesota Press, 1990); and Andrea Walsh, *Women's Film and Female
Experience, 1940–1950* (New York: Praeger, 1984). An important note
of caution is sounded by Tania Modleski in *Feminism without Women:
Culture and Criticism in a 'Postfeminist' Age* (New York: Routledge, 1991)
when she cautions against the unspoken syllogism underlying some
feminist analysis of popular culture: "I like *Dallas;* I am a feminist;
Dallas must have progressive potential [p. 45]".

6. This is not to say that a "liberal feminist" response is the only way that
a woman (or a man) might react to Earhart. To follow through on the
recognition that all meanings in popular culture are fluid rather than
fixed, it is arguable that there were other ways in which these messages
could be read than in feminist terms. Older women could have seen in
Earhart hopes for their daughters. Working-class people or the unemployed may have identified with her calls for hard work and self-help
as a prescription to improve their desperate position during the Great
Depression. Lesbians, or women groping toward that self-definition,
could have identified with Earhart, whose demeanor, exploits, and
dress all could be construed as an alternative to traditional norms of
feminine heterosexual behavior. In other words, there is not just "one"
way to read Amelia Earhart. My focus on its connections to feminism
and women's aspirations is derived from the set of questions that I as
a historian am asking.

7. Inez Haynes Irwin, "What the Movies Are Doing to Our Children,"
Photoplay (November 1936), p. 84; Eleanor Roosevelt, "Why We Roosevelts Are Movie Fans," *Photoplay* (July 1938), pp. 16–17.

8. All this background is from Raymond Fielding, *The American Newsreel, 1911–1967* (Norman: University of Oklahoma Press, 1972).

9. Ibid., pp. 48, 228, 205.

10. Joseph J. Corn, *The Winged Gospel: America's Romance with Aviation,
1900–1950* (New York: Oxford University Press, 1983), p. 84. See
also Jacqueline Cochran and Maryann Bucknum Brinley, *Jackie Cochran: An Autobiography* (New York: Bantam Books, 1987).

11. In 1932 Paramount had bought exclusive rights to Earhart's Atlantic
solo. Needless to say, it missed the unplanned landing in Ireland. To

facilitate its coverage, AE later donned her flying suit, started up the plane, and taxied, actions which the newsreels somewhat ingenuously portrayed as her actual landing. Mary S. Lovell, *Amelia Earhart: The Sound of Wings* (New York: St. Martin's Press, 1989), p. 186.

12. Ibid., p. 188.

13. I consulted newsreels at both the Schlesinger Library and the National Archives. Schlesinger's Amelia Earhart collection includes miscellaneous audiovisual sources, including a video from the Women's Air and Space Museum in Ohio (which contains the dialogue quoted in the text), and a documentary done by the National Video Industries. The National Archives contain the extensive Universal Newsreels collection. Of special help was a computerized listing of citations to Amelia Earhart called CineScan by Newsreel Access Systems, Inc. (1990) which was kindly made available to me by the documentary filmmakers at Blackside, Inc., Boston, Massachusetts.

14. For example, the CineScan printout contains printed versions of some of the sound text that accompanied the film, although not always a verbatim rendition.

15. Quoted in GPP, "The Forgotten Husband," *Pictorial Review* 34 (December 1932), pp. 12–13. See also *St. Louis Post-Dispatch,* June 21, 1932, p. 3a.

16. GPP, "The Forgotten Husband," p. 12; NYT, June 13, 1931, p. 1; NYHT, May 22, 1932, p. 1. Putnam uses the designation in the foreword to *Last Flight* and all his subsequent biographical writings about his wife. In *The Fun of It* (New York: Harcourt, Brace, and Company, 1932), the photograph next to the frontispiece is captioned simply "A. E." so the initials were already used then.

17. *Chicago Tribune,* July 19, 1928, p. 1. Many of these usages have now been expunged from popular usage, replaced by gender-neutral terms. One which seems to endure is the distinction between actress and actor. That it seems less slighting to refer to a woman as an actress may be linked to the general parity that women enjoyed in much of Hollywood's history, indeed in the theater as a whole.

18. *Universal News,* March 15, 1937, CineScan; *New York Daily News,* July 4, 1937; NYT, June 5, 1928, p. 1; NYHT, June 4, 1928, p. 1; *Chicago Tribune,* June 4, 1928, p. 2; NYT, June 5, 1928, p. 1; NYHT, June 6, 1928, p. 1; *Paramount News,* June 6, 1928, June 20, 1928, and June 27, 1928, *British Pathé Gazette,* June 21, 1928, *American Pathé News,* July 4, 1928, all in CineScan; *New York Daily News,* June 4, 1928. These headlines are not totally the fault of the sexist press. George Putnam noted that he had been commissioned to find "an American girl" for the flight. GPP, *Soaring Wings: A Biography of Amelia Earhart* (New York: Harcourt, Brace and Company, 1939), p. 52. And to be fair, Amelia Earhart referred to her pilot and navigator as the "boys who did all the work." AE, *20 Hrs. 40 Min.: Our Flight in the Friendship* (New York: G. P. Putnam's Sons, 1928), p. 201.

19. NYHT, June 21, 1928, p. 1; Elinor Smith, always quick to find fault with George Palmer Putnam's promotions of his wife, pointed this out in *Aviatrix* (New York: Harcourt Brace Jovanovich, 1981), p. 73.

20. Clipping found in AOE papers, SL; *Universal News,* May 23, 1932, *British Pathé Gazette,* May 26, 1932, *American Pathé News,* July 24, 1936, *Hearst News of the Day,* March 20, 1937, *Paramount News,* December 11, 1937, all in CineScan.

21. Barry Paris, *Louise Brooks* (New York: Alfred A. Knopf, 1989), p. 203.

22. For general background, see Valerie Steele, *Fashion and Eroticism: Ideals of Feminine Beauty from the Victorian Era to the Jazz Age* (New York: Oxford University Press, 1985); Anne Hollander, *Seeing through Clothes* (New York: Penguin, 1975); Alison Lurie, *The Language of Clothes* (New York: Random House, 1981); Elizabeth Wilson, *Adorned in Dreams: Fashion and Modernity* (Berkeley: University of California Press, 1985); Erving Goffman, *Gender Advertisements* (Cambridge: Harvard University Press, 1979); and Lois Banner, *American Beauty* (Chicago: University of Chicago Press, 1983).

23. NYT, July 24, 1931, p. 16. This citation was brought to my attention by Tina Press in a New York University seminar paper on coverage of Babe Didrikson at the 1932 Olympics.

24. Hollander, *Seeing through Clothes,* pp. 152–53. See also Steele, *Fashion and Eroticism;* Wilson, *Adorned in Dreams;* and Helen Wills Moody, "Sport and Beauty," *Cosmopolitan* (October 1931), p. 152.

25. Roland Marchand, *Advertising the American Dream: Making Way for Modernity, 1920–1940* (Berkeley: University of California Press, 1985), p. 184; Donald J. Bush, *The Streamlined Decade* (New York: George Braziller, 1975), and Jeffrey L. Meikle, *Twentieth-Century Limited: Industrial Design in America, 1925–1939* (Philadelphia: Temple University Press, 1979). Both books pay prominent attention to the airplanes of the 1930s, which, alongside trains, were some of the most streamlined products of the decade.

26. Rich, *Amelia Earhart,* p. 79.

27. See Banner, *American Beauty,* p. 277, and Lurie, *The Language of Clothes,* p. 235.

28. Hollander, *Seeing through Clothes,* pp. xv–xvi; Steele, *Fashion and Eroticism,* pp. 39, 45–46; Lurie, *The Language of Clothes,* p. 4.

29. GPP, *Soaring Wings,* p. 78.

30. David Binney Putnam quoted in Rich, *Amelia Earhart,* p. 118; Helen Schleman quoted in Shirley Dobson Gilroy, *Amelia: Pilot in Pearls* (McLean, Va.: Link Press, 1985), p. 49.

31. GPP, *Soaring Wings,* pp. 96, 216.

32. Susan Brownmiller, *Femininity* (New York: Fawcett Columbine, 1984), p. 65, which also includes the Charlotte Perkins Gilman quote. See also Iris M. Fanger, "Irene Castle," *Notable American Women: The Modern Period,* ed. Barbara Sicherman and Carol Hurd Green (Cambridge, Mass.: Harvard University Press, 1980), pp. 142–43.

33. *St. Louis Post-Dispatch,* June 22, 1928, p. 1. This major news event occurred after Earhart had landed in Wales and been feted in London, but before she returned to the United States. For more on Hollywood and hair, see Adela Rogers St. Johns, "Why Mary Pickford Bobbed Her Hair," *Photoplay* (September 1928), p. 33f.; and Harry D. Wilson, "Long Hair or Short?," *Photoplay* (October 1931), p. 28f.

34. AE, *The Fun of It,* p. 26. MEM and Carol L. Osborne, *Amelia, My Courageous Sister* (Santa Clara, Calif.: Osborne Publisher, 1987) contains the barbershop photograph. Amelia also got a trim from a cowboy while on a Wyoming dude ranch in 1934.

35. *Los Angeles Times,* June 19, 1928, p. 1; NYHT, June 20, 1928, p. 1; NYHT, June 18, 1928, p. 1; NYT, June 4, 1928, p. 2; NYT, June 26, 1928, p. 26; Boston newspaper clipping about 1932 reception, found in MEM papers, SL; NYT, June 21, 1932, p. 1; *Los Angeles Times,* April 20, 1935, p. 1.

36. Crank letter to AE (no date), found in Purdue Special Collections.

37. Fay Gillis Wells quoted in Gilroy, *Amelia: Pilot in Pearls,* p. 49; unidentified Washington journalist quoted in GPP, *Soaring Wings,* p. 91; "Miss Earhart is striking in physique and personality and decidedly feminine," noted the NYT's original biographical blurb, June 4, 1928, p. 2. In another example, a six-page prose and poetry tribute from Mae Noble Rineman to Amy Otis Earhart, the correspondent, who was clearly very enamored of the aviator, noted that AE was not masculine at all: "The boyish attire she wears is for sensible convenience around her ship. Because we know you are feminine to the utmost in your love of dainty personal things, and in your fine mind where beauty of thought prevails." No date, AOE papers, SL.

38. GPP, *Soaring Wings,* p. 156. Along similar lines an article in *Photoplay* cautioned against getting too much exercise because muscles were antithetical to beauty. Swimmer Gertrude Ederle, golfer Helen Hicks, and tennis player Helen Wills all were pointed out as bad examples of too much musculature—certainly more than Hollywood would tolerate. All that was allowed was twenty minutes of tennis a day, not too strenuous, nine holes of leisurely golf every other day, but not combined with tennis, with perhaps a bit of swimming. Horseback riding only once a week for an hour, and so forth. See Lois Shirley, "The Enemy of Beauty—Over-Exercise," *Photoplay* (August 1931), p. 30f.

39. AE *The Fun of It,* p. 83; AE quoted in *New York Sun,* June 20, 1928, clipping found in Purdue Special Collections. Recalled Ruth Nichols: "Well, I always made a point of trying to be the same as the men, in other words, to be very casual. They felt that anybody who got very much dressed up wasn't the kind of person who was a real born flyer. Therefore, if you wanted to join the fraternity, so to speak, and be well thought of, you wanted to be just as casual as possible about it." Nichols, who usually wore sports dresses and occasionally large-

brimmed hats, added, "I think another reason we did that was because we wanted, even at that early time, to have the public feel that there wasn't anything very dangerous, very daredevil about flying. Because that's the way people made money; it was to get the public to fly. So the more causal you were, the more you'd be apt to get people to fly with you." "The Reminiscences of Ruth Nichols" (1960), COHC, p. 6.

Blanche Noyes wore skirts, with very few exceptions, because she did not want to imitate men. "And I had long hair, I didn't wear short hair, and I didn't in any way imitate the men. I was a female, and was happy that I was, and I felt that there was a place for women in aviation—but, as women." "The Reminiscences of Blanche Noyes" (1960), COHC, pp. 44–45.

40. NYT, March 5, 1937, p. 23, and March 14, 1937, p. 34.
41. For information on women's fashions and pants, see Lurie, *The Language of Clothes,* p. 225. For Dietrich's influence, see "The Passing Show of '33," *Photoplay* (February 1934), p. 50, which has this line: "Fat, or skinny, they all wear pants like Marlene."
42. Rich, *Amelia Earhart,* p. 212.
43. *New York Post,* December 20, 1934, p. 3.
44. *Vanity Fair* (November 1931). The caption identified her as just having married George Palmer Putnam.
45. Clipping from *Boston Herald* (no date), found in MEM papers, SL.
46. Typescript notes about 1928 flight, Purdue Special Collections; NYHT, June 21, 1928, p. 1; NYT, June 20, 1928, p. 1.
47. NYT, June 22, 1928, p. 1. For more on cross dressing, see Marjorie Garber, *Vested Interests: Cross-Dressing and Cultural Anxiety* (New York: Routledge, 1992).
48. See, for example, Annie Woodhouse, *Fantastic Women: Sex, Gender, and Transvestism* (New Brunswick, N.J.: Rutgers University Press, 1989).
49. Lillian Faderman has called this life-style, which also included bisexual experimentation, "lesbian chic." These women often looked like men, although they were usually not trying to "pass" the way cross-dressing men were. This clothing style was part of a larger statement about their sexual orientation; generally the only women who dressed that way were lesbians, although the reverse was not true, since not all lesbians adopted such styles. This stylized and recognizable lesbian identity was entirely different from the image projected by Earhart.

For material on the history of lesbians, including patterns of dress and socialization, see Lillian Faderman, *Odd Girls and Twilight Lovers* (New York: Colombia University Press, 1991) and *Surpassing the Love of Men* (New York: William Morrow, 1981); John D'Emilio and Estelle Freedman, *Intimate Matters: A History of Sexuality in America* (New York: Harper & Row, 1988); and Shari Benstock, *Women of the Left Bank, Paris, 1900–1950* (Austin: University of Texas Press, 1986). Paris, *Louise*

Brooks, contains references to the Hollywood homosexual and bisexual scene in the 1920s.

50. Brownmiller, *Femininity,* p. 94; Carolyn G. Heilbrun, *Toward a Recognition of Androgyny* (New York: Harper & Row, 1973), p. x. Here is the rest of Brownmiller's quote: "Wearing a brown leather flight jacket and grinning shyly from the cockpit of her airplane, she appears to soar high in androgynous freedom."

51. Holly Devor, *Gender Blending: Confronting the Limits of Duality* (Bloomington: Indiana University Press, 1989), p. vii.

52. Eugene Vidal quoted in Lovell, *Sound of Wings,* p. 159. Garber, *Vested Interests,* makes a similar point about how transvestism calls into question the binary construction of gender.

53. Fascination with this image led Shirley Gilroy to choose the title *Amelia: Pilot in Pearls* for her book. Gilroy contains the photograph, as do many other books on AE.

54. Rich, *Amelia Earhart,* has the picture, plus a caption describing the origin of the wings.

55. Gilroy, *Amelia: Pilot in Pearls,* p. 74. The painting is credited to the William Rockhill Nelson Gallery of Art, Atkins Museum of Fine Art, Kansas City.

A cartoon by Jean Oberle from *Vanity Fair* (no date) presents a unisex AE, in bright color no less. Her head is too large for her body, and her features, especially her large lips, suggest a woman. But then the figure is given very broad shoulders, enhanced by a large, heavy coat. There is the obligatory silk scarf. But the lower half of her body is far too slim for the usual female body (sort of like Mick Jagger)— tiny, tiny hips; very slim legs, almost like the legs of a polio victim. They look especially incongruous on AE, who had very thick legs. Found in Nevin Bell, *Amelia Earhart* (London: Albany Publishers, 1970), p. 139. This painting is also so striking, perhaps, because of its color. As in the 1930s in general, almost all the surviving images of Earhart are in black and white.

56. Independent historian Karla Jay has conducted research on AE along those lines. Jay's previous publications include *Lesbian Texts and Contexts: Radical Revisions,* coedited with Joanne Glasgow (New York: New York University Press, 1990), and *Lavender Culture,* coedited with Allen Young (New York: Jove Publications, 1979).

57. Larry Engelmann, *The Goddess and the American Girl: The Story of Suzanne Lenglen and Helen Wills* (New York: Oxford University Press, 1988), p. ix.

58. Amelia Earhart's public asexuality was in keeping with the youthfulness of 1920s fashions. The flappers, for all their sexual imagery of short skirts, bare arms, and dancing all night, were not at all a sultry, glamorous, sexualized vision. They were pals, companions, good dates, not sexual seducers or bed partners. Similarly the tomboy stage was something to outgrow as the young woman graduated into more mature

heterosexual female behavior. In both cases the association of boyish-ness and youth, at least in women, connoted lack of sexual appetite or appeal. See Billie Melman, *Women and the Popular Imagination in the Twenties: Flappers and Nymphs* (New York: St. Martin's Press, 1988) and Sumiko Higashi, *Virgins, Vamps and Flappers: The American Silent Movie Heroine* (Montreal: Eden Press, 1978).

59. Wilson, *Adorned in Dreams,* p. 120; Elsa Maxwell quoted in Gilroy, *Amelia: Pilot in Pearls,* p. 49. See also Gaylan Studlar, "Masochism, Masquerade, and the Erotic Metamorphoses of Marlene Dietrich," *Fabrications: Costume and the Female Body,* ed. Jane Gaines and Charlotte Herzog (New York: Routledge, 1990), pp. 229–49, for discussion of Dietrich's "'fluidity of sexual identity" and its implications for her very large female following.

60. Frederick L. Collins, "Ziegfeld Would Have Said: 'Throw her out!,' " *Photoplay* (April 1935), pp.43–45; Hilary Lynn, "What Is This Thing Called 'X'?," *Photoplay* (April 1933), p. 26f. See also Campbell MacCulloch, "What Makes Them Stars?," *Photoplay* (October 1928), p. 44f., and Louis E. Bisch, "What Is Sex Appeal?," *Photoplay* (July 1928), p. 52f.

61. Ruth Waterbury, "What Is This 'Box-Office'?," *Photoplay* (February 1931), p.68f. The best example of box office was, of course, Greta Garbo.

62. NYHT, August 26, 1932, p.4; Janet Thumin, " 'Miss Hepburn Is Humanized': The Star Persona of Katharine Hepburn," *Feminist Review* 24 (August 1986), p. 101.

63. T. J. Clark quoted in Lisa Tickner, *The Spectacle of Women: Imagery of the Suffrage Campaign, 1907–1914* (Chicago: University of Chicago Press, 1988), p. 151.

CHAPTER 6: POPULAR HEROINES /
POPULAR CULTURE

1. The warm friendship between Earhart and Eleanor Roosevelt is the best example of such links. Earhart's path often crossed that of other well-known female figures, for example, on occasions when they were honored for awards. Eleanor Roosevelt, Dorothy Thompson, and Amelia Earhart all spoke at the 1934 *New York Herald Tribune* Wom-en's Conference on Changing Values. And AE knew many of the Hol-lywood stars, mainly through husband George Putnam's connections to Hollywood. When there was talk of making a movie in the late 1930s about Amelia Earhart, everyone agreed that Katharine Hepburn would be perfect for the part. And in a link between two of the figures discussed in this chapter, Babe Didrikson Zaharias appeared as herself in the Katharine Hepburn-Spencer Tracy movie *Pat and Mike* (1952).

2. Margaret Bourke-White quoted in Vicki Goldberg, *Margaret Bourke-White: A Biography* (New York: Harper & Row, 1986), pp. 115–16.

3. For the dominance of Hollywood from the 1920s through the 1940s, see Robert Sklar, *Movie-Made America: A Cultural History of American Movies* (New York: Random House, 1975); Leo Rosten, *Hollywood: The Movie Colony, the Movie Makers* (New York: Harcourt, Brace and Company, 1941); and Andrew Bergman, *We're in the Money: Depression America and Its Films* (New York: New York University Press, 1971). Robert S. McElvaine, *The Great Depression, 1929–1941* (New York: Times Books, 1984) also covers the cultural impact of films in depth.

4. The best source on the studio system is Thomas Schatz, *The Genius of the System: Hollywood Filmmaking in the Studio Era* (New York: Pantheon, 1988). For the influence of Jews on movie management, see Neil Gabler, *An Empire of Their Own: How the Jews Invented Hollywood* (New York: Anchor Doubleday, 1988).

5. Wendy Holliday is currently researching this topic for her New York University Ph.D. dissertation, "Hollywood's Modern Women: Work, Culture, and Politics, 1915–1940."

6. See Susan Ware, *Holding Their Own: American Women in the 1930s* (Boston: Twayne Publishers, 1982), pp. 188–92; Sklar, *Movie-Made America,* pp.75, 237; and Marjorie Rosen, *Popcorn Venus: Women, Movies, and the American Dream* (New York: Coward, McCann & Geoghegan, 1973), p. 392.

7. Elizabeth Kendall, *The Runaway Bride: Hollywood Romantic Comedies of the 1930s* (New York: Knopf, 1990), p. xvi. See also Molly Haskell, *From Reverence to Rape: The Treatment of Women in the Movies* (New York: Penguin, 1973); Sumiko Higashi, *Virgins, Vamps and Flappers: The American Silent Movie Heroine* (Montreal: Eden Press, 1976); and David Stenn, *Clara Bow: Runnin' Wild* (New York: Doubleday, 1988).

8. On the Production Code, see Sklar, *Movie-Made America;* Haskell, *From Reverence to Rape;* and Bergman, *We're in the Money*.

9. Bette Davis quoted in obituary by Albin Krebs, NYT, October 8, 1989.

10. Katharine Hepburn quoted at the Academy Awards telecast, April 1991. For Hepburn's ongoing impact, see Anna Quindlen, "Reading Hepburn," NYT, October 23, 1991. Here is another such tribute from writer Nancy Friday in *My Mother / My Self* (New York: Dell, 1977), p. 233: "Katharine Hepburn. She was one of my models too. Unmarried, childless, flat-chested—she is the antithesis of what mother and society want for us. And yet my mother adores her, and men too seem to sense something heroic in her. She transcends looks, style, or whatever particular circumstances the scriptwriter places her in; through force of character, by making it on her own, by never giving up and keeping her integrity intact, she wins us all. She is an image of the separate person."

11. Richard Dyer cited in Maria LaPlace, "Producing and Consuming the Woman's Film: Discursive Struggle in *Now, Voyager,*" *Home is Where*

the Heart Is, ed. Christine Gledhill (London: BFI Publishing, 1987), pp. 145–47. See also Richard Dyer, *Star* (London: BFI Publishing, 1979).

12. Leo Rosten, *Hollywood,* appendix, pp. 409–13.

13. Lois Banner, *American Beauty* (Chicago: University of Chicago Press, 1983), p. 276; Allen Guttmann, *Women's Sports: A History* (New York: Columbia University Press, 1991) p. 134; Larry Engelmann, *The Goddess and the American Girl: The Story of Suzanne Lenglen and Helen Wills* (New York: Oxford University Press, 1988), p. 240.

14. Quoted in Donald J. Mrozek, "The 'Amazon' and the American 'Lady': Sexual Fears of Women as Athletes," *From "Fair Sex" to Feminism: Sport and the Socialization of Women in Industrial and Post-Industrial Eras,* ed. J. A. Mangan and Roberta J. Park (London: Frank Cass, 1987), p. 294.

15. Quoted in Guttmann, *Women's Sports,* p. 145. See also Helen Wills Moody, "Sports and Beauty," *Cosmopolitan* (October 1931), pp. 80–81. Sally Guard, "Still Very Much in the Swim," *Sports Illustrated* (June 15, 1992), provides a lively summary of Holm's career pre- and post-Olympics.

16. AE to Mother, August 5, 1932, AOE papers, SL. A photograph of the visit portrays them dressed for a friendly game of archery.

17. General sources on the Babe include William Oscar Johnson and Nancy J. Williamson, *"Whatta-Gal": The Babe Didrikson Story* (Boston: Little, Brown / Sports Illustrated, 1975); Babe Didrikson Zaharias, *This Life I've Led: My Autobiography, as Told to Harry Paxton* (London: Robert Hale Limited, 1956); Nancy Norton, "Mildred Ella Didrikson Zaharias," *Notable American Women: The Modern Period,* ed. Barbara Sicherman and Carol Hurd Green (Cambridge, Mass.: Harvard University Press, 1980), pp. 756–57.

18. Gallico (1932) quoted in Guttmann, *Women's Sports,* p. 145. Gallico continues: "She was a tomboy who never wore make-up, who shingled her hair until it was as short as a boy's and never bothered to comb it, who didn't care about clothes and who despised silk underthings. . . . She had a boy's body, slim, straight, curveless, and she looked her best in a track suit. She hated women and loved to beat them. She was not, at that time, pretty. . . . She had good, clear, gray-green eyes, but she was what is commonly described as hatchet-faced. She looked and acted more like a boy than a girl, but she was in every respect a wholesome, normal female. She was tough as rawhide leather." The next to last sentence was supposed to reassure readers that she was not a lesbian.

19. Johnson and Williamson, *"Whatta-Gal,"* p. 190.

20. Engelmann, *The Goddess and the American Girl* provides an excellent introduction to women's tennis in the decade. See also Helen Wills, *Fifteen-Thirty: The Story of a Tennis Player* (New York: Charles Scribner's Sons, 1937). For her main rivals, see Helen Hull Jacobs, *Beyond*

the Game: An Autobiography (Philadelphia: J. P. Lippincott, 1936) and Alice Marble, *The Road to Wimbledon* (New York: Charles Scribner's Sons, 1946).

21. Wills, *Fifteen-Thirty,* pp. 218–19. Wills and Earhart had met previously, probably in California, although there is no record of their having played tennis together.

22. Charley Paddock, "Why Athletes Fail in Pictures," *Photoplay* (September 1928), p. 52f.; Engelmann, *The Goddess and the American Girl,* pp. 297–300. For Sonja Henie's career, see Robert Markel and Nancy Brooks, *For the Record: Women in Sports* (New York: World Almanac Publications, 1985), p. 74. For her Hollywood career, see Douglas Portmann, "Why Sonja Won't Marry," *Photoplay* (April 1938), p. 25.

23. See Guard, "Still Very Much in the Swim," and Markel and Brooks, *For the Record,* p. 113.

24. On linking Parker with Thompson, see Anna Quindlen, "Reading Hepburn," in which, when discussing her childhood role models, Quindlen says, "I was enamored of the two Dorothys, Thompson and Parker, the columnist and the wit, although neither had a happy life." For more on Parker, see Ann Douglas, "Dorothy Rothschild Parker," in *Notable American Women: The Modern Period,* pp. 522–25. In one of Parker's famous one-liners, she said to a young man complaining he could not bear fools, "That's odd. Your mother could." Another legendary Parker witticism was the statement that Katharine Hepburn's acting ran the gamut of emotions from A to B.

25. Peter Kurth, *American Cassandra: The Life of Dorothy Thompson* (Boston: Little, Brown, 1990), p. 50.

26. Sandra Gioia Treadway, "Anne O'Hare McCormick," *Notable American Women: The Modern Period,* pp. 439–440. See also Julia Edwards, *Women of the World: The Great Foreign Correspondents* (New York: Ballantine, 1988).

27. Goldberg, *Margaret Bourke-White,* pp. 137, 249, 361, 145. See also Margaret Bourke-White, *Portrait of Myself* (New York: Simon & Schuster, 1963). At age twenty-three (1927), Bourke-White made this entry in her diary: "I want to become famous and I want to become wealthy." Quoted in Goldberg, *Margaret Bourke-White,* p. 77.

28. Kurth, *American Cassandra,* p. 340; Ishbel Ross, *Ladies of the Press* (New York: Harper and Brothers, 1936); and Wendy Holliday, "The Woman Newspaperman: Gender, Work, and Identity in the 1920s," unpublished seminar paper, New York University, 1990.

29. Anita Pollitzer, *A Woman on Paper: Georgia O'Keeffe* (New York: Simon & Schuster, 1988), p. xxiii. See also Roxana Robinson, *Georgia O'Keeffe: A Life* (New York: Harper & Row, 1989), and Jack Cowart, Juan Hamilton, and Sarah Greenough, *Georgia O'Keeffe: Art and Letters* (Washington, D.C.: National Gallery of Art, 1987).

30. Appreciations of Graham include an obituary by Anna Kisselgoff, NYT, April 2, 1991; Agnes de Mille, NYT, April 7, 1991; and Christine

Temin, *Boston Globe,* April 2, 1991. An interpretation which influenced my understanding of Graham and her dancers was Jennifer Copaken, "From the Domestic Sphere to the Artistic Cube: The Feminist Impulse in the Modern American Dance Movement," senior honors thesis, Harvard College, 1990.

31. Sources on Eleanor Roosevelt include Joseph Lash, *Eleanor and Franklin* (New York: W. W. Norton, 1971); Joan Hoff-Wilson and Marjorie Lightman, *Without Precedent: The Life and Career of Eleanor Roosevelt* (Bloomington: Indiana University Press, 1984); William H. Chafe, "Anna Eleanor Roosevelt," *Notable American Women: The Modern Period,* pp. 595–601; and Blanche Wiesen Cook, *Eleanor Roosevelt,* Volume I, *1884–1933* (New York: Viking, 1992).

32. Hazel Carby, " 'It Just Be's Dat Way Sometime': The Sexual Politics of Women's Blues," *Unequal Sisters,* ed. Ellen Du Bois and Vicki Ruiz (New York: Routledge, 1990), p. 247.

33. Linda Dahl, *Stormy Weather: The Music and Lives of a Century of Jazzwomen* (New York: Pantheon, 1984), p. 117. Similarly, because of racism and prejudice, Josephine Baker found far more success and fame in Paris for her singing and dancing than she ever would have in the United States. See Phyllis Rose, *Jazz Cleopatra: Josephine Baker in Her Time* (New York: Doubleday, 1989).

34. For the Marian Anderson story, see Ware, *Holding Their Own,* p. 172.

35. Christopher Anderson, *Young Kate* (New York: Henry Holt, 1988), p. 140; Wills, *Fifteen-Thirty,* pp. 2–3; Marble, *The Road to Wimbledon;* Mangan and Park, *From "Fair Sex" to Feminism,* p. 282; Johnson and Williamson, *"Whatta-Gal,"* p. 51.

36. See Nancy Cott, *The Grounding of Modern Feminism* (New Haven: Yale University Press, 1987), pp. 78, 171.

37. Bourke-White, *Portrait of Myself,* pp. 308, 309; *Photoplay* (August 1938), p. 84. According to historian Elaine Tyler May, Hollywood presented marriage and career as highly problematic for actresses. Hollywood's independent women were primarily admired as women, not as wives, even though many of them were married, often several times. See May, *Homeward Bound: American Families in the Cold War Era* (New York: Basic Books, 1988).

38. Robinson, *Georgia O'Keeffe,* pp. 235, 259. Of the women most prominently discussed in the text (excluding Eleanor Roosevelt, who had a fairly traditional marriage and bore six children, five whom survived), only Dorothy Thompson and Bette Davis bore children. Each had one child, although Davis adopted another child. Babe Didrikson Zaharias tried to have children but miscarried. All the rest remained childless, a rather striking commentary on the difficulty of combining a career with child raising in the 1920s and 1930s.

39. Katharine Hepburn was married briefly and then divorced, before entering a long-term relationship with Spencer Tracy, whose wife would not divorce him. Bette Davis was married and divorced three times.

Dorothy Thompson was divorced twice (including from Sinclair Lewis) and outlived her third husband. Margaret Bourke-White had an early marriage and divorce, before her marriage to writer Erskine Caldwell also ended in divorce. Martha Graham was married in the 1940s and then divorced. And Helen Wills's marriage to Frederick Moody in 1929 did not last; by the time she published her autobiography in 1936, she had reclaimed her given name, rather than the Helen Wills Moody that she played under in the early 1930s.

40. Katharine Hepburn, *Me: Stories of My Life* (New York, Knopf, 1991), p. 154; *Ladies' Home Journal* (March 1977), p. 54; *People* (October 11, 1976), p. 66.

41. Katharine Hepburn quoted in NYT, May 2, 1981, and *Esquire* (December 1983), p. 574; interview with Charles Higham, NYT, December 9, 1973, p. 3; Margaret Fuller quoted in Robinson, *Georgia O'Keeffe,* p. 71; Susan Ware, "Katharine Hepburn—Her Mother's Daughter," *History Today* (April 1990), p. 52.

42. Bette Davis obituary, NYT, October 8, 1989; Goldberg, *Margaret Bourke-White,* p. 325.

43. Robinson, *Georgia O'Keeffe,* pp. 508–09; O'Keeffe to Eleanor Roosevelt, February 10, 1944, quoted in Cowart, Hamilton, and Greenough, *Georgia O'Keeffe: Art and Letters,* p. 235.

44. National Woman's Party flyer from 1942 in author's possession.

45. Eleanor Roosevelt quoted in Ruby Black, "Is Mrs. Roosevelt a Feminist?," *Equal Rights* (July 27, 1935), p. 163.

46. Hepburn, *Me,* p. 225. One of Hepburn's stated reasons for writing her 1991 autobiography was precisely to confront what she saw as the gulf between the public's image of her and who she thought she really was. In fact, she had been thinking about this gap for quite a while, as seen in this 1985 interview: "I'm very different from the one everyone seems to know. She's a legend, that is, a creation of, by, and for the public. But I really don't know her. I'm sort of like the man who cleans the furnace. I just keep her going." Gregory Speck interview with Katharine Hepburn, *Interview* (September 1985), pp. 217–21.

47. An enthusiastic fan, Mary Louise Frost of Shelbyville, Kentucky, is unusual in discussing several of the popular figures she could have identified with besides Amelia Earhart: "She was my inspiration, and to have one's inspiration suddenly disappear leaves a void. She was the only person I determined to meet some day. As much as I love children, seeing the Dionne quints in the movies satisfies me. I would not drive a hundred miles to see the President. But I was looking forward to 'crash' someway and meeting Amelia when I visited in Los Angeles this spring." One of the things she missed was "seeing her frequent picture in news reels and newspapers." Frost to AOE, November 27, 1937, AOE papers, SL.

48. AE, *20 Hrs. 40 Min.: Our Flight in the Friendship* (New York: G. P. Putnam's Sons, 1928), pp. 281–82.

49. See, for example, Alicia Curnutt (age fifteen) to George Palmer Putnam, July 23, 1937, in Purdue Special Collections. Very few such "fan" letters are found at Purdue; a few more (some forwarded on by GPP) ended up in Amy Otis Earhart's papers at the Schlesinger Library. Many of the letters from admirers that survive were written after Earhart's disappearance, mainly to Earhart's mother. She kept up an extensive correspondence with those who wrote to her.

50. Edith June Wilmer to AOE, September 17, 1940, and Margaret O'Neal to AOE, July 26, 1937, found in AOE papers, SL. It is possible that some of the young women drawn to Earhart's model were lesbians. Certainly many aspects of Earhart's demeanor and dress could have been construed as an alternative to traditional norms of feminine heterosexual behavior.

51. Wilmer to AOE, September 17, 1940; Florence Porter to George Putnam, December 10, 1937; Charlotte Page to AOE, July 11, 1937, Louise Bode to AOE, September 8, 1937, all found in AOE papers, SL.

52. Rachel M. Brownstein, *Becoming a Heroine: Reading about Women in Novels* (New York: Viking, 1982), pp. xxiv, xix.

53. George Lipsitz, *Time Passages: Collective Memory and American Popular Culture* (Minneapolis: University of Minnesota Press, 1990), p. 16.

CHAPTER 7: THE LAST FLIGHT

1. Quoted in NYT, September 11, 1938, p. 49. See also Hilton Howell Railey, *Touch'd with Madness* (New York: Carrick and Evans, 1938), pp. 109–10.

2. "A.E.," *Aviation* (August 1937), p. 22.

3. Railey, *Touch'd with Madness,* p. 110; *Herald Tribune* syndicate press release, July 3, 1937, found in Purdue Special Collections.

4. Here is how the *New York Herald Tribune* advertised its exclusive rights to her story: "not as a barnstorming adventure but as a practical test—a limit test—of all that is modern in scientific and aerial invention pitted against the longest world flight ever contemplated." Found in AE papers, SL.

5. A May 21, 1932, story datelined New York called her Atlantic solo flight "an almost entirely silly and useless performance." Comparing Lindbergh's nonstop trip to Paris with her forced landing in Ireland, it remarked, "About all she has proved is that well-known phenomenon of nature that a girl can't jump quite as far as a boy can." Clipping found in Purdue Special Collections.

6. GPP, *Soaring Wings: A Biography of Amelia Earhart* (New York: Harcourt, Brace and Company, 1939), pp. 198–99.

7. Editorial in the *Honolulu Star-Bulletin* quoted in NYT, December 30, 1934, p. 15; AE quoted in NYT, January 13, 1935, p. 29; GPP quoted in NYT, December 30, 1934, p. 15.

8. Franklin Roosevelt quoted in NYT, January 20, 1935, p. 28; "Amelia Earhart's Own Story of the Flight over Pacific," NYT, January 13, 1935, p. 1.

9. "A Useless Adventure," January 16, 1935, unidentified editorial found in the American Institute of Aeronautics and Astronautics Collection, LC; GPP, *Soaring Wings,* p. 201. She did in fact make what seem like plugs for Hawaii in her statements. "Anything I can do to help close the gap between Hawaii, as an integral part of the United States, and the mainland will be work into which I can throw myself wholeheartedly." NYT, January 13, 1935, p. 28. She had originally planned to fly straight through to Washington, symbolically linking Hawaii with the nation's capital, but weather and fatigue prevented her from trying. NYT, January 15, 1935, p. 4.

10. "Sticky Business," *Nation* 140, No. 3 (January 30, 1935), p. 118; copyrighted AE story, NYT, January 13, 1935, p. 1.

11. According to *Newsweek,* Earhart's flight coincided with an NBC radio campaign to promote tourism to Mexico. While in Mexico to meet his wife, Putnam had proposed an even more ambitious program which he himself would head. Gasped one of the officials when he heard its expense: "There isn't that much money in Mexico." "Philatelists Fly into Rage over Flyer's Stamp Cover," *Newsweek* 5 (May 11, 1935), pp. 15–16.

12. Gimbel's advertisement in AOE papers, SL; "Philatelists Fly into Rage," pp. 15–16; GPP, *Soaring Wings,* p. 188.

13. Doris L. Rich, *Amelia Earhart: A Biography* (Washington, D.C.: Smithsonian Institution Press, 1989), pp. 182–184, 187.

14. Mary S. Lovell, *The Sound of Wings: The Life of Amelia Earhart* (New York: St. Martin's Press, 1989), p. 205; Jean L. Backus, *Letters from Amelia, 1901–1937* (Boston: Beacon Press, 1982), p. 118. Their lack of accumulated wealth was very apparent when George probated Amelia's estate after she was declared legally dead. Except for their jointly owned house, there wasn't much else, except a car and some small bank accounts. Of course, they had put money into the last flight, assuming they could recoup the investment afterward with endorsements and lectures.

15. Typescript notes for speech, no date (1935), Purdue Special Collections. General information on the university is found in Ruth W. Freehafer, *R. B. Steward and Purdue University* (Lafayette, Ind.: Purdue University Press, 1983), and Frank K. Burrin, *Edward Charles Elliott, Educator* (Lafayette, Ind.: Purdue University Press, 1970).

16. Rich, *Amelia Earhart,* p. 252; Lovell, *Sound of Wings,* pp. 222–23, 230.

17. Lovell, *Sound of Wings,* pp. 222–23; AE to AOE, November 23, 1935, AOE papers, SL. Lovell drew on a personal recollection of AE written by Schleman, April 13, 1975, as well as a personal letter, October 1988. As one of those students training to be an engineer recalled, "She didn't see why if a woman had special talents along that line, she couldn't

go out and show 'em." Marguerite Colt cited in GPP, *Soaring Wings,*
pp. 251–52.

18. Lovell, *Sound of Wings,* p. 224; Rich, *Amelia Earhart,* pp. 225, 227;
GPP, *Soaring Wings,* p. 273. AE's quote continues: "Aviation is a business to me, and my ambition is that this project shall produce practical
results."

19. NYHT, March 7, 1937, clipping found in Clarence Strong Williams
papers, SL.

20. For example, Putnam made Earhart available for a lecture at the Naval
Academy at Annapolis in November 1936, even though he had to
"tear her lecture schedule to pieces" to do it. This was done in part to
make it more likely that the navy would cooperate in the world flight
plans, as it did. See Elliott to GPP, October 24, 1936; GPP to Elliott,
October 21, 1936; and Carroll S. Alden to Elliott, November 9, 1936,
all found in Purdue Special Collections.

21. AE to FDR, November 10, 1936, found in MEM papers, SL. This
plan was abandoned because it would have meant she had to fly for
more than twenty-four hours without a break. Noonan was only a
navigator. He could not spell her at the controls.

22. Telegram from AE to FDR, January 8, 1937, found in Purdue Special
Collections.

23. Backus, *Letters from Amelia,* p. 188; NYT, February 13, 1937, p. 3. She
took ten thousand covers total, half of them autographed. The unau-
tographed ones sold for $2.50 at Gimbel's. They were postmarked in
Oakland, and then were to be postmarked again for the stamp collec-
tors in either Australia or India. They were also to bear the Howland
Island cachet, a first. When the route was changed and the flight delayed,
all the covers were re-marked with a "World Flight—Second Attempt"
logo. See *Airport Journal* 8 (February 1937), for an ad from Gimbel's
for the flight covers. See *Newsweek* 9 (February 29, 1937), p. 33, for
general information on the stamps.

24. Carl B. Allen article in NYHT, March 15, 1937, p. 1. Allen noted that
she had spent practically every spare moment autographing stamp
covers: "So accustomed is she to the task that long ago it became a
sort of reflex action; as she writes she carries on conversations about
her forthcoming flight or on any other topic with complete detachment from what her hands are doing." See also Rich, *Amelia Earhart,*
p. 240.

25. "Sick and Tired of Ocean Flights," *Literary Digest* 114 (August 13,
1932), p. 30.

26. *Time* 29 (March 29, 1937), p. 36. Said GPP: "We will be competing
with no previous records. It will be straight pioneering. It is replete
with resultful research potentialities. It is newsworthy to the nth
degree—personnel, route, direction, equipment, scientific experimentation. All plus the finest kind of sponsorship." Putnam to Elliott,
January 2, 1936, Purdue Special Collections.

27. NYT, February 12, 1937, p. 25. The article was headed, "Amelia Earhart to Circle Globe in Her 'Flying Laboratory.' "

28 Major Al Williams quoted in clipping from the *Cleveland Press*, March 31, 1937, found in Purdue Special Collections. The column appeared after the first attempt was aborted in Hawaii (see below). For AE's response, see Rich, *Amelia Earhart*, p. 248. A slightly different wording—"I'm glad it wasn't a woman who wrote it"—is found in Lovell, *Sound of Wings*, p. 252.

29. AE to FDR, November 10, 1936, found in MEM papers, SL; AE quoted in NYT, May 30, 1937, p. 16; Louise Thaden, *High, Wide and Frightened* (New York: Stackpole Sons, 1938), pp. 262–63.

30. NYHT, March 17, 1937, p. 12; NYT, March 18, 1937, p. 1.

31. *Time* (March 29, 1937), p. 36; AE, *Last Flight* (New York: Harcourt, Brace and Company, 1937), p. 63. See also the *Los Angeles Times,* March 21, 1937, p. 1.

32. GPP, *Soaring Wings*, p. 283; GPP quoted in *Los Angeles Times,* March 21, 1937, p. 1; GPP to Elliott, March 25, 1937, Purdue Special Collections. See also Rich, *Amelia Earhart*, pp. 248–49.

33. Rich, *Amelia Earhart*, p. 247; Lovell, *Sound of Wings*, p. 254.

34. Bradford Washburn, "Amelia Earhart's Last Flight,"*Boston Museum of Science Newsletter* 33 (January–February 1984), p. 3; GPP, *Soaring Wings*, p. 288. She and George truly did sink most of their assets into this flight, hoping for the payback at the end. The main financial reward besides publicity would have been outright ownership of the Lockheed Electra.

35. On Noonan, see Rich, *Amelia Earhart*, p. 241, and Lovell, *Sound of Wings*, p. 245.

36. AE, *Last Flight*, p. 120. Episodes like this are cited by those who question the piloting and navigational abilities of the Earhart-Noonan team.

37. AE, *Last Flight*, p. 90; NHYT, March 20, 1937.

38. See, for example, pp. 137, 174, and 184 in AE, *Last Flight*. Lovell, *Sound of Wings*, pp. 301–02, describes the writing of the book and provides examples of how GPP embellished the text.

39. AE quoted in *Chicago Tribune*, July 4, 1937, p. 1; AE, *Last Flight*, p. 93; NYHT, June 5, 1937, p. 1.

40. Telegram from Helen Rogers Reid to George Palmer Putnam, March 16, 1937, Purdue Special Collections.

41. AE, *Last Flight*, p. 195.

42. Gerry Bruder, "The Enduring Mystery of Amelia Earhart," *American History Illustrated* 22 (May 1987), pp. 10–19.

43. When criticized in Congress for the expenditure, President Roosevelt defended it as an important exercise in naval training and pointed out that the ships were out there cruising around anyway, so why not put them to use looking for Earhart? This was not quite true, but the search was in fact good practice. See NYT, July 21, 1937, p. 23, as well as

MEM and Carol L. Osborne, *Amelia, My Courageous Sister* (Santa Clara, Calif.: Osborne Publisher, 1987).

44. Raymond Fielding, *The American Newsreel, 1911–1967* (Norman: University of Oklahoma Press, 1972), p. 205.
45. Alicia Curnutt to GPP, July 23, 1937, Purdue Special Collections; Mary Louise Frost to AOE, November 27, 1937, Edith June Wilmer to AOE, September 17, 1940, and Margaret O'Neal to GPP, July 21, 1937, all found in AOE papers, SL.
46. MEM to Boston radio audience, c. July 13, 1937, found in MEM papers, SL.
47. For example, an unidentified newspaper clipping concluded in a eulogy entitled "Among Flying Immortals": "Careers like Amelia Earhart Putnam's, although they end tragically at times, often end magnificently, and prove, if nothing else, that women, as well as men, can rise to any challenge civilization can provide." Found in Purdue Special Collections.
48. See M. Elisabeth McFarland to George Putnam: "I have not been able to reconcile myself to her disappearance. I feel that some way, some where she must be still carrying on, that she cannot be gone from the world of women to whom she was such an example of courage and strength." January 20, 1938, found in AOE papers, SL.
49. Helen Jones to MEM, July 16, 1937, AOE papers, SL.
50. Florence Hilles to Alma Lutz, May 7, 1938, in Alma Lutz papers, SL. Hilles was very discouraged at the response that the AE name was having. "So many persons either don't care about her, or are definitely critical of her. 'She should have stayed at home,' 'A married woman has no right to fly' etc, I am unable to get from the Duponts *[sic]* or any other rich persons up to this moment any contribution. Her name— what she accomplished for women—her courage, her charm (to those who came in contact with her) make little or no appeal."
51. Lovell, *Sound of Wings,* p. 318.
52. The appendix to Lovell, *Sound of Wings,* provides a useful summary of the disappearance historiography and theories. Also useful were Bruder, "The Enduring Mystery of Amelia Earhart," and J. Gordon Waeth, "What Happened to Amelia Earhart?", *NOAA [National Oceanic and Atmospheric Administration] Magazine* (July 1977), found in MEM papers, SL.
53. The clippings file and pressbook at the Lincoln Center Archives, New York Public Library, show conclusively how the reviews played up the Amelia Earhart connection to the hilt, although the studio publicity does not mention her by name. There were also very explicit references in the publicity to the war going on, as in this typical ad copy: "Before Pearl Harbor, officialdom said: 'That story is dynamite! Don't dare tell a word of it.' . . . Now you can see it on the screen. Now you can know the secret of this girl's mysterious mission over the Jap-

mandated islands. Now you can live the flaming adventure drama of
her courage, and of the two loves that tore at her heart!" The film was
based on a fictional treatment by Horace McCoy published in the
Woman's Home Companion (January 1943), pp. 14–16. Hollywood fueled
the rumors, but the idea for the film in the first place must have had
some credibility.

54. Eleanor Roosevelt quoted in AE biography file, SL; Lovell, *Sound of
Wings*, pp. 353–54.
55. Waeth, "What Happened to Amelia Earhart?," MEM papers, SL.
56. Statements by ex-GIs (names blacked out) found in "Tokyo Rose"
file, Serial 300, pp. 91-92, Federal Bureau of Investigation Archives,
Washington, D.C. My thanks to Professor Marilynn Johnson of
Southern Methodist University for bringing this material to my attention.
57. Bruder, "The Enduring Mystery of Amelia Earhart," pp. 17–18; Gore
Vidal, "Love of Flying," *New York Review of Books* (January 17, 1985),
pp. 19, 20.
58. Lovell, *Sound of Wings*, pp. 323–32; Rich, *Amelia Earhart*, pp. 271–73.
59. Richard Gillespie, "The Mystery of Amelia Earhart," *Life* 15, No. 4
(April 1992), pp. 69–73. The release of this material rated front-page
newspaper coverage throughout the United States. See NYT, March
16, 1992, p. 1, and *USA Today*, March 17, 1992, p.1.
60. A.E. quoted in GPP, *Soaring Wings*, p. 291.
61. The latest contribution to the disappearance theories is Randall Brink,
Lost Star (New York: W. W. Norton & Company, 1994).
62. See GPP to Elliott, June 23, 1937, Purdue Special Collections. Putnam
said that Baruch had one hundred thousand dollars available for a project similar to AE's world flight—that is, combining some real scientific attainment with opportunities for "personal fun and experience."
Baruch was interested in having Amelia and George on this projected
expedition, at least some of the time, and asked GPP to prepare a
prospectus.
63. See Rich, *Amelia Earhart*, pp. 230–33, and Lovell, *Sound of Wings*, p.
225, for speculation on the state of the marriage.
64. Lovell, *Sound of Wings* covers the rest of GPP's life. See also GPP, *Wide
Margins: A Publisher's Autobiography* (New York: Harcourt, Brace and
Company, 1942).
65. See *Weekly World News* (April 28, 1992), which was accompanied by a
charming picture of an elderly woman having a picnic wearing an old
leather flying cap similar to those which Amelia Earhart was often
photographed in. *Weekly World News* (March 23, 1993) then announced
that AE had returned to the United States for medical treatment, leaving behind 165 descendants on the South Pacific island where she had
lived since the crash.
66. Quoted as postscript to AE, *Last Flight;* Eleanor Roosevelt quoted in
NYT, July 20, 1937, p. 24.

EPILOGUE: WHERE DID THEY ALL GO?

1. Betty Friedan, *The Feminine Mystique* (New York: W. W. Norton, 1963), pp. 32, 34, 35. Friedan is not always the most accurate chronicler of women's lives. Her book, while powerful, is written entirely from the perspective of white, upper-middle-class, educated women and has little awareness that many American women, because of class and race, did not live the life she savagely condemns. And her portrait of disaffected housewives does not even apply to all middle-class women in the decade, many of whom found satisfying lives in volunteer work and professional activities in suburbia. See Susan Ware, "American Women in the 1950s: Nonpartisan Politics and Women's Politicization," *Women, Politics, and Change,* ed. Louise A. Tilly and Patricia Gurin (New York: Russell Sage Foundation, 1990), pp. 281–99.

2. See Joanne Meyerowitz, "Beyond the Feminine Mystique: A Reassessment of Postwar Popular Culture, 1946–1958," *Journal of American History,* Vol. 79, No. 4 (March 1993), pp. 1455–82.

3. See Eugenia Kaledin, *Mothers and More: American Women in the 1950s* (Boston: Twayne Publishers, 1984), which is full of lists of women.

4. Young, white, middle-class women often expressed their restlessness and disaffection with dominant political and social values not through popular heroines but through rock and roll music and fascination with beatniks and other rebels. See Wini Breines, *Young, White, and Miserable: Growing Up Female in the Fifties* (Boston: Beacon Press, 1992).

5. See Denise Mann, "The Spectacularization of Everyday Life: Recycling Hollywood Stars and Fans in Early Television Variety Shows,"*Private Screenings: Television and The Female Consumer,* ed. Lynn Spigel and Denise Mann (Minneapolis: University of Minnesota Press, 1992), pp. 41–70.

6. See, for example, Ellen Goodman, "Earhart's Life—Not Her Fate—Is Intriguing," *Boston Globe,* March 19, 1992, and Anna Quindlen, "Reading Hepburn," NYT, October 23, 1991.

7. Gloria Steinem, *Marilyn / Norma Jean* (New York: Henry Holt and Company, 1986), p. 12.

8. See Tom Wolfe, *The Right Stuff* (New York: Farrar, Straus, Giroux, 1979). By definition, having the "right stuff" meant being a man.

9. Daniel Boorstin, *The Image: A Guide to Pseudo-Events in America* (New York: Atheneum, 1961), p. 57; see also p. 48 for the distinction between heroes and celebrities. See also Richard Schickel, *Intimate Strangers: The Culture of Celebrity* (Garden City, N.Y.: Doubleday, 1985).

Credits

p. 17 National Air and Space Museum, Smithsonian Institution, Photo
       No. 78-16945
p. 20 National Air and Space Museum, Smithsonian Institution, Photo
       No. A336
p. 32 The Schlesinger Library, Radcliffe College
p. 34 The Schlesinger Library, Radcliffe College
p. 41 National Air and Space Museum, Smithsonian Institution, Photo
       No. 82-8666
p. 55 National Air and Space Museum, Smithsonian Institution, Photo
       No. 76-16558
p. 58 UPI/Bettmann
p. 66 National Air and Space Museum, Smithsonian Institution, Photo
       No. 87-6052.
p. 69 National Air and Space Museum, Smithsonian Institution, Photo
       No. 87-2489
p. 77 National Air and Space Museum, Smithsonian Institution, Photo
       No. A45874
p. 85 The Schlesinger Library, Radcliffe College

p. 100 National Air and Space Museum, Smithsonian Institution, Photo No. 82-11884

p. 104 UPI/Bettmann

p. 113 The Schlesinger Library, Radcliffe College

p. 122 The Schlesinger Library, Radcliffe College

p. 132 The Schlesinger Library, Radcliffe College

p. 138 National Air and Space Museum, Smithsonian Institution, Photo No. 82-8669

p. 154 The Schlesinger Library, Radcliffe College

p. 162 National Air and Space Museum, Smithsonian Institution, Photo No. 86-145

p. 165 National Air and Space Museum, Smithsonian Institution, Photo No. 71-1050

p. 172 The Schlesinger Library, Radcliffe College

p. 181 UPI/Bettmann

p. 184 UPI/Bettmann

p. 186 UPI/Bettmann

p. 190 The Estate of Margaret Bourke-White

p. 210 National Air and Space Museum, Smithsonian Institution, Photo No. 90-5970

p. 214 National Air and Space Museum, Smithsonian Institution, Photo No. 71-1056

p. 217 The Schlesinger Library, Radcliffe College

p. 231 National Air and Space Museum, Smithsonian Institution

Excerpts from *Soaring Wings: A Biography of Amelia Earhart*, copyright 1939 by George P. Putnam and renewed 1966 by Margaret H. Lewis, reprinted by permission of Sally Putnam Chapman.

Index

Page numbers in *italics* refer to illustrations.